*f*P

LANNY J. DAVIS

TRUTH TO TELL

Tell It Early, Tell It All,
Tell It Yourself

Notes from
My White House Education

THE FREE PRESS

THE FREE PRESS
A Division of Simon & Schuster Inc.
1230 Avenue of the Americas
New York, NY 10020

Designed by Carla Bolte

Manufactured in the United States of America

10   9   8   7   6   5   4   3   2   1

Library of Congress Cataloging-in-Publication Data

Davis, Lanny J.
    Truth to tell : tell it early, tell it all, tell it yourself :
notes from my White House education / Lanny J. Davis.
        p.   cm.
      1. Presidents—United States—Press conferences.   2. Presidents—
Press coverage—United States.   3. United States—Politics and
government—1993–   I. Title.
JK554.D37   1999
070.1'95—dc21   99-22419
                                                          CIP

ISBN 0-684-86278-6

To my wife, Carolyn,
who made it all possible, and who speaks the truth,
early, all, and herself.

Contents

Author's Note

THIS BOOK DERIVES FROM MY EXPERIENCES WORKING IN THE White House. Other than transcriptions of press briefings and television appearances, the incidents and conversations recounted—whether through description, paraphrase, or reconstructed dialogue—are as I best remember them, based on my own personal observation or participation.

Prologue

The Monica Lewinsky Story:
The First Ten Days

IT WAS ABOUT 9:00 P.M. ON FRIDAY, JANUARY 30, 1998.

I walked through the Secret Service trailer at the northwest gate of the White House for the last time as special counsel to the president. I said goodbye to each of the agents, whom I had come to know pretty well during the previous fourteen months. They were supposed to be completely apolitical, but during my tenure as the White House's chief spokesman on all "scandal" issues, they had joshed me each morning and evening about how I was surviving the ordeal. "You okay, Mr. Davis?" they used to ask me. "Don't let those bastards get you down."

"You're lucky you're getting out when you are, Mr. Davis," said one.

I wasn't so sure. I walked outside into the cold night air, thought about those words, and felt a terrible inner conflict. I had come to the White House in December of 1996 because I had been a friend of Hillary Rodham Clinton at Yale Law School and because of my support for President Clinton and his policies. At the White House I worked with the press primarily on the allegations of improper campaign fundraising and on the administration's response to congressional hearings and investigations on the subject, which by the end of

1997 had basically fizzled out with little lasting damage to the president or his administration.

I had announced my departure in December 1997, primarily because my wife Carolyn was pregnant, and I wanted to spend more time at home with my family. I also was convinced, as I told the president prior to the White House Christmas party when I informed him I planned to leave by the end of January, "I think it's okay for me to return to my law practice, Mr. President, because all the worst scandal stories are behind us."

I guess I was wrong.

THOUGH MOST OF MY DUTIES as a White House spokesman revolved around finance and politics, on one occasion I was asked to comment on a story concerning a possible encounter in the White House between the president and a woman—in this case, a volunteer named Kathleen Willey, who claimed the president had groped her during a visit she had paid to him in late November of 1993.

In early July 1997, a colleague in the White House counsel's office asked me to call Michael Isikoff of *Newsweek* magazine to find out, if I could, whether he was working on a story about the president and another woman. I had known Isikoff for many years, from the days when I had been active in Maryland politics and he was a reporter for the *Washington Post*. He was feisty, with a razor-sharp intellect, and he was relentless if he smelled a good story—especially if he sensed that the target of his reporting was being evasive or disingenuous. Isikoff reportedly had left the *Post* three years earlier in part because of disagreements with his editors over the news value of his reporting on Paula Jones's allegations against the president. The *Post*'s editors had decided that Isikoff's story was neither substantial nor legitimate enough to run, and he left the paper for a position at *Newsweek*.

I reached Isikoff at home on a Friday morning, the Fourth of July, and asked him whether he was working on a story about Clinton and another woman. He said, "Not right now." I said that was an ambiguous reply. He was silent. He asked me who was asking the question in the White House. I didn't tell him. I reported the conversation back to the counsel's office.

The following Monday, someone told me that the "Drudge Report"—an Internet Web site that focuses almost exclusively on negative rumors and developing negative stories about the Clintons and their allies—had reported that Michael Isikoff was "hot on the trail" of a story involving a "federal employee sexually propositioned by the president on federal property." I subsequently learned that Drudge had posted the allegation on July 4—the very day that I had called Isikoff.

In late July, Isikoff called to inform me that he was about to break a story naming Kathleen Willey as having been involved with the president. I asked him whether this was the same story that Drudge had reported, and why he was going with it now when he hadn't before. He said cryptically that he had more now than he had before, that there was someone else who might be corroborative. He wanted me to confirm or deny the allegations, but he also seemed worried about my going into a full-court press to try to get an official White House comment, because if I did so the word might get out to one of his competitors. He therefore refused to go into any details as to why he was taking this story seriously. The reporter's dilemma can be seen here: he needs help and information from a source to complete his story accurately, but he wants to reveal as little as possible so that he doesn't lose his scoop. In this case, because Isikoff and I had known each other for so many years he knew he could trust me not to deliberately bust his exclusive story.

I went through the motions of trying to check the story out, but given the little information Isikoff had been willing to share with me, I knew I wouldn't get very far. In fact, no one I spoke to in the counsel's office or elsewhere was even willing to check out whether someone named Kathleen Willey had ever worked at the White House as a volunteer or otherwise, much less whether the president had had an intimate incident involving her.

I don't believe I ever called Isikoff back. I just couldn't take this story seriously. I didn't understand why *Newsweek* was crossing the line into alleged private conduct by the president, a line not crossed in previous White Houses. After all, as I understood it from talking to Isikoff, in this instance there was no legal proceeding, no grand jury—and, significantly, Ms. Willey was unwilling to go on record with Isikoff. I wondered: Will Isikoff and *Newsweek* become the first mainstream national media organization perhaps in U.S. history willing to publish allegations of extramarital sexual activity by a president of the United States without anything else to justify the publication of the story?

After the story broke on August 4, the White House decision was not to comment on it at all, though we had to prepare a response because the president had a "press availability" scheduled that day or the next. (A "press availability," as distinguished from a full-blown press conference, is an event at which the president is performing some official function, such as meeting with a head of state or making an announcement of a policy initiative, and a few questions of the president on unrelated matters are permitted from representatives of the press corps.) Those of us on the White House counsel's investigations team joined the prep session with the president customarily conducted by press secretary Michael McCurry and other senior White House political advisors. McCurry turned to me and asked whether the Willey story had any "significant legs." On the scandal beat, the test of viability of a breaking story is whether other news organizations treat it seriously, get concerned or irritated that they have been beaten, and thus launch their own investigative energies and resources into finding new news to break beyond the original story. The quick shorthand expression to describe this phenomenon is "legs"; if a story has legs, other news organizations will report it, and sometimes, if it is a huge story, expand on it over additional news cycles. In response to McCurry, I said no, it had no legs, that I had heard from few reporters about it. McCurry turned to the president and asked him a hostile question about the incident—posing, as he usually did at these sessions, as an aggressive reporter. The president smiled and cracked a joke; we all laughed nervously. Then, changing to a serious tone, he denied that the incident alleged by Ms. Willey had ever happened.

When I left the room, I sought guidance from a member of the counsel's office as to how I should respond to inquiries about the *Newsweek* report. "Just refuse to answer any questions," was the response. This, I knew, was not a useful tactic. If anything, it would infuriate the press and drive them further, perhaps giving legs to the story. I caught up with McCurry after the briefing. He gave me permission, based on the president's answer, to deny that the Willey incident had ever happened as described by *Newsweek*—and to do it "on background," which meant I could be quoted, but not by name. My words would be attributed instead to an anonymous "senior White House official."

It was when I read Isikoff's story that I first came across the name Linda Tripp. Isikoff identified her as a former Bush White House employee who had worked for a time in the Clinton counsel's office as an executive assistant to then White House Counsel Bernard Nussbaum. Isikoff quoted Tripp as saying that she had seen Willey after she left her meeting with President Clinton, that her lipstick was smeared and her blouse "disheveled," and that her demeanor was "flustered, happy, and joyful." Tripp, portrayed by Isikoff as trying to be helpful to the White House, said that Willey was not distressed. I remember thinking that there was something disingenuous about Tripp's motives. Why would she go on record with Isikoff about this incident and how could she consider it "helpful" to confirm that the incident had occurred—regardless of Willey's reaction to it?

Robert Bennett, the president's personal attorney in the *Paula*

Corbin Jones case, apparently also reacted to Tripp's real motives as I had. He was quoted in the *Newsweek* story, and on television and in the press, as saying that Linda Tripp was "not to be believed" and that the incident alleged by Willey had never happened.

I received a flurry of phone calls from reporters about the Willey story, mostly about Linda Tripp and her prior service in the Clinton White House. Again I ran up against a virtual information shutdown within the place as I tried to answer these press inquiries. Attorneys in the counsel's office who were there at the time she worked as an executive assistant to Nussbaum either said that they did not remember Tripp or would not tell me whether they knew anything about her claim to have some knowledge of the Willey allegations. Several people told me that they knew Tripp to be a fairly active office gossip. Some recalled that during the aftermath of Vincent Foster's suicide in 1993 (she worked in the same office suite as Foster in the counsel's office), she was very critical of the way the White House had handled that matter, and had testified at a Senate hearing to that effect.

In any event, the information blackout seemed to work. The Willey story had no legs. We were amazed and delighted. It appeared that we had lucked out for several reasons: the fortuitous timing of a scheduled presidential press conference, permitting Clinton himself to deny the story within days of its publication; Bennett's quick public slap-down of Linda Tripp; the timing of the story in August, when most press and political people are out of town on vacation; and, most important, the fact that it was just another rumor story about Clinton and sexual liaisons, and the alleged corroboration by Tripp was suspect at best.

So we learned a very important lesson from the Willey episode: ignore or downplay stories about the president's alleged sexual liaisons; get the president to deny them as soon as possible; in any event, refuse to comment on the record or to cooperate with anyone pursuing the story. The result: We could kill the legs on such a story if we followed that strategy.

Of course we didn't realize that about five months later we would be applying the same lessons to another presidential sexual liaison story—but this time with different results.

L ATE ON FRIDAY AFTERNOON, January 16, 1998, I was preparing to leave my office when Michael Weisskopf, a political reporter for *Time* magazine, called me.

"Hear anything about the president coaching a witness who has been called before a grand jury, something relating to notes or tapes regarding the *Jones* case?" he asked. He made a cryptic reference to a young woman possibly being involved.

In the rhythms of the journalistic work cycle among Washington political reporters, Friday afternoons and evenings, I had learned, were critical for reporters at the newsweeklies. Their drop-dead deadlines were late Saturday afternoon. They went to press Saturday night and by early Sunday morning they were able to fax out their hottest political stories to the Sunday morning talk shows as a means of getting into the journalistic "buzz" for Sunday's TV news broadcasts and Monday morning's newspapers. To try to stay current, most of the newsweekly reporters worked right up to the last minute, looking for news nuggets or rumors about what their competitors were working on right up to Saturday evening's deadline.

"How strong is your source of information?" I asked. I knew Weisskopf to be one of the best in the business—a middle-of-the-road journalist, without an ideological or personal ax to grind, with a level of integrity and a concern for accuracy and fairness that were as high as those of any journalist I had encountered over the years. But sometimes he was in the Friday afternoon "trolling" mode—calling me to pick up the latest tidbit or to try to figure out what his main competition, *Newsweek*, might be working on.

"Pretty good—but won't go on the record," Weisskopf responded. "This is worth your checking it out."

I trusted Weisskopf completely. On an earlier story about the campaign-finance scandals, he had been willing to correct a mistake in his reporting on a story that could have had plenty of "legs" (and would have, therefore, earned him much credit) after I presented some new, exculpatory information that he was able to verify. I knew that he would not be pursuing this lead unless he had a serious source and a firm basis for doing so.

"Can you tell me anything more?" I pressed. "Otherwise, you know, I'll have difficulty getting people to help me."

"Can't tell you much more right now. Get back to me."

My first reaction was that there couldn't be a basis for this rumor. The only grand-jury proceedings involving the president were the Whitewater issues and their progeny under the supervision of Independent Counsel Kenneth Starr. It was inconceivable to me that President Clinton would be involved in coaching or suborning perjury of any of those witnesses. In any event, I had the strong impression that Starr's efforts to implicate the president and the first lady in these matters had come to a virtual dead end.

On the other hand, in light of my previous experiences with Weisskopf, I knew I couldn't blow off the question, especially with the possibility that his indefatigable competitor, Michael Isikoff of *Newsweek*, was undoubtedly working on a similar story. Learning when to treat a rumor inquiry seriously and when not to, learning which reporters knew the difference between a reliable source and an unreliable one, was one of the most important lessons I had learned during my year at the White House.

I had had lunch earlier in the afternoon with Isikoff—a strange lunch, now that I look back on it. Isikoff usually pumped me for information about stories he was working on. But on this Friday, he was more interested in what I was hearing around town, what other reporters were working on. And he asked me again why I had called him the previous July 4 to ask him whether he was working on a story about the president and another woman—the call I made just before he broke the Kathleen Willey story. Who asked you to call? he prodded. Why? What had you heard at that point? From whom?

I wouldn't answer any of those questions, but I said something offhanded, like "These womanizing stories are old hat and still haven't gone anywhere." He was suddenly very coy. "They're more real than you think," he said. I did not take him seriously—again remembering both how insubstantial the Willey story had been and the indifferent press reaction to it.

Pursuing Weisskopf's query, I made a few calls to colleagues in the counsel's office, then one or two to senior aides in the political and press sectors of the White House. I had to be careful. In this type of situation, helping a reporter to confirm a story or to get additional facts was always very tricky. Once I start making calls and asking questions, the grapevine begins to operate, increasing the chances that someone will mention my inquiry—sometimes quite innocently, sometimes not—to another reporter, thus unfairly busting the original reporter's exclusive.

As I had discovered during the previous year, leaks to other journalists based on inquiries from one news organization were not uncommon at the Clinton White House. An unfortunate consequence was that some reporters, having been burned in this way before, would tend to wait until the last minute before calling the White House for confirmation or comment on a story about to be published. This was a dangerous practice since it could mean that, in the name of protecting an exclusive, a story could get published before there was a fair opportunity to check it out for accuracy or to give the White House an opportunity to comment.

To each person I called, I said up front that this was confidential and should not be repeated to anyone. Then I mentioned my conversation with "a reporter" and asked whether they had heard anything along those lines. The answer each time was negative.

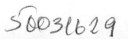

Since the president's deposition in the *Jones* case was scheduled for the next morning, however, I guessed that the source could be someone from the Jones camp and that somehow it was related not to grand-jury testimony but to a deposition in the *Jones* case. I knew from past experiences that in the earliest stages of a story, reporters were often picking up pieces of information based on a kernel of truth—which was then distorted in the repeating from one source to another—much like the old grade-school game of "telephone," where the first whispered message gets passed from one person to another. Though the final iteration of the message might be quite distorted, there was often a core of accuracy. And this felt like one of those instances, so I wasn't willing to blow it off completely.

I decided to press on. I asked someone high up in the counsel's office, "Any chance you could check this out with the president or Bob Bennett?"

"You know we don't go to the president with press questions on something like this," was the response.

I persisted. I tried calling David Kendall, another private attorney hired by the president, in this case to represent him on Whitewater and other matters under investigation by Independent Counsel Kenneth Starr. Kendall and I had been at Yale Law School together. But Kendall was out, and I left a message on his voice mail. I then called Bob Bennett. He was not in either. I assumed he would not be easy to reach, since undoubtedly he was with the president preparing for the next day's deposition.

For one instant, I remember thinking, "I've got to get to Bennett and make sure he and the president know about this inquiry." But I didn't. Inwardly, I suppose, I regarded this particular subject matter as so distasteful and illegitimate that I did not wish to dignify it by asking the president for a response.

So I called Weisskopf back and told him I couldn't confirm or deny the story, and asked him to call me if he could give me any more information, so I could make use of it to prod my colleagues to look into the story further. I went home, and heard nothing more over the weekend. None of the major news magazines had anything relating to this story or the *Jones* case when they were published on Sunday morning.

ON MONDAY MORNING, January 19, I arrived at the White House early, prepared to field press inquiries about the president's deposition in the *Jones* case on Saturday. One of the first calls I received was from Weisskopf.

"Did you see the 'Drudge Report' over the weekend?"

"No. I don't read the 'Drudge Report,'" I answered.

"Drudge says that a young intern, Monica Lewinsky, may have had an affair with the president." The report also stated that Isikoff and *Newsweek* were working on this story.

I said I had never heard the name Monica Lewinsky before and asked whether anyone was taking Drudge seriously.

"Something's popping. Can't tell you any more right now."

Even so, I received only a few phone calls that Monday and Tuesday concerning the swirling rumors generated by Drudge about the president and a White House intern.

On Tuesday evening, I was at home when, at about 9:00 P.M., I received a page from John Podesta's office to call immediately. When I did, his assistant told me that Podesta, the deputy chief of staff, had received a phone call from Peter Baker of the *Washington Post*. He wanted me to return it. I remember wondering why Baker had called Podesta rather than me. That was unusual. Perhaps, I thought, it was because I was due to leave the White House on January 30 and Baker considered me to be already out the door. I returned Baker's call.

"Are you seated or standing?" Baker asked me.

"Seated."

"We have a pretty important story and we need White House comment right away."

"What's your deadline?" I asked.

"About ten-thirty, but we might be able to extend that if you can get us a reaction."

He proceeded to tell me what he had. "Have you ever heard the name Monica Lewinsky?" he began.

Baker's story literally took my breath away. I hung up the phone and sat for a couple of minutes, thinking, trying to absorb what I had just heard. My heart was thumping. Carolyn looked at me, concerned. "What's wrong?" she asked.

"This could be the worst story of the Clinton presidency. It could threaten the Clinton presidency itself."

I suffered from the "boy who cried wolf" syndrome with Carolyn. "Oh, come on," she said. "You always are concerned when these stories first break, and then they always turn out to be less serious than you thought they would be."

"I don't think this one can be worked with the same rules," I remember saying, hardly realizing the extent of the understatement.

I immediately called John Podesta back. He picked up immediately—also unusual for Podesta, who is almost always on the phone with two calls waiting.

"John, the *Post* is running a story with three key facts confirmed, and they want our comment," I began.

"What are they?"

"First, they've confirmed that a White House intern named Monica Lewinsky claims to have had an affair with the president, and this is corroborated by tape recordings between Ms. Lewinsky and a friend."

An audible intake of breath.

"Second, they've confirmed that Ken Starr got the tapes, went to the attorney general, and has received authority from the three-judge panel to investigate the president's role, which includes possible perjury, subornation of perjury, and obstruction of justice."

Another more audible intake of breath.

"Finally, they've confirmed that as a result of suspicions about this affair someone at the White House caused Ms. Lewinsky to be transferred to a job in the Pentagon."

A long silence, another, quieter intake of breath, and then . . . a sigh.

"You better come down here right away," Podesta said quietly.

"They have about an hour to an hour and a half before deadline. Where is the president? Can we get to him and find out what we should say?"

"I doubt it—he's with Prime Minister Netanyahu in the Oval." The Israeli leader was in town on a state visit.

"I'm on my way," I said. "By the way, I suspect others may have this story too."

I was right. As I drove along the Potomac to the White House, there was little traffic on the road. It was quiet, serene. I tried to absorb the significance of what I had just heard. I remember the one thought that struck me the hardest: Ken Starr finally had the grand-jury subpoena power to investigate Bill Clinton personally—specifically, his sex life. It was frightening.

I was interrupted in my thoughts by the vibration of my pager. I looked at the lit-up message as I drove. "Call David Willman, *Los Angeles Times*. Urgent."

I called Willman back. He had the same story as the *Post*—but with a few more details about the chain of events that had led Starr to seek, and obtain, authority to investigate the president's possible affair with an intern named Monica Lewinsky, including the possibility that Vernon Jordan had assisted the president in finding Lewinsky a job in order to keep her quiet about the relationship.

As I arrived at the White House, I was paged by several other news organizations that had bits and pieces of the story. Frank Murray of the *Washington Times* apparently had spoken to Monica Lewinsky's attorney or someone close to him about the alleged affair, with a critical characterization of President Clinton. I also heard from Wolf Blitzer, the omnipresent chief White House correspondent for CNN, asking me whether I was in a position to confirm a story about the president having an affair with a White House intern. He had also heard that the FBI had interviewed Lewinsky but they denied there was any coercion involved. I warned him I couldn't confirm, and urged him not to rush onto television until I could get back to him. The rumor mill was beginning to grind. I heard from one of the reporters I spoke to that one of the television networks also had the story. (It turned out to be ABC.)

A small group of us assembled in the spacious second-floor office of White House Counsel Charles Ruff, including Podesta, Special Counsel Lanny A. Breuer, and several other senior White House aides. Press Secretary Mike McCurry had been called and was waiting for word on what we could find out. Ruff called David Kendall to see what he knew.

A few minutes later Kendall called back. Chuck Ruff murmured a few times inaudibly, hung up the phone, and confirmed that the *Post* had the basic facts right.

At about that point, Peter Baker called me and said that the *Post* couldn't wait any longer. Did we have a response? On my own, without asking anyone's permission, on "deep background" (i.e., I was not to be quoted directly in any manner), I told him that we had confirmed that Starr had been granted jurisdiction to investigate the president on the matter, but that I couldn't go any further than that.

A brief discussion ensued within the group gathered in Ruff's office as to whether the president could or should be disturbed. If the allegations of an affair are completely false, shouldn't we get our denial into the first *Post* story? I asked. But no one argued in favor of disturbing the president's meeting with Prime Minister Netanyahu.

We sent Adam Goldberg, a brilliant Harvard Law School gradu-ate who served as my deputy in the counsel's office, to the *Post*'s load-ing dock to pick up a copy of the 10:30 P.M. early edition. By the time Goldberg had returned empty-handed, we had learned that the *Post* had decided it wasn't ready to publish the story in its early edition. Finally, at around 12:30 A.M., the story was posted on the *Post*'s Web site—just about the time, I learned afterward, that ABC had broken the story on a radio broadcast.

And so it began.

I drove home at around 4:00 A.M. to try to catch a couple of hours of sleep. It was hopeless. I had the first of many sleepless nights.

EARLY THE NEXT MORNING, Wednesday, January 21, the same small group of White House lawyers met again in Charles Ruff's office, this time joined by White House press secretary Mike McCurry. McCurry wanted our reaction to what he intended to say about the Monica Lewinsky allegations to the daily 9:00 A.M. press "gaggle"—an informal press briefing around his half-circle desk in the press secretary's office. He had apparently just come from the Oval Office, where he had talked to the president.

He looked down at a scrap of paper and said, "I'm going to deny that there was any sexual relationship between the president and Ms. Lewinsky." He indicated that he had cleared the statement with the president. Someone in the room said, "Why not say 'improper,' rather than 'sexual'?"

Ordinarily there would have been a debate about the advisability of using an obviously ambiguous word like "improper" at the first moment of a major breaking story. But on this occasion, the usual atmosphere and routine in our damage-control sessions seemed to be virtually inoperative. It was a different, almost surreal atmosphere. All our usual instincts were frozen. This was not about politics or public-relations damage control, I thought. This is about a prosecutor who seemed hell-bent to bring down a president, a federal grand jury with the power of subpoena and indictment, and—potentially—the possibility of impeachment. I am sure that many people in the room were also well aware that anything they said in this meeting could some day be the subject of a grand-jury subpoena.

We were also skittish about the subject matter, the issue of a possible sexual relationship between the president and a woman other than his wife. By general unspoken consensus, this was the one subject that was rarely discussed in the Clinton White House. It was one thing to not be bashful about asking the president about campaign-finance issues, quite another to ask him about matters involving a possible extramarital relationship.

And so, we started to act and think differently. It was noticeable. Instead of the usual discussion at this critical moment about effective damage control—plans to get the facts out, shape them, put them in context, prepare for the opposition attack—we just sat in silence. There was no real debate about what the president should say, about the ramifications of using a coy word like "improper," no expression of concern that we needed to obtain all the details of the story before we allowed the president to speak. We were frozen.

Mike McCurry did not resist the suggestion that we change the denial from "no sexual" relationship to "no improper" one. "Okay, I'll use the word 'improper,'" he said, scratching out and writing the word on the back of a folded piece of paper. I was surprised by McCurry's willingness to go along. It was, well, un-McCurry-like. He knew, and I knew that he knew, that he (and the president) would never get away with the word "improper"; so why was he so passive? This was the first moment when I understood that McCurry had been forced into a different mode: now there was a grand jury, Kenneth Starr, and allegations of a sexual relationship. All the rules, it seemed, would be different from this point on.

Someone briefly argued that such a substitution would simply prod the press into asking whether the word "improper" included "sexual" or excluded it, and that if anything, it would draw attention to the issue, suggesting there was something to hide. Yet, although I am sure we all had the same doubts at that particular moment, no one was willing to say so. Someone else again insisted that the word "improper" should be used by McCurry.

No response. More silence.

The president had previously scheduled interviews for that day with reporters from National Public Radio's *All Things Considered* program, with Jim Lehrer of public television's nightly *News Hour,* and with Mort Kondracke of *Roll Call.* Someone asked whether it was a good idea for these interviews to proceed. It was obvious that to cancel them would have conveyed the message that the Lewinsky charges were serious and problematic for the president. On the other hand, there were serious dangers in allowing the president to make a public response to this story before he had an opportunity to share all the facts with his attorneys and his political/press team.

Yet there was virtually no debate about this significant decision to let the interviews take place under these circumstances. The atmosphere of intellectual and political paralysis was palpable.

Most of the White House staff were watching when the interview with Jim Lehrer was broadcast on the early evening of January 21. The president was asked about whether he had had an "affair" with Monica Lewinsky, and he answered, using the same expression McCurry had used, that there was no improper relationship. Predictably, Lehrer was not satisfied with the word "improper." What did he mean by that? "Well, I think you know what it means. It means that there is not a sexual relationship, an improper sexual relationship, or any other kind of improper relationship."

I watched the president closely on the television screen. He was unsure of himself. Unsettled. Obviously uncomfortable, evasive, and legalistic. He wasn't the Bill Clinton I knew, not the Bill Clinton in command, his mind rapidly computing the three-part answer with two subparts even before the questioner had completed the question. I was very shaken.

I immediately received a flurry of press calls. "Did you notice he used the present tense?" asked Claire Shipman, an NBC White House correspondent.

I hadn't noticed. "Come on, Claire, give me a break. That wasn't intentional. He's denying there was a sexual relationship. Period."

Then several other reporters pointed out the same issue—the use of the present tense. I couldn't believe the press had reached this level of cynicism. I used a few expletives to express my reaction to their questions.

"Why did McCurry and Clinton at first use the word 'improper' rather than 'sexual'?" was another question asked by many reporters. "Isn't it obvious that Clinton is trying to avoid answering whether he had a sexual relationship with Lewinsky?"

My heart was sinking fast. I had no answers. I tried contacting my usual sources in the counsel's office and elsewhere to find out why the president had used the present tense in his answers to Lehrer. Still no answers—though everyone assumed, with me, that this was unintentional.

I had another sleepless night. I knew that there was something very wrong here, something that was causing Clinton not to be himself, something that seemed to be embarrassing to him. I feared that the Clinton presidency was very much at risk.

The next morning, January 22, we had a senior staff meeting of the White House lawyers, press and political people in Deputy Chief of Staff John Podesta's office. No one knew much, and no one had much of a strategy to talk about. We were tense and we had little to say. Few people in the room were willing to look one another in the eye. I especially noticed how tense John Podesta was, how worried. That worried me even more.

Afterward, about 8:45 A.M., as I was leaving the meeting, I saw

White House Chief of Staff Erskine Bowles coming out of his office, which was in the same suite of offices as Podesta's. I asked if I could talk with him privately. He took me into the expansive chief of staff's office, with its luxurious living room, sitting area, and fireplace, as well as a large conference table and desk. Bowles is one of those rare people who is exactly what he appears to be the first time you meet him. He is a decent, kind-hearted, honest man. He has simple values and a direct way of speaking to you. He tells you what he thinks. There are no secret agendas. He has tremendous inner integrity and balance.

I shared my concerns with him about the president's performance in the Lehrer and NPR interviews. After hearing me out, he nodded, and said simply, "I agree with you. You should say all this to the president." He picked up the phone and called the president's personal secretary, Betty Currie. "I'm sending Lanny Davis down to see the president."

I walked down the hallway from the chief of staff's office, past the small foyer and office on the right occupied by senior adviser Rahm Emanuel. I passed the steward's passageway, the one leading to the president's private study, then passed the closed front door to the Oval Office, nodding to the uniformed Secret Service officer sitting in front of the door, and then to the right, through the visitors' doorway, into the reception area that leads to the Oval Office's side entrance. There, Betty Currie was sitting at her desk. She smiled. "He's on the phone," she told me. "As soon as he gets off, you can go in."

Betty had been my friend—more accurately, my mother-protector—since my earliest days in the White House. In fact, she had a delightful quality—a warmth, a ready smile, a softness—that engendered a similar reaction from most others at the White House who encountered her. Whenever I was having a bad day, she would be there for a quick smile, a hug, and a kind word.

I sat on a chair in front of her desk. Usually when I stuck my head into her office to say hello, she would banter with me. "Uh-oh, Lanny's here—must be bad news," she'd say. This morning, somehow, such banter did not seem appropriate. I sat silently, waiting. At one point, after about ten minutes, I thought to myself, "This is a mistake—I might be called before a grand jury for going through with this meeting," and I thought about leaving. But I stayed.

Finally Betty said, "Go on in. He's off the phone."

President Clinton was sitting at his desk. I noticed that his eyes were puffy, with bags under them, a condition that in the past I had attributed to his sensitivity to allergies. I also had seen them when I thought he was under stress. Here is my recollection of our conversation.

Hello, Mr. President.

He nodded and motioned me to sit in the chair right next to his desk.

I'm not here as your lawyer, or as a White House lawyer, I went on. I'm here as your friend.

I also cautioned him that there might not be attorney-client privilege in our conversation. The president nodded his head, leading me to think he knew why I was concerned about his telling me any new factual information.

I took a deep breath. I told him that in the previous day's interview with Jim Lehrer he had looked more like a defendant under the heel of a criminal defense attorney than a president of the United States. I said he had looked evasive, untruthful, and, worst of all, unsure of himself.

I said that he had a great deal of support in the country for his presidency, for what he had accomplished, and that he had a reservoir of goodwill and significant political capital in his Democratic base. I understood that he was concerned about his situation; I could tell it from his body language during the Lehrer interview. But I thought he could afford to take risks—if there were risks that had to be taken.

Do what you do best, I said, better, perhaps, than any president in modern history: Take your case to the American people, tell them everything, everything there is to tell. Let them judge. Give them credit for being able to put it in perspective.

Let your lawyers do the law, I added. You do politics—what you were born to do.

He nodded his head, as if agreeing. He then spoke for a few minutes and seemed very much in pain. He was concerned about the political fallout.

I said it would be bad.

And the press?

I said the press assumed he had had the affair—that he was presumed guilty.

He shrugged his shoulders, then said that there was nothing new there.

I told the president that most of the press were clamoring for Lewinsky's WAVES records, the Secret Service computer records recording visitor entries and exits. ("WAVES" is an acronym for "Worker and Visitor Entry System.") Some reporters had already heard that she had visited him as many as three dozen times, I said.

He shook his head, indicating that she had not been to visit with him that many times since she left the White House to work at the Pentagon.

Then let's get those records out now, I said, before they are leaked and distorted by the opposition. I reminded him that it was always better if we put them out ourselves first, and thus had a chance to frame the story.

He left me with the impression that, as a politician, as a keen observer of American history, he agreed that it was important to get as much information out as possible as early as possible, that to resist would only make matters worse.

But he also left me with a strong impression that he was very uncomfortable about something, something causing him a deep, deep internal conflict, something tearing at him from different directions, something very elemental. I saw the pain, the fatigue, in his eyes.

There wasn't much more to say, I realized, certainly not now.

As I walked out of the Oval Office, I looked back to wave goodbye, the last time, I knew, for me as a White House official. I was struck by how lonely the president of the United States seemed to be.

That afternoon, the president had a televised photo opportunity in the Oval Office with Palestinian leader Yasir Arafat. He was asked by a member of the press pool whether he would answer all the questions about the Lewinsky matter. He stated:

> The American people have a right to get answers. We are working very hard to comply, get all the requests for information up here. . . . I'd like for you to have more rather than less, sooner rather than later.

I was watching on closed-circuit White House television when he said this. This is the real Bill Clinton speaking, I thought, speaking as president, not as someone dominated by his lawyers.

IT WAS INEVITABLE. They all wanted the WAVES records for Monica Lewinsky.

Beginning on the first day the story broke, my phone kept ringing repeatedly. All the reporters were all asking for the same thing: the Secret Service records on the dates and times of the entries and exits of Monica Lewinsky since she left the White House in April 1996. These records also list the sponsor of the visitor—the person who enters the information into the White House computers ahead of time to permit a brief verification of the information (such as date of birth and social security number) identifying the individual.

A few days later, I was standing in the hallway with a White House colleague after a morning staff meeting. One of the president's outside attorneys, accompanied by some attorneys from the White House counsel's office, was coming down the hallway from the Oval Office.

"We've got to put out the WAVES information as soon as possible," I said. "The pressure is immense from the press and every day we delay will look like we're trying to hide something. It's going to get out at some point anyway."

The answer was simple, to the point, and without any suggestion of further discussion:

"No."

"Why? We've always put out WAVES records preemptively—so we could be sure to get our context and interpretation as part of the story," I argued. "Starr is going to get them anyway. They speak for themselves. Whatever they say, they say."

"No information is going to be put out to the press by the White House about this matter—period."

I was stunned. I literally couldn't believe what I had just heard. I knew that this situation was different from any we had faced before, now that a grand jury had been impaneled to conduct a criminal investigation of the president of the United States. I also knew that criminal defense attorneys ordinarily shut down all information flowing to the press regarding their clients. But still, an independent counsel and a grand jury had been investigating the president on the Whitewater matter since 1994. At that time, then Deputy Chief of Staff Harold Ickes, an attorney, assembled a damage-control legal team led by Jane Sherburne, with Mark Fabiani and Christopher Lehane primarily responsible for dealing with the press. Sherburne, Fabiani, and Lehane, in the middle of Kenneth Starr's investigation and the congressional Whitewater hearings, still pushed out stories, responded to press inquiries, and gained a reputation for forthrightness that ultimately was given credit for minimizing the political impact of Whitewater and the various other matters under investigation. Even if there was a difference here, given Kenneth Starr's singular new jurisdiction and focus on President Clinton and his personal conduct, there had to be a distinction made between putting information out, such as documents that would likely be leaked or released at some point anyway, and allowing the president himself to answer detailed questions before it was clear where the independent counsel was headed. The complete cutoff of all information to the press, imposed on McCurry and everyone else in the White House by the attorneys, was unprecedented; moreover, as became painfully obvious in the days ahead, it simply added pressure to the cooker, making an inevitably bad story much worse.

I appealed to as many people in the White House leadership hierarchy as I could find—the chief of staff's office, the White House counsel's office, the press secretary's office, the senior political advisers—in short, all the places and people in the White House where in the past there would be levers of influence and power concerning the appropriate damage control strategy when the president faced a crisis. One senior White House official, someone who had the right combination of legal and political skills and ongoing direct access to the president, someone with whom I had worked closely on the campaign-finance issues and who understood the need to get information out to the press as quickly and as comprehensively as possible, was sitting glumly in his office when I walked in without knocking to make my pitch for at least getting the records out on Lewinsky's White House visits as early as possible. He nodded his head in seeming agreement at my argument that we could make a distinction between putting documents out that Ken Starr would get anyway versus putting the president out for detailed questioning, which no responsible criminal defense attorney would allow. Yet as I left I had the firm impression that even he would not push this viewpoint, and that everything was different now.

I was right. The information shutdown was complete. No one was willing to second-guess the attorneys. As one senior official said to me, "Do you want to be the one responsible for saying something, or putting something out, that leads to the impeachment of a president?" Another said, "This is different. We don't know enough to make a judgment." A third said, "You don't want to know the facts here. It could cost you a grand-jury subpoena and hundreds of thousands of dollars of legal fees."

I went back to my office and looked at the list of seventy-five press calls that I had received by midday. And I decided not to return any of them. The information shutdown, I thought, was total.

MY RESOLVE NOT TO RETURN CALLS was short-lived. A press feeding frenzy was underway as hordes of hungry journalists chased tidbits of information. My phone continued to ring incessantly, even after I told reporters that I had nothing to say.

It was clear that the old classroom whisper game was operating at its insidious worst. I would get a call from a reporter, asking me whether I had heard about a particular rumor. I would call several White House people to ask them whether they had any knowledge of this. Often those whom I called had already heard about the rumor from the same reporter, but wouldn't tell me that, only that they had heard the same rumor. Or sometimes the same reporter would call the individual whom I had just called, and get some type of confirmation that the individual had heard the same rumor. Every so often, a new piece of information would be leaked, its origins and reliability uncertain, further stoking the flames. And around and around, within virtually a closed loop of the same people talking to each other, we would go again and again. Often, to my astonishment, at least initially, the next morning I would actually find these rumors printed in certain newspapers, attributed only to anonymous "sources."

In the next several days, several reporters got burned by the rush to print new stories, not always based on reliable or corroborated sources. On Sunday morning, January 25, Jackie Judd of ABC News called me to say she had a source telling her that there was an eyewitness to an "intimate incident" between the president and Ms. Lewinsky. She went on the air with the report after I told her I could not help her one way or the other.

The same thing happened with David Jackson of the *Dallas Morning News*. He called me early the following evening, with a source telling him that a Secret Service agent had seen the president and Ms. Lewinsky in a "compromising situation." I had to tell Jackson the same thing: couldn't help him, either to confirm or deny.

The next morning I found out that overnight Jackson and the *Dallas Morning News* had had to withdraw the story, which they had rushed to post on the *News's* Web site, because their single source had called them back—after the posting—to tell them he had it wrong. (Months later, after the grand jury testimony was released to the press by the House Judiciary Committee, it was apparent that Judd had gotten it wrong too; no Secret Service agent had ever seen any "intimate incident," although there had been reasons for some agents to guess that such an incident was occurring.)

I felt sorry for Jackson. He was one of the better journalists on the scandal watch, and I knew he was scrupulous about getting it right and about being fair. As I hung up the phone, I also knew that we had made it difficult for Jackson and the others to write these stories. Our walls had gone up and we were in shutdown. This did not excuse reporters pushing beyond the facts under the pressure to beat the competition. But I thought: Didn't our shutdown invite, if not make inevitable, that kind of journalism?

I WAS THINKING ABOUT David Jackson, and the *Dallas Morning News* incident, and our at least partial responsibility for it, as I left the White House for the last time on Friday evening, January 30.

I turned to look back at the White House—brilliantly white under floodlights. Not for the first time it reminded me of a fairy castle floating somewhere in the center of the universe, the place where Andrew Jackson and Abraham Lincoln and Theodore and Franklin Roosevelt and John Kennedy had lived and worked and walked on the same stones I had.

I remembered how thrilled I felt the first morning, and indeed every morning, that I walked through the Northwest Secret Service gate, down the driveway, bearing right toward the West Wing, where the president and the Oval Office and the Roosevelt Room were, to the left the driveway bending in front of the main residence, with its white colonnades, heavy with history.

I remembered the day in mid–November 1996 when I was first offered the job of "scandal spokesman" for the White House by Jack Quinn, who was then White House counsel. I told him the charge I had felt when I walked down that driveway that morning, and he smiled and said, "If you ever lose that thrill as you come to work in this house, it's time to leave."

I remembered how much I believed in the Clinton presidency, and still do as these words are written—how Bill Clinton had remade the Democratic party into a new, centrist party, a party speaking to the concerns of both the middle class and the underclass; a party that could attract supporters in the South and in the suburbs as well as in the North and in the inner cities; a party that could keep the faith with the liberal values and concern for the poor that my father taught me was the difference between us and the Republicans; yet also a party that could balance the budget and take tough stands on crime, welfare, and family values.

But tonight my heart was heavy, burdened, sad.

I thought about all the damage-control rules we had learned, usually the hard way after making many mistakes, over the last fourteen months in dealing with scandal stories and bad stories and damaging stories; how we learned to get all the facts out, good and bad, early, often, and in context, thereby giving us a reasonable opportunity to comment and have our perspective on those facts reflected in the stories.

I thought about the rules we had learned for coping with the scandal-beat reporters, by fighting back against their inclination to "connect the dots" and jump to premature conclusions—not by making it difficult for them to report and get the facts, but rather by making it easy for them.

I thought about the tensions inherent in most public-relations crises—between lawyers thinking like litigators and the press and political people worrying about public opinion—and how an essential rule for effective damage control and crisis management required some balance and consensus between the two viewpoints and, most important, equal access for both to the facts.

And then I thought about my last ten days, about the way it appeared that the White House—now almost completely dominated by the president's attorneys and legal considerations—seemed to be embarked on a path regarding the Monica Lewinsky story that ignored every one of those rules. Every one.

And I felt sick to my stomach.

I

Whose Side Are You On?

MIKE McCURRY WAS IN A GOOD MOOD. I WAS IN HIS OFFICE ON December 10, 1996, my second day in the White House, and he was trying to explain my job as the press's point man on scandal. He was grinning like a Cheshire cat—as if he knew something I didn't know, saw something I didn't see. His feet were on his half-moon desk. Behind him were watercolor paintings by his children, giving a surreal impressionistic backdrop for a tutorial on how to handle the scandal machine.

This is going to be fun, he said, watching me suffer.

Some fun, I said.

I remembered the first time I talked to McCurry about whether I should take the job, just a month or so before. My title was supposed to be "special counsel to the president," but my central responsibility was to deal with the press on behalf of the president and the White House on a variety of "scandal" stories, primarily the ones dealing with the allegations of Democratic campaign-finance abuses. My concern was that since McCurry spoke for the president and the White House, and since I was supposed to do the same, if I took the job how would I know where his job ended and mine began?

"That's easy," he said. "Have you ever seen the bumper sticker, 'Shit Happens'?"

"Yes."

"Well, when shit happens—you speak."

We both laughed—the kind of nervous laughter, however, when a joke cuts just too close to the bone of truth. McCurry got suddenly serious. He told me, Your work on the scandal watch is more important than you realize, and has serious implications. Every time I am able to shovel a bad scandal-story question over to you, you'll be helping me—and the president—to put public focus on the president's agenda, on issues that the American people care about and elected him to work on. That means, he reminded me, that it's your job to take the poison, to catch the flak. (Whatever the metaphor, I got the point.) Your role, he went on, will be to separate the president and his press secretary from these scandal stories so that we can concentrate on doing the business of the country. This will be critical to the president's success in his second term. Remember that, he repeated, the stakes are enormous.

Then we talked about the strategic rules for damage control that we had both come to understand through more than two decades of experience in national politics, political campaigns, and dealings with the press corps. We did not invent these rules; they are well known to corporate crisis managers and to political consultants and press secretaries who try to minimize the damage of a negative breaking story. My predecessors at the White House—Harold Ickes, Jane Sherburne, Mark Fabiani, and Christopher Lehane—had had great success following these rules as well.

You can't help the president, McCurry said, unless you are credible to the press. In this place, there are some people who don't get it and will accuse you of consorting with the enemy, of forgetting whose side you're supposed to be on, and worst of all, of pandering to the press. Forget them. To help your client the most, you have work to do to establish your credibility with the press. Right now, he said, most of the reporters think you're a partisan pit bull for Clinton. (I winced inwardly, hearing that, realizing it was largely true.) You need to prove to them that you can defend your client while still being straight with them and helping them do their jobs.

He reminded me of the one absolute rule, with no exceptions: Never, never lie or mislead the press. If you are under pressure to, then refuse or resign. If you can't answer a question completely and honestly, then tell the reporter exactly that. If giving them half the information is going to mislead them into writing an inaccurate story, then give them nothing.

In this context, we then talked about the difference between "good spin" and "bad spin." The rules for dealing with bad news are not about turning bad news into good news. Facts are facts—and no amount of spinning will alter those facts. We can't change bad facts or avoid all damage. Rather, good spinning aims to minimize the damage—by surrounding bad facts with context, with good facts (if there are any), and, if possible, with a credible, favorable (or less damaging) interpretation of these facts. Even if there is no such damage-limiting interpretation of the information available, there is still a good chance that reporters and the public will discount the impact of the story if the object of the bad news proactively puts the facts out: "If they helped put the story out, how bad could it be?"

In recent years, the word "spinning" has been given a somewhat pejorative connotation. But this fails to distinguish good from bad. Bad spinning is essentially a strategy of deception. It attempts to turn a bad story into a good story by hiding or obscuring bad facts, by releasing information selectively and misleadingly, and sometimes by being less than completely forthright in answering media questions. As I was to learn, bad spinning is not only dishonest, it is ineffective. Sooner or later, the reporters will catch up with the omitted facts or, ultimately, with the misleading information. Then the story will be written with the additional "Gotcha!" element that always makes it worse—and the reporters who were the victims of the deception will almost certainly find a way to enjoy their revenge.

It was clear that McCurry and I spoke the same language, had the same philosophy about disclosure and accuracy. We talked for a while about his unhappy experiences the preceding fall, in the last few weeks before the November elections, when the Democratic campaign-finance stories first broke. He warned me that because the White House had mounted such an effective blocking action before the election to stop the press from writing stories about controversial Asian American Democratic fundraisers like John Huang and Charlie Trie, the press was out for blood and I would be the recipient of their ire. Which brought him to the next point, the core of our strategy in handling the campaign-finance scandal: I had to get all the bad stories written before the opening day of the Senate hearings, if possible over the Christmas holidays, when the politicians would be out of town and most normal people would be more concerned about their families and Christmas shopping than about John Huang and Charlie Trie. The key premise was that all these bad and embarrassing campaign finance stories are coming out anyway. By definition, the worse they were the more certain it was that they would come out. Better that they get written now so that they will be old news by the time the Senate hearings begin. People will be bored with this stuff by the time the TV cameras are turned on.

I'm going to be helping reporters write bad stories? I asked. Stories that will embarrass us, even damage us politically?

That's the inherent paradox in your job, McCurry said.

And you'll back me up when I am criticized for being on the wrong side—for consorting with the enemy? I asked. I knew that charge would be made early and often.

Yes, I will.

This is a job where I am certain to make mistakes, I said. I'm going to hold you to that.

We then discussed the importance of the baseline or "predicate" story: Help the reporter writing the first story, make sure it's complete, with everything in it—and in all likelihood the story will be over. From that point on, other reporters will find it when they search the LEXIS-NEXIS database of published newspaper stories, and so it will become the starting point for all future reporting. If you let the story dribble out in pieces, we agreed, there'll be ten bad stories, each half right and incomplete, rather than one bad story.

There are different ways of getting these predicate stories written, he pointed out. Sometimes there will be reasons why the White House will not want to officially put a story out on the record. I'd have to figure out a way to put them out anyway without asking permission.

Such as?

Learn how to place stories with individual reporters on background, he said—be fair, rotate so that each news organization gets a fair shot—and make sure they have enough information to write the stories fairly and completely.

He said he wanted to be kept informed at all times, but he would trust me to use my judgment, given my legal training, as to how much he should know or needed to know. If the leaks get you in trouble with some of your colleagues, he said, remember: As long as you are following the strategy of getting these campaign-finance stories that are coming out anyway written before the hearings, then taking the flak inside this place is as much your job as taking it from outside. He added, pointedly, Some people will seem unhappy with your leaks while knowing you are doing the right thing and giving them deniability.

Which brought him to his final point: The toughest part of your job is that you have three constituencies to be worried about, who at various times will be at cross-purposes: Your client, the president of the United States; the press; and your fellow lawyers in the counsel's office. When you are in the room with your fellow lawyers in the counsel's office, you have to be vocal in representing the White House's political and press interests. You will be the only person in this place who wears all three hats, he said. You will have to run the risk of angering some of your fellow attorneys by playing that role, but that's your job.

I was growing more and more anxious. It seemed as if he was prescribing a role for me destined to fail: one with a high risk of alienating my legal colleagues in the counsel's office; one of possibly angering the president by helping the press write bad stories about him; and, inevitably, one of being cut up in the press through anonymous leaks as being ineffective in obtaining information and lacking support from within the White House. And that would be the end of me. I said as much to McCurry.

He grinned, mischievously. Everyone who is a friend of Mike McCurry knows that grin—somewhere between childlike and evil.

He said I'd be fine, waving me out of the office, his feet back up on the half-moon desk. I tried to smile back. As I walked through the door, I was asking myself how the hell I had ever said yes to this job.

Hey, Lanny, one more thing, he called out. I turned around.

I'll back you up, he said. But don't fuck up.

There was that grin again.

I QUICKLY LEARNED, THE HARD WAY, that it's not enough simply to take the rules for damage control and start applying them. There was another set of rules that had to be learned too—the press's rules. A press secretary has to know these rules, just as a lawyer has to know the law. I had to learn the vocabulary for conversations with the press corps, their ethical values, the work habits and rhythms and pressures of their professional life. I had to learn how to argue without offending, how to concede the point and yield damaging information without being disloyal to the president. I had to learn how to be fair and avoid giving unfair advantages among hard-driving, ambitious competitors, while also grasping the subtleties of helping reporters who have given you a fair shake and not going out of your way to help those who haven't.

Vocabulary training was my first lesson. Unfortunately, when I arrived at the White House, no one, including McCurry, thought to teach me the difference between "off the record," "background," and "deep background." I guess they assumed I knew the difference. I guess I assumed I knew the difference. We were all wrong.

Less than two weeks into my job in the White House, on Sunday afternoon, December 22, 1996, I received a call from Ruth Marcus of the *Washington Post*. As I had already discovered, if there was a reporter anywhere working on a scandal story relating to the Clinton White House, the system McCurry had already put into place was that they would now be calling me, not him; and it would be my responsibility to listen to their questions, prod them into telling me as much information as possible to enable me to get them the accurate answers, and then get back to them. In this capacity, in the ordinary course of a day, I would receive twenty-five to fifty phone calls. In the middle of a breaking hot story, the calls would balloon to almost twice that number—all of them from reporters asking questions, needing information, public comment, or background comment, and needing it within hours or sometimes within minutes to meet their deadlines.

Ruth Marcus of the *Post* was interested in what had been discussed at a spring 1996 meeting between Michael Cardozo, director of the Presidential Legal Defense Fund (established to help the Clintons pay their legal bills), and senior White House staff. Specifically, she wanted to know whether the White House officials attending that meeting had advised Cardozo on what to do about returning hundreds of thousands of dollars in suspicious checks raised by Charlie Trie, a Little Rock restaurateur who knew Bill Clinton from his days as governor of Arkansas. Some of the checks, delivered by Trie in a brown paper bag, seemed to be legal, but many were written in the same handwriting, with the same misspellings, although each was signed with a different person's name. The issue of whether White House officials had advised Cardozo had important legal and political implications, because the Legal Defense Fund was established to be completely independent of and insulated from the White House, with a bipartisan board of trustees.

It had been reported in various newspapers that such a meeting had been held, and reporters were suspicious that senior White House officials had indeed been very much involved in the decision to return the checks, and then, remarkably, had kept the Trie checks secret from the press until after the November elections. Marcus was specifically interested in whether any White House official had argued to Cardozo that the nonsuspicious checks raised by Trie did not need to be returned, especially given the fact that the Clintons owed millions in legal fees. I had the impression from Marcus's questions and tone that she had a source telling her that such an argument had been made by someone at the meeting with Cardozo.

I hung up the phone and called one of the White House attorneys who was assigned to supervise my fact-finding in response to press inquiries. During my first days at the White House, I was informed by my supervisors in the counsel's office that I was not permitted to do any independent fact-finding to answer reporters' questions. I had to ask one of the White House attorneys to do the fact-finding for me. In this instance, I was told I could not call anyone directly who attended that meeting to ask Marcus's questions myself. The explanation for this two-stage process was that there might be information that I could not reveal to the press, and thus I might be compromised if I found such information out.

This rationale made no sense to me. If, for example, I received information that was subject to a legal privilege, I could always tell the reporter that I could not answer the question. In any event, this was one of the early arguments I lost or, more accurately, chose not to press at the moment. I was too uncertain of my position, my leverage,

or my ability to obtain reliable facts within the multilayered bureau-
cracies that constituted the White House complex. But I made a
mental note that at some point I would probably have to break out of
this prohibition and do fact-finding myself. I perceived that the real
reason for limiting my fact-finding powers was to keep information
closely held and to avoid leaks. It was also obvious that there must
have been some perception that I might leak some information that
was nonprivileged but embarrassing. In fact, that was precisely
what McCurry and I had agreed I was supposed to do—get the bad
stories out.

The fact-finding attorney called me back in a few minutes and
said that the subject of not returning all the checks had been debated
at the meeting, but that no White House official had taken a particular position one way or another. That sounded okay to me, so I called
Marcus back. I told her that I didn't have a certain answer yet, since
we were still trying to contact other people who had been at the meeting, but that for now, "on background," I could tell her that the subject of not returning some of the checks had been debated.

Several hours later the White House attorney called me and
said that after making several more calls to participants in the meeting, I needed to refine somewhat the answer that I had given to the
Post reporter. The subject of not returning the checks had not been
debated, but rather, a "question had been raised" as to whether the
checks needed to be returned. I was puzzled; I did not perceive a significant difference between having a debate and raising a question.
Aren't we asking for trouble by hairsplitting words like that? I asked.
No, was the answer, a debate implies that White House people were
taking a position on this matter, and that's not accurate. I called Ruth
Marcus back and gave her the refinement.

"But that's different from what you told me earlier," she said,
agreeing with the White House attorney that there was in fact a significant difference between my two statements.

"It's really not that different," I responded. "Debating something, versus raising a question whether something should be done—that's not really that different. Anyway, I was talking on background, and I told you we were trying to confirm this by talking to other people at the meeting."

After some back-and-forth discussion, in which I attempted to persuade Marcus that there really wasn't too much difference between the two formulations, she reluctantly agreed to use the second one.

A short time later, the White House attorney called me again. After talking to still more people who attended the meeting, the consensus was that the question that was raised at the meeting by a White House official was not *whether* the good checks needed to be returned, but rather how it would *look* to the public if the good checks were returned. The concern seemed to be that there might appear to be an ethnic slight if perfectly legal checks, all drawn by people with Asian surnames, were returned to the donors.

I thought this was a valid point to be concerned about, and I said so, but I also commented that this formulation was quite different from the previous two. Well, came the response, that is the most accurate answer, and you need to call Ruth Marcus back. I respected this attorney's devotion to accuracy and factual precision. But I worried that at this point I would be pushing Ruth Marcus one step too far. The attorney was adamant. I called Marcus back and told her the new formulation. "This is clearly the one most people remember, Ruth," I said.

Her reaction was not very positive, to say the least. She suggested that I had changed my story to avoid admitting that the White House had gotten involved in a substantive discussion with the Defense Fund trustees, and that she found it very interesting that I had given her three different versions within a few hours. That in and of itself, she said, was newsworthy.

"Wait a minute," I said, my stomach beginning to roll as I sensed that I was starting to get into very troubled waters. "We were on background. I told you I was trying to confirm this information each time we talked."

"I won't quote you by name, just as a White House official," she said. "That's what 'on background' means."

"I thought it meant off the record until I can confirm it," I answered, trying to hide my panic.

"Sorry, it doesn't."

"But you've got to use my last comment to you, because I am told that is the most accurate consensus of people's memories," I said, hearing a note of pleading in my voice.

There was a pause. I half held my breath, waiting.

"Okay," Marcus said. "I'll put into the story your last formulation—someone asking about how it would look to return all the good checks if they are all from Asian American names."

"Thank you, Ruth," I said, relieved.

"But I will also quote the first two statements you gave me on background," she said.

My stomach began to roll again. "What? You can't do that. That wouldn't be fair—I told you, I thought 'on background' meant 'off the record,'" I said.

Marcus was unrelenting: She believed that I had been tugged around by White House participants, who were concerned about a news report that some had, in fact, urged Cardozo not to send the good checks back and, now that the story had come out, were trying to blur what happened. Again I was struck with the impression that she had other sources on this, and that she knew more than I did.

I knew it was my fault for not knowing the difference between "off the record" and "on background," but I felt that in the first couple of weeks on the job, I should have been given some slack by Marcus. I asked her if I could appeal to her editor. She was very amenable to that, to her credit. Some time later, in the early evening, I had a conference call with Marcus and her editor, Sharon LaFraniere. I explained what had happened, but I could not convince LaFraniere that the *Post* should not print the fact that I had given out three different versions.

The next day's story headlined and led with the fact that the White House had described in "three different ways" what was discussed about the return of Charlie Trie's checks at the spring 1996 White House meeting. Clearly, a reader would be left to conclude that the anonymous "White House official" who put out those three versions was incompetent or dissembling or both. When I arrived at the White House that morning, the White House counsel, Jack Quinn, summoned me into his office and, in the presence of several other White House attorneys, told me there had been a great deal of unhappiness with my performance on the *Post* story expressed at that morning's senior staff meeting. I took the responsibility for not knowing the difference between "off the record" and "on background" and said nothing more. But as I left, I wasn't very happy about being forced to rely on others to do fact-finding and then to be left hanging alone when things turned out badly. I resolved that from this point on, I would do my own fact-finding when I felt the need to—without footprints, if necessary.

I went down to McCurry's office to commiserate and to complain that he had forgotten to teach me the difference between "on background" and "off the record." He agreed it was an oversight. He explained that "on background," as I had learned from Ruth Marcus, meant that the source would be identified not by name but by some generic job description or identifier, such as "a White House official," an "administration official," a "White House lawyer." And "deep background"—a term made famous by Bob Woodward's agreement with "Deep Throat" during his reporting on Watergate—means that the information or facts may be used, but the source cannot be identified, even generically, or quoted directly.

I never forgot during the rest of my White House tenure that it was necessary, indeed imperative, to start every conversation with a reporter with the question, "What are our ground rules?" Then I discovered that some reporters interpreted "off the record" as allowing them to report what I told them, but without attribution—which is what I understood "deep background" to mean. So I realized that I had to be clear what *I* meant by "off the record." I would frequently add the expression "not to be used at all," or "no pencil please"— meaning "no notes" and the reporter could not use what I told him or her, not even as a way to provoke another source to confirm it. Similarly, I discovered that there were different possible definitions of the expression "deep background," and it was wise to discuss what our understanding was when we agreed on this ground rule. For example, "deep background" can mean that the information cannot be used unless it can be confirmed by another source, or that it *can* be used, but only with a completely anonymous attribution such as "sources say," or with no attribution at all.

Just as I came to learn from on-the-job experience working with reporters that there were shades of gray in the definitions of key words and phrases, so I learned from experience that McCurry's absolute rule about not lying to or misleading a reporter might not be so absolute when, for example, it conflicts with another equally important imperative: to keep your word and protect another reporter's exclusive story.

During my first few days at the White House, McCurry called and told me to call the *Washington Post* and invite them to come over for an exclusive release of John Huang's correspondence with the White House. Huang was the controversial fundraiser for the Democratic National Committee whose suspect campaign fundraising had triggered the Democratic campaign-finance scandal. McCurry explained that the *Post* had been inadvertently left off a list of news organizations who had received information about Huang's visits to the White House, so he owed them one. The correspondence did not contain anything significant, as far as I could tell, but because of Huang's high profile and the increasing press interest in anything to do with the Democratic campaign-finance story, it would still have some news value.

We guided two *Post* reporters to a conference room in a corner office of the Old Executive Office Building and let them take notes while reading the correspondence. I was instructed by a White House attorney not to allow them to make copies so they could work back at their offices. I could not understand that, but I didn't argue. The reporters grumbled about it but went along. Since we had already turned these papers over to the congressional committees, which would be leaking them soon anyway, I saw no reason to make things difficult for the reporters.

I left the *Post* reporters in the conference room, attended to by my colleagues, and went back to my office for introductory appointments with two network broadcast journalists—Jackie Judd of ABC and Rita Braver of CBS. Each asked me whether there was any news breaking that evening, or anything new that the White House was releasing. I had to look them both in the eyes and say, No, there wasn't. In other words, I lied.

The next morning, after the *Post's* John Huang scoop was published, I received a not very friendly phone call from Jackie Judd and an even less friendly call from Rita Braver. I explained to both of them why I couldn't answer their question honestly. "If it had been your exclusive, I would have had to be dishonest with another reporter who asked me the question," I explained.

Both seemed to appreciate the difficult position I was in, but they were still angry that we had favored a print organization with an exclusive. Rita Braver pointedly reminded me that the White House frequently released documents and other news items after the evening deadlines for the network news shows, preventing her from broadcasting the story until the next evening, when it might be old news. She asked me to promise that I would never deliberately do that.

I had to be careful. I knew that we had to reserve the right to try to lessen the impact of a bad story by releasing it after the networks' deadlines—or, for that matter, the daily newspapers' deadlines. I promised Braver only that we would treat the networks and the news organizations fairly and, if we were doing a generalized release of information, I would try my best to do it early in the day so that the networks would have equal opportunity to report it. I used the expression "generalized release" to leave us the option of selective placements of news stories with particular news organizations and at particular times.

I learned some important early lessons about the disadvantage of these preferential placements, even if they were driven by valid damage control reasons. There is a serious equity imperative when a reporter or a news organization has developed proprietary information from its own investigations—meaning information derived from its investigative reporting that no one else has. However, in the case of McCurry's leak of the Huang correspondence exclusively to the *Washington Post,* there was no proprietary interest to protect. The exclusive was a present from McCurry, evidently because he had burned them on a previous occasion and felt that he owed them one. I learned that if I chose to give an exclusive story to one news organization, I ran a great risk of alienating the others and losing my credibility. At the very least, as McCurry had previously advised, I would have to rotate those leaks so everyone got a fair chance.

This was my first insight into the importance, and fragility, of the mutual trust between me and the reporters, which became a mandatory, indispensable staple of my ability to do my job effectively—and of theirs as well. An oral agreement that something is off the record, or a commitment to protect a proprietary work product by an investigative reporter, or an agreement by a reporter to protect my anonymity—these were the daily, mutual acts of faith that bound me to the reporter and vice versa. The fact that over time a culture of trust developed between me and the reporters with whom I did ardent combat each day on behalf of my client is still, in retrospect, a significant component of my White House education.

The need to protect the proprietary work product of the various reporters I dealt with was often complicated. Investigative reporters are often in a bind—if they seek White House help, or reaction, to a particular story, they run the risk that someone at the White House will tell one of their competitors about the information. Unless they could be confident that I would do my utmost to protect the information they had given me, they would not confide in me. A lack of such trust would have hurt the White House and the president, since it would have meant that we would not be able to comment or react to correct possible inaccuracies in a story until after it had been published. Sometimes the commitment to protect a proprietary piece of information meant that I was barred from conveying the information to anyone in the White House. I realized that I needed to be able to assure a reporter of this commitment, or else I would not learn the information at all. But I also worried that in such circumstances I could find myself in a clear conflict of interest, especially if I learned something very damaging about the president, something that the White House counsel's office clearly needed to know.

Another difficult problem was to sort out the protection of a reporter's proprietary work product when there were several reporters working on similar but not identical stories. One example of this related to the series of stories that were published in the first few months of 1997 concerning efforts by White House officials and friends of the Clintons to help former associate attorney general Webster Hubbell find clients for his law practice after he was forced to resign under a cloud in March 1994. The investigative journalists were operating under the theory (unproved to this day) that Hubbell had received all this assistance in order to keep him quiet concerning his knowledge of wrongdoing by the Clintons in Whitewater-related matters. It didn't seem to matter that no one could produce specific evidence to support this theory—no evidence at all that Hubbell knew anything that could hurt the Clintons, or that the individuals who hired Hubbell (or helped arrange the retainers) did so in order to keep him quiet.

In the first few months of 1997, virtually every major investigative journalist on the scandal watch was chasing leads to locate any new example of someone close to the Clintons hiring or trying to help Webb Hubbell. In early March, I heard from two of the best of them: Jeff Gerth of the *New York Times,* who had broken the Whitewater story five years earlier, and Glenn Simpson of the *Wall Street Journal,* who (along with Alan Miller of the *Los Angeles Times*) had broken the first Democratic campaign-finance stories in September and October 1996. First Gerth called and said he had information that Chief of Staff Erskine Bowles, when he had been head of the Small Business Administration in 1994, had made a couple of phone calls to try to get work for Webb Hubbell but that it hadn't amounted to anything. I argued strenuously to Gerth that there was no news in that and that this frenzy to write about people who helped Hubbell out of friendship was nuts. I made a note to follow up on Gerth's request, but perhaps because I gave so little credence to the seriousness of the story I put the request aside, knowing that Gerth was about to go on vacation.

Then Glenn Simpson of the *Wall Street Journal* called to say that he had heard that Mack McLarty had also made a few calls to help Hubbell during the same time period, and that McLarty had briefly told the first lady of his efforts to help Hubbell. Simpson was pretty close to writing, so this time I had to respond immediately. In the past several weeks other reporters from the *Los Angeles Times* and the *Washington Post* had also asked more general questions about who else at the White House might have helped Hubbell, and I had never responded.

At a senior staff meeting to decide what to do, McCurry and I argued strenuously that we needed to get this Hubbell story behind us and that Gerth's and Simpson's inquires gave us an opportunity to put it all out at once: that McLarty and Bowles had both acted out of friendship, innocently. We also learned that former U.S. trade representative and commerce secretary Mickey Kantor, a close friend of Hubbell's, had also helped him get some legal contracts. That did it. Now we could put out all three helpers in the same story and get it over with. And that was the decision. While one of my colleagues prepared the background "fact sheets" about the circumstances of each man's help to Hubbell, I repaired to McCurry's office to sort out the proprietary-work-product dilemma.

If we did a general release to all reporters, then the investigative work of Gerth and Simpson—which had triggered our decision to put out the story—would be busted. And that seemed wrong. Gerth had asked us about Bowles, not McLarty; Simpson had asked us about McLarty, not Bowles. If we gave Simpson the piece about Bowles, that would be unfair to Gerth; if we gave Gerth the piece about McLarty, that would be unfair to Simpson. Meanwhile, if we gave anything out to Gerth or Simpson that the other did not have, to some extent we would be unfair to the *Los Angeles Times* and the *Washington Post*, which had been asking for some time about other White House officials helping Hubbell. What to do? To make matters even more difficult, Gerth was out of the office on personal matters and would not be returning until the following day.

I proposed a solution to McCurry, and he agreed: We do an on-the-record selective placement with the four news organizations that had invested the most in this particular story—the *New York Times*, the *Wall Street Journal*, the *Washington Post*, and the *Los Angeles Times*. And we wait a day for Gerth to return. Waiting a day would be dangerous, McCurry warned; the story could bust by then, especially now that it had been the subject of a formal meeting. But I said it seemed unfair to Jeff Gerth, who was first to call, if he were to end up losing out on any participation in the story.

As it turned out, McCurry was right about the danger of waiting a day. The next afternoon, with Gerth back, we held a conference call in the late afternoon for just the four news organizations and gave them all the information we had about Hubbell. We finished the call about 5:00 P.M. At 5:30, I received a phone call from Pete Yost of the Associated Press. Yost had some of the best sources on the various scandal stories on the beat, including good sources in the newsrooms as to what other people were working on. "We're about to put a story over the wire about McLarty, Bowles, and Kantor helping Hubbell," he said. I was sure, knowing Yost, that he was enjoying the vision of the look of horror that had just taken over my face. "Does the White House have any comment?" he asked.

I knew that once the story hit the AP wire, everyone—including the TV networks—would be calling. Our efforts to protect the proprietary investments of the four news organizations in the Hubbell story had just gone up in smoke and we were going to catch hell from everyone else for not including them. I had no choice but to respond to Yost's question with the various statements and background information that we had just shared selectively on the conference call. I called McCurry to be sure he agreed, and he did. We called all four reporters to forewarn them that their exclusive was no more. Glenn Simpson had more reason than anyone to be upset that I had waited the additional day for Gerth's return, since he had uncovered more specific information than anyone else, and he reminded me of that, but he was gracious about conceding that we had no choice but to respond to the AP. I also called each of the network reporters to let them know in time to permit them to prepare a story by air time (fulfilling my earlier commitment to Rita Braver of CBS). As for those reporters who complained about not being included in the original conference call, I reminded them that if it had been their proprietary work product, I would have protected them as well.

I sensed, once again, that it was important for me to justify myself and my ability to be fair and to be trusted among these reporters. It was not about trying to please them, or even trying to look good in their eyes. It was about my effectiveness in doing my job. If they didn't trust me, they wouldn't confide in me and let me help them write their stories accurately and completely. If I couldn't do that, then my client's interests would be injured—and, most assuredly, my viewpoint on behalf of my client would not always be prominently mentioned in the stories they wrote. Of course, for the same reasons, they needed my trust in them to be fair and balanced in their reporting if I was going to help them get the information and sources they needed to do their jobs.

THERE WERE TWO MAJOR TECHNIQUES that we used to implement McCurry's strategy of getting all the bad news out early and helping reporters write bad stories.

The first was overt and fully approved within the White House chain of command, at least in the first few months of 1997: Documents would be released to the press at the same time as they were handed over to the Congress. Over time the press came to call these episodes "document dumps." The second method was covert, both to the outside world and within the "official" channels of the White House—the selective placement of certain stories and hot documents with a particular news organization, on "deep background," in a manner designed to minimize damage.

The trumping argument used by McCurry and me for doing these document dumps was directly out of the rules: that the hot documents were going to be leaked anyway, or, worse, they would *not* be leaked, but would be released for the first time during nationally televised Senate and House campaign-finance hearings. Better that we put the story out ourselves, with plenty of opportunity to answer questions and to characterize the documents favorably, or at least accurately.

We first used this technique in late January 1997 when we released, all at once, thousands of pages of documents from the political files of former Deputy Chief of Staff Harold M. Ickes, who had served as the president's *de facto* campaign manager during the 1996 reelection campaign. And when we made these and subsequent "dumps" of large volumes of documents and materials all at once, we also decided, contrary to conventional wisdom and recent White House practices, to make it easy, not hard, for the reporters to write their story. We made multiple copies, gave them plenty of time to review them before deadlines, and stayed nearby to answer all their questions and give them on-the-record comments whenever possible. We did this not to be nice guys to the press, but in our own self-interest. By making it easier, we would maximize the chance that the stories would be written comprehensively, accurately, and with our viewpoint expressed.

The experience of standing in front of the room and trying to respond to questions from fifty to seventy-five reporters poring through thousands of pages of documents, each person focusing on different documents or different angles, is not easy to describe. I felt as if I were being cross-examined on the witness stand during a trial, except that rather than having one lawyer working on one case trying to trip me up, there were seventy-five lawyers working on multiple cases. And talk about pressure: If I made a mistake or used the wrong word or phrase, my mistake would instantaneously be made public and conceivably could do grievous harm to the political standing of the president and his administration.

My young colleague and deputy, Adam Goldberg, was my secret weapon. He prepped me, gave me talking points, cross-examined me and challenged me, so that by the time I stood in front of the assembled press corps there was little I could be asked that I wasn't prepared for. I was also blessed by the arrival of Rochester "Ches" Johnson, who served as press and communications assistant. Johnson had been part of the original Ickes-Sherburne damage-control team in the early days of Whitewater and the ensuing investigations. He knew where all the paper, facts, documents, and files were in the White House better than almost anyone—and there was simply no one better at searching LEXIS-NEXIS or making a quick phone call or a trip to the WAVES records room to obtain information or to confirm facts quickly and reliably.

EVEN THOUGH WE WERE SUCCESSFUL in getting many stories written immediately after each dump, in January and February 1997 Goldberg, Johnson, and I experienced an exponential explosion of follow-up questions, and new lines and subjects of inquiry. These included requests for particular documents that led to other documents that led to other areas of possible campaign-finance abuses. We were receiving as many as fifteen to twenty-five requests for new information every day concerning Democratic donors: WAVES records, correspondence, attendance at political and fundraising events, interactions with the president. But we were still required to rely on a small crew of White House attorneys to get us answers. And they were spread very, very thin, trying to keep up with the slew of subpoenas from congressional committees and the Justice Department. We also ran into some resistance to our counterintuitive notion that we should help reporters write bad stories. We struggled under a daily, growing backlog of unanswered inquiries from the press, usually averaging over fifty, and faced increasing frustration and unhappiness from the press corps with our nonresponsiveness. And so in spite of our efforts at openness, in these early months stories were nonetheless starting to appear about White House "stonewalling," as if we had something to hide.

But we kept trying. In addition to the document dumps, our second device for getting bad stories written early and accurately was the so-called "deep-background private placement." This device had to be used covertly, hidden not only from the outside world but even within the official White House chain of command, since there were at times reasons why, as a matter of policy, the White House would not release a document—for example, if it had not yet been turned over to a congressional investigating committee that had requested it and there was a concern that Republican committee chairs would be offended by the premature leak. We did this rarely; this method was almost always limited to a potentially very damaging story that was complicated, and therefore needed a baseline or "predicate" story to frame the issue. I never did a deep-background private placement without at least someone at a high level of the White House chain of command at least generally aware of what I was doing.

The advantages of the predicate story as a critical tool of damage control cannot be overstated. For damaging stories that have complicated facts, particularly ones mixing facts and legal issues—as was almost always the case in the campaign-finance stories for which I was responsible—the predicate story is simply mandatory. If it is complete and accurate, it will likely kill or at least diminish follow-up stories, since there won't be much more to report. If it is incomplete and wrong, then the LEXIS-NEXIS database will cause it to repeat and grow, like a virus, more and more difficult to catch up with, correct, and cure.

By its very nature, a predicate story takes time to investigate and time to write, and thus does not lend itself to the competitive pressures and imminent deadlines that are inevitable when there is a general release to all news organizations. That is why it was necessary to select a single reporter or news organization to help generate such a story. This offered us the luxury of being able to take as much time as necessary to work with the reporter, give him or her all the facts and documents, get all the questions answered, and engage in an ongoing back-and-forth dialogue to sort out the facts and legal issues accurately. Finally, this procedure offered us the maximum chance to get into the story our interpretation or characterization of the facts most favorable (or least damaging) to the president.

Of course the main disadvantage of the deep-background private placement was that it pissed off the other reporters who were not the recipients of the exclusive. Under McCurry's guidance, when possible, I tried to rotate these placements so that all felt they were being treated equally. However, in certain instances, when we were trying to kill the impact of a story, we used certain news organizations for this purpose. And we chose certain time periods or days of the week to place these stories with the same purpose in mind. Usually our first choice was the Associated Press. Not only was the AP's team of investigative reporters first-rate and notoriously fact-oriented and fair, but we found that when an AP story went out on the overnight wires the major daily national newspapers, such as the *Washington Post* or the *New York Times,* would not be inclined to give it front-page play. If they printed it at all, it was often buried on an inside page. More important, if an AP story was comprehensive and accurate—meaning, if it was an effective predicate story—it was less likely that the major dailies would have much left to report the following day.

Two other news organizations of choice for placement of our deep-background predicate stories were the *Wall Street Journal* and the *Los Angeles Times.* It might seem odd that the *Journal* was one of our favorites, given the ideological hostility towards Clinton and his administration regularly reflected on its editorial page. But the *Journal* had some of the best reporters in the city—led by Glenn Simpson and Phil Kuntz—covering these scandal stories. And the *Journal* almost never put current political news on the front page; it usually got placed on the back page of the front section, which often diminished the impact of the story. We liked the *Los Angeles Times* for similar reasons. The *Times* also had three reporters who were very highly regarded for their fairness and balanced reporting: Alan Miller, Glenn Bunting, and David Willman. And for reasons that again seemed to us based more on institutional pride than anything else, the major national daily newspapers resisted repeating stories broken by an "out-of-town" newspaper such as the *Los Angeles Times.*

A good example of such a private placement is the way we handled documents suggesting that President Clinton had made fundraising calls from the White House residence. It appeared, according to the call sheets and surrounding information we had about those calls, that the president's purposes and words during the phone calls had been ambiguous. He had not clearly asked for money, but in his usual elliptical fashion had thanked people for their "support." The fact that in some cases donations had followed the call clearly implied that the president would be suspected of having solicited campaign contributions. The call sheets also suggested, but did not definitively prove, that the president's phone calls took place on phones in the White House residence. If so, this would have made them legal even if they were direct solicitations. The Justice Department had long ago held that the residential part of the White House was not a "federal building," and thus not intended to be covered by the federal restrictions against making political solicitations on federal property.

The call sheets had been uncovered in May or early June 1997 and would have to be turned over to congressional committees. Clearly, this would make a very big story—one that, if not reported accurately and comprehensively, could damage the president and perhaps even lead to the appointment of an independent counsel.

So we decided to call John Solomon at the AP and invited him to come over to the White House to look over the call sheets and to answer any other questions he might have. My colleagues and I had come to regard Solomon as a factually-oriented and fair journalist. He would kill us with stories, for sure; but he usually went the extra mile to be fair and complete in his reporting. Several members of the White House counsel's office were present to help me walk Solomon through all the documents, explain the underlying laws and rulings, and respond to his questions. One other tactical decision needs mentioning: We called Solomon on Thursday, July 3—so that the story would go out over the wires just in time for the newspapers on Friday, July 4.

Solomon wrote the story as comprehensively and completely as we had hoped—and included comments from me that the calls would have been legal even if there had been a direct solicitation. By the time the Fourth of July's fireworks and picnics and celebrations were completed, we hoped, there would be little interest among journalists—and less among nonjournalists—in whether the president had made a few ambiguous and completely legal phone calls. Maybe there might be a follow-up story in Saturday's or Sunday's papers, but since Solomon's story was so complete, there really wouldn't be much to report. By Monday, we hoped, the story would have died down almost completely. As it turned out, we were right. Manipulative and strategic in the choice and timing of the publication of this story? I guess. But though we were obligated to be honest with reporters, we were not required to be suicidal.

This is a perfect example of good spinning: the facts got out, in context, and we helped diminish the impact of the story not by deceiving but by ensuring a comprehensive and accurate treatment of those facts.

One delicious aspect of the deep-background private placement is the awkward position in which it puts rival news organizations, who might otherwise bitterly complain about not being the recipient of the placement. "Why did you give Solomon that story?" one reporter asked me on July 5. "It's not fair to favor the AP over the rest of us."

I waited, sensing what was coming next. I was not disappointed. "You should have placed that story with me."

2

Making Waves

MY FIRST REACTION WHEN I READ THE STORY WAS: HOW DID HE get into the White House so many times? I had only been there twice—and then accompanied by several hundred perfect strangers who were on the public tour with me. This guy John Huang has been there *seventy-six times in fifteen months*! That is unbelievable, I thought. And very suspicious.

If I had this reaction, I could only imagine the reaction of others less favorably inclined toward the president.

The date was October 31, 1996—just five days before the election. John Huang had been in the newspapers a lot over the past few weeks, along with several other Asian Americans who had raised campaign funds for the Democratic National Committee. Much of the money they had raised had questionable sources; some of it apparently had come from foreign bank accounts.

The story of Huang's White House visits appeared to have been leaked by Republican staffers on a House subcommittee that had subpoenaed Huang's Secret Service WAVES records. The way the White House handled, or, more accurately, mishandled the story of his WAVES records, and the nature and purpose of his visits, is a classic example of how *not* to do effective damage control—proof of the adverse consequences of allowing the opposition to put the story out first and of withholding all the facts from the press until they dribble out over time.

First a brief explanation of those WAVES records. One cannot fully appreciate how badly the White House handled the John Huang WAVES story unless one understands what information is stored in these records, including how it gets put in and how it gets retrieved for analysis.

When someone is scheduled to visit the White House, he or she has to be "WAVEd in," to use the White House jargon. A "sponsor" must enter information into a White House computer hooked into the Secret Service computer, providing the visitor's full name, birth date, social security number, citizenship status—or, if not a U.S. citizen, his or her passport number and country of birth, the expected date and time of arrival, and the name and location of the office to be visited (called the "visitee" on the WAVES record). When the visitor arrives and departs, Secret Service officers record the time of entry and exit.

So finding out who visited the White House, how many times, and when, should be as simple as typing the person's name into the computer database, hitting the "search" key and, bingo, there it is. Right? Wrong. As incredible as it may seem, when I first arrived at the White House in late 1996, there was no simple database information-retrieval system to break out WAVES information about a particular individual.

Instead, if a reporter wanted to know how many times someone had visited the White House and when, a staff member would have to sit and read the small-print hard-copy printouts—day by day, line by line—to look for a particular name. The records were recorded not in alphabetical order but were sorted by month, last name, first name, and date of entry. If John Jones came to the White House on October 1 at 10:00 A.M., left, and came back in the afternoon at 2:00 P.M., you would have to go to the WAVES records room and look up October 1; the name John Jones would be found twice, once in the morning and once in the afternoon. If someone asked how many times John Jones came to the White House over four years, you would have to sit and comb through every day's records for those four years, looking for the name John Jones, line by line.

Only in midsummer of 1997 did we discover that there was a way to pull up a particular name from the WAVES records using a software database program—but even then, we could not trust the results and still had to resort to untold hours of looking through every day's WAVES records to track a particular individual's visits to the White House. There are also a lot of pitfalls along the way. If two people with the same name are visitors, the only way to differentiate them is to compare birth dates and social security numbers. Of course, if you are searching thousands of names at a time, you may not remember to do that. You might also find the person's name in the WAVES record, but you may notice that he or she is not recorded as ever having arrived—perhaps meaning that this person was scheduled to come but didn't make it. Or there may be no record of someone who did actually attend an event. It is also possible that the "sponsor"—the person who "WAVEd in" the visitor—was not the actual "visitee," meaning that the visitor had an appointment with someone other than the sponsor.

Finally, unless you look at all the WAVES records data, you will not know what part of the White House complex the visitor visited. When most Americans hear that someone visited the White House, they think of the famous white mansion with the huge white-columned portico and West Wing facing Pennsylvania Avenue where the president lives and works. They imagine important high policy meetings between the visitor and the president and his top aides, and assume that such rarefied access is limited to only the most important and influential visitors. But WAVES records fail to distinguish between visits to the main White House residences, visits to the West Wing, and visits to the Old Executive Office Building.

The Old Executive Office Building, or OEOB, was completed in the late nineteenth century to house the State, War, and Navy

departments. Today it is considered part of the White House complex; thus, to enter the OEOB, all visitors must go through the Secret
Service White House WAVES procedure just as if they were going to
the White House residence or the West Wing. The OEOB is home to
some two thousand White House employees who work for various
agencies of the Executive Office of the President, such as the Office of
Management and Budget, the National Security Council, and the
Council of Economic Advisers. It is also where my office was located.
The building has several large rooms and auditoriums where briefings
can be held for large numbers of people and one room, the Indian
Treaty Room, that is the traditional site for large social receptions. On
several days every week briefings and receptions are held for various
organizations and constituencies that the White House hopes will
support the president's programs.

Thus, visits that take place at the OEOB have a connotation to
journalists and most Americans far different from visits to see someone in the actual White House or the West Wing. The West Wing is
where the Oval Office, the Cabinet Room, and the Situation Room
are. Approximately fifty senior staff have working offices there—as
does the vice president, whose office is just down the hall from the
Oval Office. A visit to the West Wing would have the appearance, if
not the reality, of a substantive meeting with senior advisors and possibly with the president, a meeting that could affect policy. Certainly,
from a political standpoint, there would be an implication of much
less significance if someone is said to have visited the OEOB many
times for large group receptions or briefings in an auditorium than if
he or she attended meetings in the West Wing with senior White
House officials.

IT WAS NOT JUST THE FAILURE to appreciate the intricacies of the
WAVES data that got the Clinton administration on the wrong
track in the early days of the Huang story. The rule about proactive

factual disclosure requires, first and foremost, an appreciation of the danger that the *negative message* of a story might pose, and then the search for the appropriate facts to be able to counter such a negative message. No damage control operation can be effective unless that evaluation and search occur first.

The political danger of the Huang story was not really about the unusually large number of visits to the White House by a big Democratic Party fundraiser. The fact that big donors receive invitations to the White House was neither unusual nor especially harmful politically. The real dangerous combination evoked by the John Huang story was *foreign money plus access* equaling a foreign power's influence on foreign policy or national security. The White House damage-control strategy should have been to put out a maximum amount of information about John Huang's White House visits in order to knock down the notion that Huang was given special influence over *policy.* Instead, the opposite occurred: information was withheld, or dribbled out, under circumstances making it more difficult for reporters to write the stories. The predictable result: the story ended up being much worse than it needed to be.

John Huang was a Chinese American who had been an official in a Little Rock, Arkansas, bank owned by the Riady family, a wealthy Indonesian family who are owners of the the Lippo Group, a multinational company. James Riady and Huang had gotten to know Governor Bill Clinton in Arkansas and had helped raise money for his gubernatorial and presidential campaigns. In 1994, reportedly in part due to the intercession of James Riady, Huang received an appointment as a deputy assistant secretary in the Commerce Department. In late 1995, Huang was appointed a deputy finance director for the Democratic National Committee, with responsibility to raise money from the Asian American community.

Beginning in the early fall of 1996, the first stories about fundraising excesses by Huang and the Riadys were broken by Glenn Simpson of the *Wall Street Journal* and Glenn F. Bunting and Alan Miller of the *Los Angeles Times*; this was essentially the beginning of the Democratic campaign-finance scandal. These and subsequent stories chronicled Huang's continued closeness to Lippo and the Riadys even after he joined the administration as a deputy assistant secretary of commerce. The stories also alleged numerous substantial contributions raised by Huang and other Asian Americans associated with him and the Riadys that appeared to be legally questionable, in that they were given by individuals who seemed to have little or no personal resources themselves or by companies that had no operating income from U.S. operations. These allegations, if true, would imply violations of U.S. campaign-finance laws.

The more controversial Huang became in the closing days of the 1996 campaign, the more the White House press corps clamored for John Huang's WAVES records to learn the frequency and purpose of his visits. The press strongly suspected that Huang had purchased unusual special access to the Clinton White House through his campaign fundraising and his connection to the Riadys, and that he had used this access to influence policy for the benefit of the Riadys. The White House knew that reporters were trying to make this connection—and mightily resisted giving the reporters even a morsel that might help them. For some time reporters had been asking what the president had discussed with James Riady at a September 13, 1995, meeting in the Oval Office. Also attending were John Huang and senior presidential aide and counsel Bruce Lindsey, who had known Riady and Huang from his days as an attorney in Little Rock. The suspicion was that Riady was there to promote policies for the Pacific Rim that would benefit the Lippo Group, particularly about opening up trade opportunities with China.

On October 16, 1996, *Los Angeles Times* reporters Jim Mann and Glenn F. Bunting reported that Bruce Lindsey had described this September 1995 Clinton-Riady-Huang meeting as "basically a drop-by social visit." The reporters added that "Lindsey said no issues of U.S. policy were discussed." Most of the press read Lindsey's comments as a categorical denial that any policy issue or anything else of substance had been discussed at that meeting. No one at the White House did anything to disabuse them of that impression in the days leading up to the election.

The *Los Angeles Times* reporters also asked Lindsey whether there was any discussion about fundraising, but Lindsey replied, "I'm not going to tell you what the meeting was about." You don't have to be a rocket scientist or a damage-control expert to know that an answer like that will drive reporters to find out what the meeting was about—and on from there, to fill in all the other blanks of the information that they suspect is being withheld from them.

And that is exactly what happened. The pressure to produce the WAVES information documenting the number and dates of Huang's visits to the White House grew exponentially as Election Day approached. Finally, the inevitable occurred. On October 31, portions of Huang's WAVES information were apparently leaked from a Republican-controlled House committee that had previously subpoenaed them. The information showed that Huang had visited the White House 76 times within a fifteen-month period from July 1994 to October 1995—the period of time when Huang had served as a deputy assistant secretary at the Commerce Department.

The White House had no choice but to respond, but it was not prepared. It did not have all the facts at hand about the Huang visits, nor enough information about those visits to explain them. Most important, it did not have a message ready to refute the notion that these visits proved that Huang (and implicitly the Riadys) had been granted unusual access to the White House and had been able to influence policy.

On the key issue of money for policy, all Mike McCurry could say was he was "unaware" of Huang having "sat in policy meetings." He also said that Huang had not been involved in any White House meetings about "fundraising." At his White House press briefing, he was asked whether the White House would provide more complete

WAVES records. He responded, "We don't have an exhaustive list of Mr. Huang's visits to the White House; in fact, we don't have possession of the records. . . . They're in the custody of the Secret Service." Later a McCurry deputy was quoted as saying that those records were "not available."

As things turned out, unbeknownst to McCurry, every one of these statements was essentially inaccurate. In the next several weeks, it was disclosed that Huang had, in fact, sat in on policy discussions between James Riady and the president in September 1995 and that the possibility of sending John Huang to the DNC as a fundraiser in the Asian American community had also been discussed. Moreover, the WAVES records were certainly "available," albeit in the "possession" of the Secret Service. The truth was, at that point the White House was not prepared to give out all the information it had on Huang, either proactively or reactively. And at the end of a campaign in which the president was ahead, it seemed to make sense to hold the line and get past the elections.

The initial round of stories from these Republican leaks of Huang's visits could not have been worse from the White House's viewpoint. The simple negative message established by the opposition's spin was that there was something wrong about all those visits—specifically, that Huang and the Riadys had bought unusual access as a result of Democratic fundraising and were attempting to influence policy in a direction favorable to the Lippo Group's commercial interests. It is a telling political fact that once this negative first impression was established, it lived on for the White House all the way through the campaign-finance congressional hearings, which were held in the summer of 1997. And indeed, it could be argued, it still lives on today. No clearer argument can be made for releasing the predicate story yourself, especially if it's a bad story.

On the second day of the story, November 1, unfortunately too late to be included in the first day's story, the White House did discover one semi-exculpatory fact. In reviewing John Huang's WAVES records, the White House discovered that—hard as it may be to believe—there had been, in fact, two visitors named John Huang. (The other one worked for Vice President Gore's Reinventing Government effort.) The result was that the John Huang who was the Democratic fundraiser had been to the White House 42 times, not 76 times. (I think at one point McCurry quipped, "This only proves two Huangs don't make a right.")

This confusion by the Republicans and the press caused some temporary chortling in the White House. But even so, 42 visits in fifteen months still seemed like a large number. And all the unanswered questions remained: What about other visits from before July 1994? What were his visits about? What about Huang's sponsors, the Riadys? When were they there? Who was talked to—and what policy issues were discussed? How many visits with the president himself? The reporters were as angry and as frustrated as they were energized. If the White House was holding all this information back, then by definition it must be bad.

WITHHOLDING INFORMATION is like a pressure cooker. If the heat gets too high, the story is going to blow. On November 15, 1996, ten days after President Clinton's reelection, White House officials thought they could relieve the pressure by releasing information on the total number of Huang's visits between 1993 and 1996. But they violated a basic rule of effective damage control: they tried to be half pregnant, putting out some, but not all, of the facts. This of course did nothing but guarantee greater pressure by the journalists to fill in the rest of the story. The White House chose to release the information on a Friday afternoon—through background briefings to the *Washington Post,* the *New York Times,* and the *Los Angeles Times*—so that the story would be published on a Saturday, a day when most people tend to disregard newspapers. Then the rest of the newspapers would be left to do follow-up stories that would get less play than if they were writing on the first day. This is a standard technique for killing the impact of a bad story. But in this case, because the information was not complete, it did not have that effect.

The White House disclosed only that between 1993 and 1996, Huang had been to the White House 94 times and had attended 15 "presidential events," that is, events that the president is scheduled to attend. No breakdown was provided differentiating the location of Huang's "White House" visits between those to the West Wing and those to the OEOB; no exposition as to who attended, what was discussed, or why the meeting or event was held. In other words, very few of the key questions journalists had been asking and were interested in were answered, most especially whether Huang had attended any meetings with President Clinton at which policy issues were discussed. Thus, McCurry's denial of knowledge of any such policy discussions remained unchanged.

But this limited release of Huang WAVES information only drove the story from bad to worse. The naked number released to the press—"94 White House visits"—seemed unusually high, as was the "15 visits with the president" (the phrase most reporters used, rather than the murkier expression, "presidential events," used by the White House). With no other information provided to fill in the gaps and provide context, these two numbers, 94 and 15, became the blank slates to be filled in by the opposition. Many reporters also noticed that the number of Huang visits acknowledged by the White House appeared to have risen from 42 before the election to 94 after. The fact that the 42 visits covered a *fifteen-month period* whereas the 94 visits took place over a *four-year period* got lost in the cacophony.

A few days later, the story got even worse, if that was possible. Now added to the money-for-access mix was the suggestion of cover-up. On November 18, Jeff Gerth and Stephen Labaton reported on the front page of the *New York Times* that "administration officials" said that Bruce Lindsey had resisted the recommendations of two White House lawyers for a "fuller disclosure" of the September 13 meeting between the president and James Riady, also attended by Huang—the meeting that Bruce Lindsey had described to the *Los Angeles Times* in the October 16, 1996, story as "basically a drop-by social visit" at which no policy had been discussed. The *New York Times* story went on: "Officials said Mr. Lindsey was the central figure behind the White House's decision to call the meetings social calls, ignoring the counsel of two White House lawyers who were part of a special team to handle sensitive inquiries." It then quoted White House special counsel Jane Sherburne as saying, "Bruce was concerned that if we overstate the case that these were much more than social, that we would be inaccurately describing them. I felt as did Mark [Fabiani] that calling them social would subject us to challenges. We recommended that the description be elaborated."

This article generated extensive follow-up coverage in the major newspapers and even on the TV networks. The editors of the *New York Times* even called for Bruce Lindsey's resignation. Two months later, in response to an inquiry from a *Los Angeles Times* reporter, Lindsey defended his characterization of the meeting as "basically" a social visit: "Mr. Riady's expression of support for a year-old trade policy and his hope that the President would continue to engage the Chinese leadership as he rose to leave an otherwise personal visit does not, in my opinion, convert the visit into a policy discussion."

It does seem rather odd that what seemed a minor semantic distinction between a meeting being "basically social" versus "basically social with one person making a policy comment" should blow up into such a big story, with serious damage to the White House's credibility with the press. Part of this was generated by serious internal disagreements, which spilled over into the press. There is no doubt that McCurry was not happy with the incomplete information he had been given on John Huang's visits on October 31, and with the fact that no one had corrected him in the intervening weeks. And it was also true that Bruce Lindsey's categorical statement to the *Los Angeles Times* in mid-October 1996 that there had been no policy discussion at all had never been modified. At bottom, this story unleashed a deep-seated and growing feeling with the press corps that the White House did not play with a straight deck.

Shortly after my arrival at the White House in December, I was called by Glenn Bunting and Alan Miller of the *Los Angeles Times,* who were working on a year-end story about the campaign-finance issues. When I read their piece I was somewhat shocked at the intensity of their conviction that the White House had manipulated and deceived the press on the campaign-finance issues before the election and continued to do so. As they wrote,

> In the weeks before the election, top White House, party and Commerce Department officials provided misleading accounts while also declining to release important details that probably would have intensified criticism of Clinton and the Democratic Party.

I did not believe in this instance that the White House had deliberately deceived the press. The reporters and the pundits often underestimated the difficulties that the White House attorneys and press office experienced in obtaining reliable information and their reluctance to put out incomplete information (with charges of obstruction of justice possible if an innocent mistake was made). But I also recognized that the instinct for self-protection often led people in the White House, especially the lawyers, to say and disclose only the bare minimum, hoping that more damaging formulations will not have to follow. As I was soon to find out, this understandable instinct for self-protection often caused more damage in the long run.

L OOKING BACK, IT IS CLEAR that the initial decision not to put out detailed and comprehensive information on John Huang's visits ultimately made this story much worse for the White House. Because there was so much mystery remaining behind his 94 visits, and with only a few factual dots on the wall, the press was left to its own natural instinct to connect the dots while driving forward to fill in all the gaps.

This realization came crashing home to me many months later, in July 1997, after the start of the Senate campaign-finance hearings, chaired by Senator Fred Thompson, Republican of Tennessee. When the subject of John Huang came up in the early days of the hearings, it was clear that the Republicans saw Huang as the linchpin of their argument that foreign money had polluted the electoral process through illegal donations to the Democrats. They saw Huang's frequent visits to the White House as proof of their theory. In large, colorful charts the Republican senators announced that the number of Huang visits between 1993 and 1996 was not 94, but actually 164! This raised further questions about the White House's credibility. The charts listed in detail each of the visits by date and "visitee": 39 visits in 1993–94 when Huang was still working for Lippo, 67 visits when he was at the Commerce Department from July 1994 to December 1995, and 58 visits when he was working in the Finance Division of the DNC. For 15 of the visits listed, the "visitee" was simply identified as "POTUS," the White House acronym for "President of the United States"—meaning, as I overheard Committee attorneys explain in the hallway outside the hearing room, that John Huang had "fifteen meetings with President Clinton" during this time period. And the number the senators kept repeating again and again—164 visits—was picked up and repeated by most of the broadcast and print media then and in subsequent weeks, and always to reinforce the same story line.

But wait! When the number "164" was first announced at Senator Thompson's hearings, I was sitting in a small anteroom near the Senate committee hearing room watching the proceedings on closed circuit television. The air conditioner was not working, and I was hot and irritable. Every time a Republican senator referred to John Huang's "164 visits to the White House," I threw a paper coffee cup at the TV screen. In a short time, there was a pile of cups on the floor. I immediately started working the phones, trying to reach press people.

"The number is not a hundred and sixty-four—it's ninety-three!" I kept telling reporters. (The original number released by the White House, 94, had been one visit too high; there was a duplicate WAVES record, for a single event that was inadvertently double-counted.) I explained that the Republicans had counted as visits the 45 times that Huang's name had been entered into the WAVES records *but there was no "time of arrival"* and—most embarrassing of all—they had also included in their count the visits by the other John Huang!

But it was hard to make much of an impact with the argument that Huang had visited the White House "only" 93 times—not the 164 times that the Republicans were arguing. It certainly was not an effective counter to the essential Republican message about Huang: money, access, and influence on foreign policy. The not-surprising unanimous response I got from most reporters about the Republicans' mistake: a big yawn.

I couldn't really blame them. Here I was playing "Gotcha!" with the Republican committee staff, but their mistake in counting was somewhat understandable. They certainly had been given even less help by the White House in trying to understand WAVES records than the reporters had. And I was still stuck with explaining away 93 Huang visits.

I wondered, in frustration: Was there any way to break down that number 93—to analyze how many of those visits had nothing to do with policy but were simply for social receptions or big group meetings? Such a breakdown was the only way, I realized, that we could counter the negative spin that had been established by the first Huang-visits story. Most people still thought of "White House visits" as visits to "the" White House—not to the Old Executive Office Building where such large meetings were traditionally held. I called Ches Johnson, my expert locator of all White House data great and small, and asked him whether it was possible to break down Huang's visits. I hoped we could do a precise count of the number of times Huang visited the West Wing versus the OEOB, and a detailed analysis of every one of Huang's 93 visits: who sponsored him in the WAVES records, whom he had really visited, and why. Johnson spent a good part of the next few days analyzing and reanalyzing all the information on the WAVES sheets. I spent time talking to individuals who had WAVEd Huang in or had met with Huang during that time period. I reviewed the president's private schedule on the relevant days to see whether I could substantiate the description used by the White House earlier—attendance at "presidential events"—as attending large group parties and receptions in the residence.

When Ches and I had finished all this research, the results were better than I could have hoped for. All those months of being pounded by the press and the Republicans about all those Huang visits—with the implication from the Bruce Lindsey/*New York Times* story that the White House had reasons to cover up a detailed explanation of all of Huang's visits—had come down to this amazing fact:

Of the 93 visits by John Huang over four years, 87 were entirely social or were part of big political group briefings in the OEOB. Only six had anything to do with policy, including the September 13, 1995, meeting at which policy was discussed for a few minutes by James Riady and the president.

I stared at the results of our efforts. The exhilaration of the discovery that this huge story had in fact been a nonstory from the beginning was somewhat dimmed by the understanding that it was probably too late in the day to get this story out. I tried, though. By now, the mid-July 1997 hearings had moved on to other topics, and John Huang was no longer in the news. I tried to interest reporters in what I had come up with, but few took the bait. Most made the obvious comment that it was a little late in the day for the White House, for the first time, to be willing to explain all of Huang's White House visits. Ouch. Only Glenn Bunting of the *Los Angeles Times* was sympathetic to my argument that the Huang–White House visits story had been hyped and misreported from the very beginning. He spent a good amount of time looking at our data and even began to prepare a story. But after he talked with a White House attorney who explained all the subtleties and complexities of the WAVES records, he got discouraged.

Out of frustration (and boredom from sitting in the little room all day long watching the Senate campaign-finance hearings on television—about as exciting as watching concrete harden), I engaged in my own spin fantasy. I imagined turning the clock back to October 1996, when the John Huang story was breaking and it would have been obvious that soon the press would be asking for his WAVES records. My colleagues and I would have completed all of our research and work well ahead of time along the lines of what we had just done in July 1997. We then would have prepared a comprehensive background fact sheet. I would have argued to the political hierarchy of the White House that we would do better to put this story out *ourselves* without delay, even before the election; the facts were on our side, and in this way we would demystify the Huang story, which was hurting us in the election in part because it seemed that we were afraid of it. Even if I lost that argument (which, in the closing days of a winning campaign, I suspect I would have), at least we would have been ready to put the story out ourselves right after the election—or at least we would have been fully prepared to respond when and if we were blind-sided by a Republican leak. Ideally we would have found a single reporter to write the predicate story, shown him or her the fact sheet and supporting information, and answered every question as best as we could. After the story was published, we would have released all the information to the entire press corps.

The fact sheet would refer to Huang's visits, not to the "White House," but to the "White House complex, including the Old Executive Office Building," so that from the very beginning, people would appreciate the distinction between the White House and the

OEOB that had been missed all these months. Here is what the fact sheet would have looked like:

John Huang Visits to White House Complex, Including the Old Executive Office Building 1993–1996

1. *Over the four-year period January 1993 through December 1996, John Huang had one meeting with President Clinton involving any substantive discussion.* That meeting occurred on September 13, 1995. It was brief and mostly social—attended by Mr. and Mrs. James Riady as well as Arkansas lawyers Joseph Giroir and Bruce Lindsey. The president knew Huang, the Riadys, and Giroir from Little Rock. For a few brief minutes at the end of the meeting, Mr. Riady, head of the U.S. branch of the Lippo Group, expressed his hope that the president would continue to try to have good relations with the government of China and encourage trade in the Pacific Rim. Also at that meeting Mr. Huang expressed an interest in leaving his Commerce Department position in order to help the president raise funds from the Asian Pacific American community through a post at the DNC. The president was supportive of that idea.

2. *There were other occasions over this four-year period when Mr. Huang attended an event where the president was present—but these were all group meetings of a political or social nature.* On one occasion, he attended a White House coffee, attended by the president and 15–20 other big Democratic donors. Thus, even though "POTUS" is listed as the "visitee," these were not actual "meetings with the president."

3. *Of Mr. Huang's 93 visits over four years, only six had anything even remotely to do with discussing any policy issues.* All occurred while Mr. Huang was a trade official at the Department of Commerce in an area of his expertise—trade affecting the Asian-Pacific nations. One was about budget issues, two about science and technology issues, one about an Asian Pacific summit meeting to be attended by President Clinton, one

relating to Indonesia issues, and one was the September 13, 1995, meeting with the president referred to in the first point, above. That was all. There is no evidence that Mr. Huang ever asked for anything as a result of those meetings or tried to influence anyone either before or after these meetings.

4. *Of the 93 visits to the White House, more than two-thirds (63) were meetings in the Old Executive Office Building*—mostly involving large group briefings, receptions, and personnel issues involving Asian Pacific American community issues.

5. *Of the 30 West Wing visits, aside from the one September 13, 1995, meeting attended by Mr. and Mrs. Riady explained in Point 1, above, none pertained to discussions of policy.* Virtually all of the rest were social lunches in the White House Mess or, after Mr Huang's move to the DNC job, a few political meetings in the Ward Room—a room in the West Wing expressly dedicated for political meetings in this and prior administrations—about increasing support from the Asian Pacific American community in the campaign.

I would have backed up this summary of the facts by a chart listing every single visit—date, time of entry and exit, person sponsored, person visited, and explanation. Then I would have tried to answer every conceivable question that any reporter had about those visits— all with the understanding that people's memories might be faulty over such a long period of time, and asking the reporters to note that caveat in their stories.

And so, because we had done it the right way, following the essential imperatives of full proactive disclosure early on, doing it ourselves, reporters would likely have given us a fair opportunity, high up in the story, to interject our interpretation of these facts:

The facts show that John Huang, though he visited the White House Complex 93 times over four years, met with the president on only one occasion when any policy was ever discussed, and then only for a few minutes. This single meeting resulted in no policy changes. Virtually all the rest of his visits, more than two-thirds of them in the Old Executive Office Building, were for social receptions, large group briefings, or about political matters after he left the Commerce Department to join the DNC. The fact that Mr. Huang, as an active fundraiser and political supporter of the president, visited the White House complex a large number of times over four years for a variety of social and political events should not strike anyone as unusual in comparison to prior administrations, or in any way inappropriate.

This is a classic example of what I have called "good spin": the assembly of all the facts—accurate, complete, and in context—and then the statement of a reasonable characterization or inference that can be drawn from those facts, one favorable to my client. In these four sentences, I would have reasonably countered (a) the hyperbole about an inordinate number of Huang visits to the White House beyond a large number of routine social receptions and big-group briefings; (b) the innuendo that Huang and Riady's fundraising prowess put them in a position to influence the president on policy issues; and (c) the sanctimonious humbug arguments by the Republicans that they were "shocked" that Huang's fundraising prowess had actually gotten him access to the White House. The bottom line was our core counterpoint message: The Republicans' attack on John Huang was nothing more than partisan politics.

Not a perfect story. Not even a good story. No matter what our spin, there would have been some political embarrassment over facts which show that money does buy access in American politics and that Huang received such substantial access essentially because of his fundraising prowess. But clearly, with all these facts laid out the story would have been less damaging than the John Huang story that actually got written—the one that in its distorted form, thanks to incomplete White House disclosures, drove the rest of the campaign-finance story so far for so long.

The ironic result, now much easier to see in hindsight: The main victim of the White House's reluctance to fully disclose everything on John Huang's visits was . . . the White House. It misjudged the seriousness of the story, with key officials wrongly believing that Huang had had an unusually large number of substantive meetings that, if revealed, would have damaging political effects. That misjudgment led to a series of counterproductive decisions: to be coy about openly discussing the substance of the September 1995 meeting involving Huang, Riady, and the president; to allow the Republicans to leak the Huang WAVES information first, and then to be ill prepared to respond; to make it difficult in the extreme for reporters to write a full and complete Huang/WAVES story once the decision was made in mid-November to put the information out; and worst of all, to permit the White House press secretary to be out there with only half a deck of information, thus allowing him to make statements that were factually incomplete or misleading.

It would not be the last time that Mike McCurry would find himself in that position.

3

Two Plus Two Equals Five

IN EARLY JANUARY 1997, JUST FOUR WEEKS INTO MY WHITE HOUSE job, I received a phone call from Alan Miller of the *Los Angeles Times*. Miller and his colleagues on the *Times* had been early in breaking the Democratic campaign-finance story, and a Republican-controlled House investigating committee had by this point subpoenaed and obtained thousands of pages of Finance Division documents from the Democratic National Committee. There was a journalistic buzz that these records conveyed overwhelmingly that the White House and the DNC had combined to produce large donations of "soft" money. These are unregulated, unlimited political contributions from individuals and corporations, which are legally permitted to be donated to a national party committee for "party-building" activities. It now appeared that White House events and facilities had sometimes been used as venues for these fundraising efforts.

Yet Miller surprised me when he asked me whether I had ever heard about a formal DNC program for "White House coffee klatches" for donors and the President.

I knew the term "coffee klatches," of course, as a political colloquialism for inviting a small group of neighborhood people into your living room to meet and have coffee with a candidate.

"I have a source telling me," Miller continued, "that a series of White House morning coffees were held in 1996 to raise money for the DNC, attended by the president."

No particular alarm bells went off. I knew a little about the Hatch Act, the federal law restricting political and fundraising activities by federal employees. I had the impression that as long as money was not solicited at an event held in a federal building, there would be nothing illegal about such an event.

"What do you want to know?"

"I'd like to get a list of the dates and attendees at the coffees."

"That shouldn't be a problem—I don't see this as a big deal."

Talk about understatement.

That afternoon, I joined a telephone conference call with DNC officials and asked about the White House coffees program. "What program?" was the first reply by the DNC's counsel.

"I'm told it was a formal program to invite in donors to have coffee with the president."

"We had lots of events at the White House, some of them coffees, some of them dinners, some of them political motivating events," was the reply. "We're not going to release a list of attendees. It will embarrass our contributors."

That struck me as an odd objection, since under federal law all campaign contributors are listed in filings that are a matter of public record. In any event, I still hadn't gotten a direct answer to my question, whether there was a coffee klatch program at the White House specifically for campaign donors. And that raised suspicions in my mind that perhaps the lawyers were hiding something because there was something dangerous about such a coffees program.

Funny, I thought—for the first but not the last time during my tenure at the White House—I was reacting the way reporters react when they can't get answers to questions.

For the next several days, more and more reporters, presumably talking to the same sources as Miller, were calling and asking about the White House coffees. It was clear that they were talking to DNC officials who were telling them about these coffees, specifically the fact that they were fundraisers. I kept asking, and re-asking, for the information, but could not get answers or even confirmation that there were such coffees. I started to realize that the resistance I was encountering in getting answers to the reporters' questions was not simply the normal political resistance to cooperating with the press. I began to think that at least some of the DNC legal and finance people were lying to me.

The first problem was practical: It was unclear where the list of all the coffees and attendees was, or indeed whether it existed at all. Many reporters think that any information they want concerning the White House is filed by subject area in some readily locatable central file. But this is often not the case in any large organization such as a big corporation, still less so in the White House, which operates under both space limitations and budgetary constraints. I was told, and it rang true to me, that there was no central list in one file of the so-called White House coffees sponsored by the DNC. It was true that there had been many different kinds of political events at the White House sponsored by the DNC, and that all of them mixed political guest lists with donor-oriented guest lists—and, most of the time, there is little basis for differentiating between these two. Since there were so many different kinds of "coffees" held at the White House during this time period—some of them for political purposes having nothing to do with fundraising—it would take time to gather the lists and be sure they were complete.

There were also political concerns about full disclosure of the White House coffees program. There was a perception that it would be politically dangerous to admit that the White House was used during the campaign not only for political purposes, but also to motivate people to give money to help reelect the president. The staff was also concerned that publishing the names of attendees might embarrass them and make it less likely that they would want to make contributions in the future. Often this concern was cloaked under the comforting mantra of protecting the "right to privacy" of visitors to the White House.

And, of course, the lawyers weighed in, warning against full disclosure of the White House coffees information. Since the files were not well organized and the list of attendees not very reliable, there was a concern about completeness and accuracy. In the environment of a White House subject to congressional subpoenas, the innocent omission of even one name or two would surely be the basis for politicians and commentators to charge cover-up.

Most significantly, the lawyers quickly made it clear that they were concerned about whether or not it was lawful to hold a fundraiser in the White House. The Hatch Act (a federal law passed in 1939 whose official name is "An Act to Prevent Pernicious Political Activities") prohibits "solicitations" of funds on federal property and by federal employees. Here's what a November 27, 1995, legal memorandum by two DNC attorneys stated on the subject:

> DNC events, whether they are fund-raisers, donor maintenance or anything else, cannot be held in any government building, including the White House. The only exception is that donor maintenance events (not fund-raisers) may be held in the Executive Residence portion of the White House. . . . No contribution can be solicited in any federal building.

That sentence became the bible for us as we decided how to handle the White House coffees story—and the parenthetical expression, "not fundraisers," also became the unquestioned and unchallenged premise that drove the entire strategy for it.

A S THE ISSUE OF THE WHITE HOUSE coffees got more and more play in the press, the role of the lawyers in the damage-control process grew commensurately. As a lawyer who was also a press-relations person, I had a unique perspective on the split that was developing between the press-political side of the White House and the legal side.

Lawyers are trained to hold back bad facts as long as possible, within the limits of the rules of professional ethics. If a question calling for damaging information is asked under oath, the lawyer is trained to answer the question asked, but as evasively and generally as possible; no lawyer ever volunteers damaging information that hasn't been directly asked. If documents are subpoenaed, the lawyer is trained to parse carefully the words of the document request; if there is any rational way to read the request as *not* calling for a particular damaging document, then that document should not be surrendered. The professional obligation is to be honest in responding to questions from any adversary in a civil proceeding, but not helpful. Under no circumstances should a lawyer volunteer damaging answers to questions or damaging documents not specifically asked for, or assist a careless questioner to clarify an ambiguous question. To do so could constitute professional malpractice.

In contrast, the political-press adviser's instinct is to do the opposite: Put the bad news out yourself—indeed, help the reporter ask the question to obtain the bad news—because, as McCurry and I discussed early on, sooner or later it's going to come out anyway so you might as well put it out yourself rather than let the opposition do it for you.

The reporters often tried to depict this split between the political-press people and the lawyers as a division between those who favor disclosure (the forces of light!) and those who want to hold it back (the forces of darkness!). But things are rarely that simple. There are legitimate issues and concerns on both sides.

Looking at it from the White House attorneys' perspective, there are practical and legal constraints on the process of gathering and proactively disclosing the facts. First, in any large organization, whether it be the White House or a big corporation, there are thousands of file cabinets where a document might be lurking, innocently overlooked, ready to explode if it turns out to be important and perhaps damaging. In private litigation, most lawyers understand the possibility that even after a diligent search for all documents in response to a subpoena, some might be missed. But the stakes are much more dangerous for White House lawyers in a politically charged environment. An innocent mistake—the explanation least believed in Washington nowadays—can, and did, lead to charges against White House attorneys of obstruction of justice along with the incurring of substantial legal fees.

The fear of being accused of obstruction of justice or witness tampering also deterred White House attorneys from making inquiries on behalf of the press to obtain facts or information from other executive-branch officials. If this seems far-fetched, this is precisely the charge that Republicans on the Senate Whitewater committee made in 1995 after it was learned that the Clinton White House counsel's office had called the Treasury Department to inquire about a rumor that the Resolution Trust Corporation had made a criminal referral concerning the president's involvement in the Whitewater land deal.

In this instance, the White House had pursued the course that McCurry and I would have chosen, calling the Treasury Department in order to prepare accurate responses to press inquiries. Yet the Whitewater committee depicted this fact-finding effort as an attempt by White House officials to influence or put political pressure on those at the RTC who were investigating the Clintons and Whitewater.

From that point on, the White House counsel's office almost never permitted any phone calls to be made to other agencies or departments to gather information in response to press inquiries. Indeed, once the congressional investigations of Democratic campaign-finance abuses began in 1997 and various subpoenas had been issued for information and documents from the White House, there were times when White House attorneys were reluctant to interview individuals in the White House itself to gather information in response to press inquiries, for fear of being accused of "witness tampering" or obstruction.

The lawyers also resisted, for many of the same reasons, the creation of any new document characterizing or summarizing information for release to the press. Compiling information in the form of a new document means not only that the document may have to be produced in response to a subpoena, but also that the compiler could face critical questioning (and huge legal fees) especially if the document turns out to be less than complete or to contain innocent mistakes. An incomplete summary could be a basis for accusing the author of deliberately withholding material information that had been subpoenaed—a potentially criminal offense. Again, as I came to understand more fully over the course of my days at the White House, it was easy enough for me to insist on a summary of WAVES information to make it easier for reporters to report; I wasn't the White House attorney who would be subpoenaed, put under oath, and asked why the document omitted or mischaracterized a particular fact that might be been damaging to the president.

Then there was the overwhelming factor of the independent-counsel statute. All dangers of criminal prosecution are fearsome, especially to the targets themselves, but the danger of a criminal prosecution by an unaccountable independent counsel is the most fearsome of all. For a White House always facing the possible triggering of an independent-counsel investigation, the stakes are far higher than a corporation's financial liability in a product-liability case. Any admissions or proactive disclosure that could lead to the appointment of an independent counsel, no matter how slight or trivial they may be, are resisted, and for good reason, by both White House lawyers and outside counsel.

This led to a *de facto* adoption of the Zero Risk Rule. As attorneys, we are trained in law school and in law practice that if there is any risk at all of civil or criminal exposure to our client in making an admission or assisting reporters in writing damaging stories, and there is no legal downside for refusing to do so, then our client should stand mute.

Note that I said "no legal downside." What gets tricky, very tricky, is if there is a significant political downside to refusing to answer questions or to refusing to put out information requested by the press, but only a small legal downside, what should the damage-control strategy be? The strict application of the Zero Risk Rule in all situations, then, becomes a counterproductive show stopper. So those on the political-press side of the discussion will have to make such a compelling political-downside case for remaining silent or refusing to be completely forthcoming that it forces acceptance of some legal risk as a price worth paying.

Striking that balance is never easy. Both sides should have some doubts, if they are being honest, no matter what the decision is—to take the risk and put it out, or to batten down the legal hatches and take the political hit.

Finally, there was the simple reality of the workload and the pressure on a small number of White House attorneys who were forced to respond to volumes of subpoenas, document requests, questions, and constant accusations and demands for meetings from as many as twenty Republican-controlled congressional committees as well as the independent counsel. My legal colleagues and I were just another pressure point on this small group, trying to get their attention and time away from all the other demands that they faced daily.

During my first few weeks at the White House, I was routinely assigned an "in-house lawyer" to do my fact-finding, with mixed results—as I learned when I wound up giving Ruth Marcus three different accounts of a single meeting back in December 1996. It was the unhappy task of these lawyers to supply me with all the information the press was demanding about dozens of stories on campaign finance, all breaking at the same time.

Among the lawyers who were assigned to me for this purpose was associate White House counsel Cheryl Mills, who had joined the administration in 1993 and knew more about the issues, personalities, and various investigations than anyone else in the counsel's office. In the early days she and I often clashed, sometimes strenuously, usually over the same issue: I would want to push out information when the press wanted it, and she would insist on accuracy and completeness, with what I sometimes felt was an excessive concern for legal risks. She gave me a headache sometimes, and I know I gave her a bigger one in return. The tension between us, with two legitimate sets of concerns tugging at us, was healthy and even indispensable in an institution like the White House. Even when we were at loggerheads, there wasn't a minute when I did not respect her greatly.

But before Cheryl and I reached the point where we would have taken each other's heads off, into the breach came another special counsel to the president, Lanny A. Breuer, who arrived in late January 1997. Breuer had been given the responsibility for organizing a staff of four young attorneys to respond to all the subpoenas, deal with congressional, Justice Department, and independent counsel's investigators, and, last but not least, put up with my constant nagging for information, answers to questions, and authority to do more document dumps.

There was something beyond coincidental, maybe karmic, about the arrival of Lanny Breuer. I had rarely met anyone else named Lanny. (His mother, like mine, had named him after the title character in the "Lanny Budd" series of novels written in the late 1930s by the famous muckraker Upton Sinclair.) There was also something very lucky for our damage-control operation about his arrival: Breuer helped us to break the logjam of unanswered press inquiries. He had the additional resources of his young legal team to help us with the variety of stories we were working on. These lawyers would be assigned to do all the document review and fact-gathering to prepare Adam Goldberg, Ches Johnson, and me for reporters' questions. Of course there were tensions. I remember one lawyer loudly complaining, within my hearing, "Why is it every document in Lanny's presence somehow gets out into the press the next day?" I think inwardly she knew the answer, knowing what my job was, and over time there grew an unspoken understanding that it was the responsibility of my team to get information out the door and the responsibility of Breuer's team to put the brakes on us to make sure we got it right. Breuer, in the cross fire, had to be the broker, the mediator among some highly egotistic and temperamental personalities, but somehow he managed to make it all work.

At the outset, Breuer had limited political experience and had little understanding of the requirements of the press. However, over time, he learned that no decision in the White House can be a purely legal one, but must reflect political and press considerations as well. Breuer also worked out with me a subtle understanding that certain decisions McCurry and I had to make regarding the placement of stories did not necessarily need his formal approval. And I made sure to keep him "in the loop" so that he would never be blind-sided by bad news. The ultimate court of appeals for conflicts between the press people and the legal people was the deputy chief of staff, John Podesta, who ran our morning strategy meetings. Aside from McCurry, there was no one in the White House I relied on more than Podesta for advice and counsel and constructive criticism.

M Y OWN INTRODUCTION TO the conflict between press and legal considerations grew out of my efforts to answer what at first seemed like a simple factual question: Were the White House coffees fundraisers?

By late January 1997, after the press had run numerous stories based on leaks from Republican sources, the White House was forced to respond to a subpoena concerning records and lists of attendees at these coffees. Now that we knew that the information would be in the hands of a Republican-controlled committee, and was thus sure to be leaked anyway, we made the decision to release the names of coffee attendees ourselves, even though from a political standpoint we felt an instinctive discomfort in admitting that the White House had been used to raise money for the campaign. Call it the "tacky factor." We felt that the aura and mystique of the White House was such that using it as a resource to raise campaign contributions would seem, well, unseemly to many people.

Our legal analysis was, unfortunately, less clear than we had initially believed. Based on the DNC legal memorandum quoted on page 88, we had unquestioningly assumed that the simple—and exclusive—legal question under the Hatch Act was whether a "solicitation" had occurred on "federal property."

Within the context of this apparently simple legal rule, however, there were still some ambiguities. What is the definition of "solicitation"? We were pretty certain, as far as we could determine, that no "solicitations" for contributions had occurred at any of these White House coffees. But what if someone said, "I hope you will continue to support the president's campaign," and the word "support" was understood to be a euphemism for "financial contribution"? Suppose a contribution was sought and obtained immediately prior to, or after, the event? If everyone knows that you are expected to give money in order to go to an event on federal property, is a contribution in effect "solicited" at the event, even though the actual request is made a minute before or a minute after? What is a "federal property," anyway?

None of the White House lawyers, myself included, were certain of the answers to these questions, not only because most of us weren't election experts but because in fact these were questions that could not be definitively answered. So much depended on the facts, intentions, and circumstances. In such a case, legal training drove us into the Zero Risk Rule mindset.

Thus, we faced a tricky problem concerning the handling of the White House coffees story—caught between the something's-tacky-here political factor and the ambiguity concerning legal risk. It was that combination, therefore, that led us to adopt what we thought was the appropriate "spin": We would never concede that the White House coffees were "fundraisers." Indeed, we would try not to refer directly to "money" or "campaign contributors," preferring instead "support" or "supporters." If we had to describe an event attended entirely by campaign contributors, we would describe it as for "donor maintenance" or "donor motivation." We couldn't even say that such an event had anything to do with raising money. I swallowed hard, and went along.

Thus, when I prepared a set of talking points in preparation for possible questions I would be asked, I wrote:

> The coffees were not fundraisers. They were events planned in part to thank and motivate prior political and financial supporters.

To address the legal issue, I would always focus on the concepts of a "requirement" to give money and "solicitation" of money at the event; I interpreted both issues as being important to address under the strictures of the Hatch Act:

> No money was *required* to be contributed in order to attend and no solicitation for funds occurred at the event.

On the afternoon of Thursday, January 23, we distributed the complete list of DNC-sponsored White House coffees and attendees; the final number came to 103 coffees, each usually attended by about twenty "supporters." That evening, I held a conference call for about fifty reporters. I said that most of the coffees had been held in the first half of 1995 and that they were all held in the Map Room, a beautiful sitting room on the ground floor of the White House Residence, so named because it had been used by Franklin Roosevelt to track troop movements during World War II.

At each coffee, the president would arrive around 9:00 A.M., walk around the room, say a few words to each of the attendees, and then, once everyone was seated, speak generally about his program and campaign themes. As far as we could tell, and apparently as a result of legal advice from the DNC's general counsel, no mention of campaign donations was made by anyone at the coffee event, and funds were never directly solicited. Nor, as far as we knew, had anyone been told that he or she had to commit to giving a certain amount of money in order to go to the event.

As we had anticipated, almost all the reporters' questions reflected a skepticism of my denial that these coffees were fundraisers. I continued to stress the two other denials in my talking points—no "requirement" to contribute and no "solicitation."

Then someone on the reporters' conference call asked whether I considered it to be "appropriate" that one of the DNC coffees, attended mostly by bank executives, had also been attended by the comptroller of the currency, Eugene Ludwig. The comptroller of the currency, I knew, was the nation's top bank regulator. I had not had an opportunity to review the list of names of attendees of all the coffees; in fact, I had not seen the list until five minutes before the call, which infuriated me. So that question caught me completely by surprise. I pushed the hold button and asked some of my colleagues from the counsel's office who were in the room with me for advice on how to answer. One of the attorneys called a senior White House attorney for advice, and I was handed the phone.

"Well, since the president was there, you can't say it was inappropriate, can you?" he responded. I didn't argue—though a voice in my head was screaming, "*Of course* it's not appropriate for the top banking regulator to be at a DNC Finance Committee event with a bunch of bankers!" I quickly punched back onto the phone line. "There was nothing inappropriate about that," I said, using a double negative formulation that reflected my sense that this might not altogether be a good answer.

"Suppose the comptroller himself said that he was never told the

DNC was the sponsor of the event and wouldn't have attended had he known?" asked Tim Weiner of the *New York Times*. Unknown to me, Ludwig's representative had said as much to another *Times* reporter.

Gulp. "My answer is the same," I said, trying not to let anyone know I was feeling a choking sensation in the back of my throat.

Why that sensation? There was no suggestion that his presence was illegal, since there was no evidence or suggestion that any of the bankers present had asked for a favor or obtained a *quid pro quo*. However, the issue was one of appearances. How does it look for the comptroller to be at an event sponsored by the fundraising arm of a national party committee? Doesn't it convey the impression that if you want favorable treatment from the comptroller's office, you ought to give money to the Democrats?

The fact is, there's a certain line out there that most people in politics know exists—the line between appropriate and inappropriate, suitable and unsuitable, a fuzzy but still definite line that is in the eye of the beholder. Having a nonpolitical federal regulator attend a political-finance related event is not only over that line—it's way, way over that line. How, I wondered, could anyone at the DNC or the White House whose idea it was to invite Ludwig or who approved the invitation not have understood that? How, I wondered, could someone as seasoned and politically astute as Bill Clinton not have seen that line?

I knew that this story was not going away. The immediate consequence of denying the obvious is that the scandal machine press will be driven, sometimes into a frenzy, to prove that the obvious is the obvious—or to put you through the maximum humiliation for continuing to deny it. Over the next several days, through the weekend, the press reaction to my statement that Ludwig's presence at the coffee was "not inappropriate" was overwhelmingly negative. On Saturday morning, a *Washington Post* editorial questioned my credibility in denying that Ludwig's attendance at a DNC finance-related event, where he was surrounded by the people he regulates, was inappropriate. I drove to the White House and went immediately to the West Wing, where I talked to several senior aides about revising my comments defending Ludwig's presence. "You can't reverse yourself now," said one senior attorney. "You'll get killed—and you just started this job." Said another: "If you say this was inappropriate, you'll be trumping the president—and yourself. You can't do that."

It was clear to me, however, that while reversing my position would be embarrassing, unless I did so we would be feeding the underlying story line that the Clinton White House saw no line between propriety and impropriety at all—and that, in turn, would feed into other stories about the campaign-finance scandal.

The president was scheduled to have a press conference on Tuesday, January 28. Prior to our usual preparatory session with him, some senior aides got together to review what would be the likely hot questions on campaign finance. I suggested that we find a way to have the president trump my position and say, basically, that Ludwig should not have been at that event. The consensus was that this would not be smart, since an admission by the president that he had done something wrong—after all, he had attended the event, too— would blow up the story and keep it going even more. I disagreed, because inwardly I knew that denying the obvious never works.

I went to see McCurry before the briefing of the president and told him what I intended to do.

At these pre–press-conference sessions with the president, those of us involved in the various scandal issues, as well as the chief of staff, Erskine Bowles, and the vice president, gathered to do a kind of dress rehearsal of what the president would likely be asked. Usually these sessions took place in the Oval Office, sometimes in the Cabinet Room. McCurry always emceed, happily playing the role of hostile reporter, asking nasty and obnoxious questions designed to get the president's goat. He was often successful in this role.

When McCurry asked the president at the January 28 briefing

to justify Ludwig's presence at the coffee, President Clinton seemed genuinely confused, indicating that he hadn't known about Ludwig being invited or being there until he had walked into the room. McCurry pointed out that throughout the preceding weekend I had been defending the decision to invite Ludwig.

I saw my opening. I told the president that that shouldn't be an issue, that it would be much better for him to say he hadn't known about Ludwig and, in retrospect, that the comptroller shouldn't have been there. The vice president agreed, suggesting a phrase or two for the answer. I had already come to appreciate the political instincts and wisdom of Al Gore when it came to advising Bill Clinton, and his critical importance in the Clinton presidency. As he often did at these pre–press-conference briefings, he would wait for the right moment, after some discussion had occurred, and then weigh in with his views—and the president would always take his advice. I looked at the vice president gratefully, although I knew that, in effect, the president of the United States would be publicly contradicting me.

At the press conference, the president responded to a question on Ludwig's presence at the coffee almost exactly as the vice president had advised: "In retrospect, since the DNC sponsored it, I do not think the comptroller of the currency should have been there. I agree with Mr. Ludwig and he should have been told who was sponsoring it. . . . It would have been better if he had not been there. Regulators should not come to meetings that are sponsored—have any kind of political sponsorship, I don't think."

As I had anticipated, the controversy over Ludwig virtually ended after the press conference. I learned three important, early lessons here about effective damage control: First, don't put anything out to the press without reviewing all the material and at least trying to anticipate problematic questions. I was put in an impossible situation by not knowing about Ludwig. Had I known, we could have sorted out a better answer, including having the time to go to the president to ask him whether he had known that Ludwig was going to be there.

Second, if you make a mistake and can correct it early, do it—even at the expense of short-term embarrassment. As it turned out, the correction of my "not inappropriate" comment on Ludwig's presence occurred in less than a week's time—not bad under the circumstances.

Third, don't underestimate your client. We all assumed that President Clinton had known about Ludwig being present and that he would defend the invitation; we didn't want to embarrass him by saying that Ludwig's presence was inappropriate. Even though at the press conference he never used the word "mistake," the "in retrospect" formulation made the point that needed to be made.

Of course, it was also an early lesson that denying the obvious never works.

UNFORTUNATELY THE CONTROVERSY over the coffees did not end there. Indeed, it got worse. The reporters now had a great incentive to prove, contrary to our denial, that the coffees were indeed fundraisers.

For the next several weeks, story after story appeared quoting "DNC sources" as saying that there *was* a price tag on attending the coffees—most with the number $25,000. Then several newspapers compared the coffee guest list to the database of DNC contributors filed with the Federal Election Commission—and found that attendees at these coffees had given a total of $27 million to the Democratic Party in 1995 and 1996.

In typical spin mode, I challenged the reporters concerning the $27 million and offered my lawyer's interpretation: "All that means is that big donors get invited to White House coffees—not necessarily that they are asked to contribute money as a price tag for going." I also pointed out that a large percentage of that $27 million (I didn't know how much) had been contributed in 1995, before the first White House coffee was scheduled.

Then, in early February, documents released from the files of former deputy chief of staff Harold Ickes added a few more facts to the equation, making it even more difficult to deny that the coffees were "fundraisers." First, one document from Evelyn Lieberman, another deputy chief of staff, explicitly described them as such. A handwritten note from the White House deputy political director, Karen Hancox, to Ickes stated: "Harold—Here are the coffee attendees (with POTUS) & amts. raised." Finally, the document I considered the killer: A spreadsheet with numerous coffees listed by date, and called "POTUS Coffee," with the number "$400,000" under the heading "Projected Revenue," and then in the next column, under the heading "Raised to Date," the number "$400,000."

When McCurry and I saw this DNC $400,000-per-coffee spreadsheet for the first time we were not happy, to say the least. We wished we had seen it earlier or, even more, that the DNC legal and finance people who obviously knew about it had brought it to our attention. But since we couldn't turn back the clock, we soldiered on. I presented the spreadsheet to a colleague in the counsel's office, and we tried to figure out whether McCurry and I could gracefully back off our denial. But after some discussion, we found that we were still nervous about the legal implications of using the White House for an overt fundraising purpose. And so, reluctantly, we stuck with the dual formulation (completely accurate, I might add) that no money had been solicited at any coffee and no one had been required to give money in order to attend. McCurry and I stayed with the script, but not very happily. Each day, during his press briefings, I would watch McCurry on closed-circuit television, as he danced around what was, or was not, a fair definition of "fundraiser." It was as pleasant as watching him scrape his fingernails across a blackboard.

For example, during one press briefing, McCurry insisted:

No, they were not fundraisers, because fundraisers—I've been to them, you've been to them— . . . you buy a ticket, you sit down, you have a bad chicken meal and you listen to the speech. But you have to buy the ticket to get in. These were not events in which you had to buy a ticket to get in, nor was there any solicitation of funds made by the president at the occasion, and that's why they were not fundraisers.

What about the reference in the documents to specific amounts that were supposed to be raised from these coffee events?

No, it doesn't turn it into a fundraiser, but it makes it part of the effort to build financial support for the party.

So now an "effort to build financial support" is not a fundraiser. Right.

McCurry also pointed out that some people who attended these events did not make a contribution afterwards—which he called "another important point" to prove they were not fundraisers.

As I tried the same verbal gymnastics in my prepared statements to the press, I began to wonder, Why are we making this argument? I went to McCurry. He grimly agreed. It was no fun. And not at all believable.

The answer still seemed to be: Because if we admit they were fundraisers, we could be admitting to an illegal act by the president, which would trigger an independent counsel investigation, which would be a disaster, perhaps for all history, and it would all be blamed on McCurry and Davis. And so we had no choice—under the mandates of the attorneys' Zero Risk Rule—but to continue to deny the obvious and insist that the White House coffees were not fundraisers.

EVEN THE PRESS GETS TIRED out if enough time goes by. Once the second set of Ickes documents had clearly established that the DNC had set specific fundraising goals of $400,000 per coffee and that those goals had been met, there wasn't too much reporting left to be done—aside from the ongoing effort to humiliate me every time I denied the obvious. The White House coffees story sort of petered out, replaced by numerous other examples of big donors buying perks and access to the White House and to the president.

Then, in the late summer of 1997, I discovered—to my utter amazement and chagrin—that the whole painful exercise in denying the obvious had been completely unnecessary. I learned that the core legal advice that had triggered the Zero Risk Rule—the November 1995 DNC memorandum warning that under federal law no fund-raisers could be held anywhere in the White House—was wrong. Just plain wrong.

First, it was simply not true that the Executive Residence of the White House was considered to be a "federal building" and thus subject to the ban on solicitations.

I learned this accidentally while researching another matter, namely, whether it was legal or illegal under the Hatch Act to "solicit" campaign contributions from the White House West Wing. I read a 1979 memorandum by the Justice Department written in response to an inquiry concerning a fundraising luncheon held on the second floor of the Executive Residence and hosted by President Jimmy Carter. During that luncheon, someone stood up and uttered words that could have been interpreted as a solicitation for campaign funds. The question presented was whether that solicitation was a violation of the Hatch Act, that is, whether the Residence area of the White House is equivalent to a federal building subject to the Hatch Act, or rather is simply the private residence of the president.

The writer analyzed the legislative history of the Hatch Act and concluded that the Act was only applicable to a government building where "official business" was intended to be conducted, and that the White House Executive Residence was the private quarters of the White House and thus was not intended to be subject to the Hatch Act.

Translated from that legalese: The president could do anything he wanted in his home, including pitching people directly for campaign money. Thus, even if the White House coffees *were* deemed "fundraisers," and a direct solicitation did occur, it would have been legal.

But was the Map Room part of the Residence? It was on the ground floor, not on the second floor, where the president and his family actually lived. And at times the president hosted diplomatic officials and other official guests in the Map Room. The Justice Department memorandum actually addressed this issue. The Executive Residence might have "dual-purpose" rooms used for both official and private purposes. In such an event, the memorandum stated, it could be legally used for political purposes so long as the costs were borne by the president personally or by his campaign or political party.

So we could have said up front, from the beginning, that the coffees were for the purpose of raising money—flat out, straight and simple. The DNC could have solicited contributions right in the middle of those events and been perfectly within the law to do so.

Which left only the political-sensitivity issue, the "tacky factor," as the reason why we went though all those semantic arguments denying the obvious about the coffees. True, there was some political risk to admitting that the Clinton campaign and the DNC were using the aura of a visit to the White House as an additional incentive to raise big money. That would undoubtedly offend some people, especially a certain slice of journalists, pundits, and editorial writers who see politics and fundraising as a dirty business, and thus see a fundraiser at the White House as inappropriate.

But in retrospect, this political downside would have had little effect. Polls consistently show that most of the American people understand that both political parties engage in relatively tacky efforts to raise political money, for such is the system. I would have reminded everyone that it shouldn't be so shocking that the Democrats, once they had a president living in the White House (a rare event over the last thirty years), tried to take advantage of that for fundraising purposes. Even with using the White House, the playing field wasn't level in terms of competing with the Republicans. In the 1995–96 election cycle, the Democrats were still out-fundraised by the Republicans by over $200 million. And, as things turned out, we subsequently discovered White House videotapes of President Ronald Reagan pitching the Republican "Eagles"—large donors to the Republican National Committee—for additional "help" during a meeting in the East Room on the main floor of the Residence. So let's not take too seriously the sanctimonious "shock" of Republicans when they heard that the White House coffees might have been about raising money.

That may sound like the old "everybody does it" defense—and we were certainly accused of that defense every time we tried to make the argument that the Republicans did it, too. But this is the key: During the Watergate era, the Nixon people tried to say that "everybody does it" and that makes it okay. What we were saying was "Everybody does it and it's not okay, so let's clean up the system." That's why in our daily strategy sessions, during and after the White House coffees story, we would always add: We've got to clean the system up, both parties, through comprehensive campaign finance reform.

Anyway, that would have been my spin—my "good" spin. Yes, the coffees were fundraisers. They were legal. And they were neither surprising nor inappropriate. Period.

THE ULTIMATE LESSON I LEARNED from handling—or more accurately, mishandling—the White House coffees story is that if you try to deny the obvious, regardless of the valid legal or political reasons for trying to do so, no one will believe you—so why try?

It's amazing that such an elementary rule should be so frequently violated by people in the middle of a public-relations crisis. The fallacy of trying to deny the obvious begins with a cynical, possibly elitist judgment about the intelligence of the average person—and the assumption that he or she can be sold something that you would never believe yourself. Even if people are sometimes that dumb and you are sometimes that smart, there is a second fallacy here: Before you get your viewpoint through to the public, you ordinarily will have to go through a communications filter called the media.

Of course there may be individuals in the media who will want to believe what you say when you insist that the obvious is not so obvious, but you can't count them on more than one hand. People in the press are like everyone else in their common-sense instincts as to what rings true and what doesn't. They are trained over the years to assume that what they are being sold by politicians is not likely to be true in all respects. Thus, their first reaction to an effort to deny an obvious fact will be to try to disprove the denial, and not to stop until they are successful.

In short, by attempting to deny the obvious, you only succeed in motivating the press corps to prove the obvious—and to prove you wrong.

The denial process is hard enough to resist for a politician or company about to face a public-relations crisis when it's just the normal instinct for self-preservation at work. Get a lawyer involved, and it becomes virtually impossible. This is because by professional training and experience we lawyers are trained, when faced with adverse facts that might endanger our client, to construct an entire denial edifice, comprising a series of building-block-by-building-block premises that neatly support the denial. The syllogism works like this: We have a problem. We define words and phrases that logically support an innocent solution to the problem, finding precedents for those definitions based on past denial edifices under similar circumstances (called precedents). We distinguish, or if possible delete, any words to the contrary and definitions inconsistent with our solution. Therefore, we tell the world (or more precisely, the judge or jury), the problem is solved—meaning that, in effect, there never was a serious problem in the first place. Within that semantic structure, all is logical, cogent, complete. How could anyone not agree?

But what happens when someone is outside the structure, unwilling (or unable) to appreciate the perfect syllogistic symmetry of the way things look from the inside? Now we switch to another metaphor—the story of the emperor's new clothes. A rose may be a rose may be a rose because a lawyer says that only a rose can solve our problem—therefore we have a rose. Everyone in the emperor's town was ordered (by the lawyers?) to see the beautiful gowns and scarlet robes on the emperor, and they saw, they saw. But the little boy, who certainly was not a lawyer, looked from outside the bubble. And he saw—a naked emperor.

Somehow, McCurry and I spun and spun, we bobbed and weaved, and we insisted that the coffees were not fundraisers because no one solicited funds and no one gave funds *at the event*—ergo, it was not a fundraiser. And that was all there was to that. Well, that was not all there was to that.

Why do we lawyers think we—and our clients—can get away with denying the obvious? The Zero Risk Rule is very much at work here. We convince our clients (and even sometimes ourselves) that even if few people will believe us when we deny the obvious, we have no choice because by admitting the obvious we are exposing ourselves and our clients to legal risk. Better to stay where you are within the legal argument structure, and force the other side to prove that the internal logic is wrong, than to volunteer anything that can lead to even greater risk. But what I learned at the White House was that if you do admit the obvious and assume the worst-case scenario, it's amazing how often the outcome turns out to be much less damaging than was initially imagined.

As PLEASURABLE AS IT IS TO blame all of our problems with the coffees story on the lawyers—and as a lawyer, I concede that even I find that pleasurable, so long as I can blame all of our problems on *other* lawyers—in this instance that would be both unfair and inaccurate. In fact, those of us responsible for dealing with the press and for spin and damage control got swept up into the legal distinctions and none of the political people at the DNC and the White House who knew better chose to correct us. We bought into the legal advice too readily and uttered and re-uttered the implausible words about the nature and purpose of the White House coffees because we enjoyed playing the game. We convinced ourselves of the internal, semantic logic of our argument. Most important, we forgot about the essential rule of effective damage control: You can't change facts; therefore you must learn to use them as friends, not enemies.

Those coffees were held to raise money during a political campaign. That's a fact. It is also a fact that no contributions were solicited and that no checks were required or collected at any of these coffees, either. And they were successful at producing contributions. No amount of linguistic gamesmanship can alter those facts. Had we known from the beginning (and had the people from the DNC been more forthcoming with us during those early conference calls and with the press) that there was a fundraising program implemented by the DNC Finance Department, with the White House coffees an important component, we would have acted very differently.

We could have had time to review all the names of people who attended, researched the ones who proved to be most embarrassing (such as Comptroller Ludwig) and then prepared our explanation or reaction to their presence.

We could have prepared our legal research to explain to reporters why, contrary to conventional wisdom and basic intuition, it was quite legal to hold a fundraiser in the Executive Residence and why, given the practices of previous presidents, it was not unusual for such fundraising events to take place there.

By putting all this information out *first*—completely, in context—we could have gotten our interpretation of these facts fairly reflected in the reporting. And by not denying the obvious, we would have avoided the "Gotcha!" reporting that set out to prove, over months of investigative reporting, that in fact the White House coffees were fundraisers.

Arguably, the problem began much, much earlier. It was not about legal concerns, really. It was about the "tacky factor." The political operatives felt that there was something not quite right about using the White House so blatantly to cultivate big donors to give money—something, well, tacky. For this reason, the political people decided to keep the White House coffees off the president's official schedule, to keep them hush-hush, not to tell the press about them or invite the press in to cover them, not even to tell several high-ranking officials in the White House about them and their true purpose, including the White House press secretary. It is amazing, in a White House that was usually the leakiest ship in Washington, that news of these coffees never leaked and they were never written about at the time they were being held.

Months after the coffees story was over and everyone knew that our denial that the coffees were about fundraising had been absurd, McCurry and I played out the hypothetical scenario: What if the White House had publicized the coffees during the campaign? We concluded that one of two things would have happened: Either the political fallout would have been so bad that they would have been canceled, or the heat would have been taken and absorbed, and the story would have been old news by the time I arrived at the White House. In either case, we both concluded, it would have been better to have described these events from the start as fundraisers and not to have attempted to deny the obvious.

That we didn't follow this course shows the power of the tacky factor. But worse was yet to come.

4

Shocked, Shocked

IT BEGAN WITH A SINGLE PIECE OF PAPER, ONE OF SEVERAL THOU-
sand that comprised the political files of Harold Ickes, White House
deputy chief of staff.

Here is what it said:

TO: MARTHA PHIPPS

IN ORDER TO REACH OUR VERY AGGRESSIVE GOAL OF $40 MIL-
LION THIS YEAR, IT WOULD BE HELPFUL IF WE COULD COORDI-
NATE THE FOLLOWING ACTIVITIES:

1. Two seats on Air Force I and II trips.
2. Six seats at all private dinners.
3. Six to eight spots at all White House events. (i.e., . . . Jazz Fest,
   Ceremonies, Official visits . . .)
4. Official delegation trips abroad.
5. Better coordination on appointments to Boards and Commis-
   sions.
6. White House mess privileges.
7. White house residence visits and overnight stays.
8. Guaranteed Kennedy Center Tickets (at least one month in
   advance).

9. Six radio address spots.

10. Photo opportunities with principles [*sic*].

NOTE: Any money above and beyond the $40 million goal would require two additional Presidential events outside of Washington, DC.

I first saw this piece of paper late on a Friday night in January 1997. I had been on my way to the airport for a weekend trip when I received an urgent page from the White House to return. When I arrived, members of the White House counsel's office were sitting among boxes of documents that Harold Ickes was about to turn over to a congressional committee—documents that the committee had subpoenaed as part of their investigation of Democratic fundraising in the 1996 campaign.

For hours we looked through this trove of political memos and detailed fundraising plans administered by Ickes and his lieutenants at the White House and the Finance Division of the Democratic National Committee. I wasn't shocked that Ickes had played such a hands-on role in political and fundraising management even while he served as the White House deputy chief of staff. I knew that the White House was a political institution. The Hatch Act, which barred most federal employees from most political activity, did not apply to White House political employees for that reason. I recalled, for example, that James Baker, chief of staff to President George Bush, had managed the president's 1992 reelection campaign from the White House. I could not recall any Republicans criticizing Bush and Baker for allowing the White House to be used for political purposes or complaining about White House staffers spending working hours doing politics.

I heard a soft whistle and someone said to me, "Hey, look at this one!" She handed me what came to be known as the "Phipps memo," the document reprinted above.

Within seconds, I realized that I held in my hand an undoubtedly "hot document"—one that would be of great interest to the press corps. Here it was, all on one page—a clear example of how the Democrats intended to use the aura of the White House and the presidency as a fundraising instrument. It was breathtaking in its simplicity and directness. I immediately knew that this document would become an emblem of the underlying Republican story line of the campaign-finance scandal story: the selling of access to the president and the White House and other "perks" for campaign money. This story would undoubtedly have legs.

It occurred to me that there might be a legal issue here if some of these perks had been granted in return for campaign donations. For example, if someone gave a contribution in explicit exchange for appointment to a governmental board or commission, that could be a crime. But we knew that the game did not work that way. Contributors were asked to contribute. Perks and special access followed.

Those of us who had been in politics for some time knew that, like it or not, big political donations led to special access for the donor. This had been so for both political parties for a very long time, probably back to George Washington—indeed, probably back to the ancient Greeks, or at least the Romans.

Why do people give money to politicians? When you boil it all down, there are really only three legal reasons.

The first is idealism and conviction: They believe in what the politician stands for and they want him to get elected so that he can fight for those ideals. For example, during the Vietnam war, there were untold numbers of people who gave money to Eugene McCarthy, who was challenging then President Lyndon B. Johnson, because of his anti–Vietnam war platform, not because they expected any special favors from him after he got elected. Similarly, a lot of business executives contributed to Ronald Reagan's presidential campaigns not because they expected a *quid pro quo,* but because they shared his belief in lower taxes and a stronger national defense system.

The second reason is ego: Big donors want special access to the politician they have given money to because they want to feel important in front of their peers and family. They want invitations to special events, photographs in their offices, special phone calls and thank-yous from the public official. This is so for lower-level offices, and it is clearly so for the presidency. Knowing the president, the possibility of being invited to the White House for a state dinner or an informal meeting, and to have a host of other personal contacts and mementos from the president of the United States is reason enough for many people to give big campaign contributions—without ever wanting or expecting any political favors or regulatory or policy decisions that might benefit themselves or their businesses. In the cynicism of today's Washington, this motivation is often discounted or disbelieved. But in my personal experience it is very real for a great many people.

The third reason is the one that gets the most attention in the press: Big donors expect that if their candidate wins, he or she will remember the contribution in some fashion and grant access to the contributor when an issue comes up that will have a commercial impact on the contributor or his business. Note that I said *access*. After such access, the donor—and the politician accepting the contribution—is supposed to believe that the politician's subsequent policy decision will be made on the merits.

I stated the third reason carefully, within parameters that should make it legal. There is, of course, a fourth reason. It is the illegal version of number three, and it is called bribery. It means giving money not only to get access, but to get results—to effect a change in a vote or policy that would not have occurred but for the contribution.

Bribery is a difficult crime to prove, which is why convictions for this offense are rare in the history of American politics. To prove that a donor has committed bribery, one has to prove that the individual intended to give a thing of value in order to produce an official act (or omission). But to prove that a politician has participated in a bribery conspiracy, one not only has to prove the intent and the acceptance of a thing of value, but also the actual performance of the *quid pro quo*.

The distinction between a legal contribution with the expectation limited only to special access, and a bribe, producing a *quid pro quo* vote or change in policy, may be a fine one and very difficult to prove. Nevertheless, that is the line the law creates, one that our democratic society has countenanced since the earliest days of the Republic.

In short, the underlying premise expressed in the Phipps memo—that to raise big money, you have to offer your big contributors special perks and access—should not have been particularly surprising. Not only did big donors expect special access; very few politicians take a large donation without knowing that at some point the contributor (or his or her lobbyist) might call to ask for a meeting on a particular issue of interest, and that such a meeting would be granted. Or perhaps the call would be seeking an ego-driven perk—such as a special tour, or visit, or dinner invitation. In any event, the politician understands that something would be expected in return for the donation—something legal, but something nonetheless.

All of us who worked in the White House on the campaign-finance investigation knew how the system works. We were there precisely because we had experience in politics; we weren't shocked that big money gains special access. And we understood that granting such access in return for money didn't necessarily mean corruption or even anything to apologize for. Yet we were still electrified by the Phipps memo. In fact, when we first read it, and passed it around to one another on that late Friday night when we first were looking through the boxes of Harold Ickes papers, we reacted as if it was—well—not quite a nuclear bomb but certainly a very hot potato.

One reason was that while everyone understood how the money-for-perks system worked, seeing it so blatantly and simply laid out in writing made us uneasy. The idea of using White House coffees and overnight stays as a way to motivate donors had a high "tacky factor." It wasn't illegal, but it didn't feel quite clean either. After all, the DNC paid for all the expenses of the White House coffees and the president and the first lady had to pay for meals and miscellaneous expenses of anyone staying overnight in the residence, including any prospective donors. However, there were certain items listed in the Phipps memo that, apart from the poor judgment of anyone writing up such a list in the context of raising $40 million in campaign contributions, could have been illegal had they ever been implemented. For example, selling a seat on Air Force One or on an official trade mission abroad in return for a campaign donation clearly could have been illegal.

The importance of the "tacky factor" in our own thinking, even our unconscious thinking, grew out of the changes in our political culture in the wake of the Watergate scandal. Although Watergate itself had little to do with the issue of money-for-access, it certainly had a lot to do with how big money could be used for corrupt purposes in a political campaign. And it led to the enactment of a series of campaign-finance reform bills that put limits on campaign contributions to federal campaigns and imposed strict disclosure requirements.

Equally important, accompanying this reform legislation was a reform mentality, an entirely new cultural attitude that regarded politics and political money as inherently suspect. This new attitude challenged the old rules and understandings, namely that it was okay for contributors to get special access so long as the politician made his or her decision on the merits. It introduced a pervasive cynicism toward politics, a cynicism so great that the constitutionally mandated principle of the presumption of innocence had effectively been reversed. Once a politician accepted a large donation, he or she was presumed to have been corrupted in some fashion. The burden was on the politician to prove the negative, to prove that no bribery had occurred. The relatively bright line of the rule of law had been replaced by the blurry one of the world of appearances.

Suzanne Garment, a scholar at the American Enterprise Institute whose 1991 book, *Scandal,* is the best study of these changes in our political culture, observes that this "culture of mistrust" has been enforced by a corps of self-appointed adjudicators of political ethics, what she collectively refers to as the "Ethics Apparat." Garment devotes two chapters of her book to an analysis of the Apparat's excesses—one focusing on the dangers of an independent counsel with unlimited and unaccountable power and the other, with the subhead "A Cast of Thousands," describing the awesome ethics combines of congressional investigators, ethics agencies and enforcers, and inspectors general. Similarly, Peter W. Morgan and Glenn H. Reynolds, in *The Appearance of Impropriety* (1997), described an "ethics establishment," comprising a "complex of interest groups, journalists, consultants, government ethics officers, and legislators owing its existence to the Watergate scandal," who have created a new "appearance ethics." David Mann, in a February 1998 *New Republic* article on the prosecution of former agriculture secretary Mike Espy by an independent counsel, noted that "watchdog groups, the press and ordinary Americans have blurred the distinction between real corruption and faux corruption, between creeps and criminals, between law and morality." Ten months later, Espy was acquitted on all counts on charges that he had accepted such gifts as football tickets and dinners from businesses regulated by the Department of Agriculture. There was no evidence whatsoever that there had been any *quid pro quo* to these gifts. Two statements issued on the day of the acquittal perfectly capture the attitude and excess of the Ethics Apparat. The independent counsel who brought the case, Donald Smaltz, declared, "The appearance of impropriety can be as damning as bribery is to public confidence. . . . The actual indictment of a public official may in fact be as great a deterrent as a conviction of that official." And Charles Lewis, executive secretary of the Center for Public Integrity, criticized Espy's acquittal, complaining that the size of the gift should not matter and suggesting that it should be a crime to accept a small gift from a regulated business even if there is no *quid pro quo*. In short, in the world of the Ethics Apparat, indictments of individuals later proven innocent serve a useful function and appearances alone should be a crime, even where there is no underlying reality.

Unfortunately, our reaction to the Phipps memo was heavily influenced by this new culture and the preoccupation with appearances of the post-Watergate Ethics Apparat. It's not just that we anticipated their negative reaction to the Phipps memo's blatant statement of money-for-access. Consciously or unconsciously, we bought into their underlying premise that there was something wrong or unusual (if not illegal) about giving big contributors special perks and access as a reward for their largesse or to motivate more largesse in the future. All of our strategy and reactions, and, significantly, all of our mistakes in effective damage control in the months to come, must be viewed in this context.

THERE WERE THREE SEPARATE "document dumps" of Harold Ickes's political files—in late January, in late February, and in early April 1997. Ickes, it will be recalled, had been the president's deputy chief of staff in 1994–96, and had served as the *de facto* campaign manager for the president's 1996 reelection campaign, essentially running the campaign from the White House, much as James Baker had done for George Bush in 1992. Ickes had taken these documents with him when he left the White House in December 1996. Rather than letting his client be subject to a subpoena, Ickes's attorney, Robert Bennett, arranged to have them turned over to the Republican-controlled congressional committee voluntarily. Thus we knew that the Ickes documents would be leaked by the Republicans; we therefore determined to dump them all as soon as we got them.

It was in the first batch, released in mid-January, that we found the Phipps memo. It was stapled, apparently inadvertently, to a DNC document that contained 1996 budget information. The DNC's counsel objected to turning over the budget document and the attached Phipps memo to the congressional committee, claiming the budget document was "confidential." He appeared also to be worried that the Phipps memo was a very hot document (it was) and would have a lot of news value (it did), and therefore he figured that if he didn't release the hot document, it would never be leaked and he could avoid the bad news. I suppose he also believed that pigs can fly.

Many of us vehemently argued at the time for the Phipps memo to be released along with everything else, but the lawyers at the White House were unwilling to overrule the DNC's lawyers. It was no surprise to us that within a few days of our release of the first batch of Ickes documents, the Phipps memo was leaked. It was first reported by Bob Franken of CNN. Within hours a feeding frenzy was in full force. Every reporter covering the campaign-finance story clamored for details about each of the perks listed—specifically, which ones had been offered and who were the people who received them.

The answers were not forthcoming from within the White House or the DNC. The first report we got from the DNC was that Ms. Phipps was someone who worked in the DNC's finance department, that these were just "wish list" items to help raise money, and that few if any of them had ever been implemented. I was told very little and so had nothing to say to the press. We did not even know the date of the memo or its author. All we knew was that the memo had been found in Harold Ickes's files.

Our lack of responsiveness to press inquiries had the predictable effect of revving them up to even further efforts to get those details and lists of the donors who received these perks. And clearly the one that aroused the most interest was the reference to "overnight stays."

I knew that this issue posed the greatest political danger when I received a phone call from my mother shortly after the Phipps memo was first reported. She was an ardent Democrat and Clinton supporter. "So how come I never got invited to stay overnight in the White House?" she asked me. It quickly hit me: She gets this story, so millions of others will as well. This was a perk that people understood and resented. That spelled trouble.

Top White House aides on the damage-control team met on Saturday morning, February 6, to sort out a disclosure plan for all the perks listed in the Phipps memo. Most of our attention was focused on overnight stays at the White House and on trips on Air Force One, the two items that appeared to have been implemented, and also the two that held the most potential for political and press interest.

After some discussion, it was clear that there were two legitimate sources of resistance to a full disclosure plan. The first, which applied to all the various perks, was the practical difficulty of finding out all this information. It appeared that there was no central person in charge of dispensing all these perks, and no single file, either at the DNC or the White House, for all the lists. The White House lawyers were reluctant to begin a full-scale investigation, including interviews of White House and DNC personnel and files, in order to release all this information to the press. Once again, the concern was the possibility that information disclosed might be incomplete or inaccurate—perhaps leading to charges of obstruction of justice by Republican-controlled investigating committees.

The second problem, specifically related to the overnights in the Lincoln Bedroom (where most of the guests stayed, as we learned), was a privacy issue. The president and the first lady had become accustomed to inviting many friends to stay overnight in the White House, including Chelsea's friends. It was not an easy task to differentiate between personal friends who were also campaign donors and campaign donors who were not personal friends. Even more difficult was dealing with the understandable sensitivity of the president and the first lady about protecting their own privacy and that of their friends.

After some debate, we concluded that there was no way to prevent this information from coming out, since Republican-controlled congressional committees would obtain it soon in response to a subpoena. After some stops and starts, the process of compiling and categorizing the list of overnight guests began. We tried to draw clear lines between private, personal guests and official or political ones, but without success. At the end of the day, the only guests that could safely be called private or personal were Chelsea's friends and the relatives of the president and the first lady. It was agreed that other than these, we would begin the effort to release a list of everyone who had stayed overnight in the Executive Residence during the previous four years. But for reasons that are unclear to this day, we were forbidden to disclose the actual dates of the overnights of particular individuals—I guess to make it more difficult for reporters to match the dates against the contributions, that is, more difficult to link a particular contribution with a particular overnight stay.

As it turned out, the very next day—Sunday, February 7—the *Los Angeles Times* broke a story on the Lincoln Bedroom overnights, one that was amazingly complete. It contained most of the information that we had been told by the counsel's office would be difficult to gather. Reporters Glenn F. Bunting and Ralph Frammolino wrote that there were "577 overnight stays in 1995 and 1996 by friends and supporters" of the Clintons, including "many major party contributors referred by the Democratic National Committee." The story made reference to "up to 900" donors as the estimate from 1993 on.

The story contained a comment by a DNC spokesperson as well as anonymous Democratic sources and current and former White House officials acknowledging the use of the Lincoln Bedroom to motivate donors. Overnight donor guest names were referred to the White House by the DNC's finance chairman and director precisely because they had previously been substantial campaign contributors to the DNC and/or to the president's 1992 campaign. The assumption was that, as a result of their overnight visit, they would be motivated to give more.

The *Times* even identified and interviewed one of the overnight guests, William Rollnick, a retired Florida executive who spent the night in April 1994 and who had donated $456,300 to the DNC. Said Mr. Rollnick: "For a kid from Cleveland, it was pretty heady stuff. It was major-league excitement." Was there a connection between the overnight and his campaign contribution—the key political issue? The *Times* report contained what looked like a smoking gun.

"Although he said the invitation was not the reason he contributed, Rollnick said he could see a causal relationship [between] being invited to stay there and then giving." He added, "I guess I never did anything right; I was already giving."

The same sources also acknowledged that the overall "perks" program outlined in the Phipps memo was for the express purpose of using the aura of the White House and access to the president to raise money.

So there it all was—all reported in one story. Money. Access. The White House. Perks. The Lincoln Bedroom. Fundraising for the Democratic Party. What more was there to say? The circumstantial evidence of a causal link between contributions and overnight stays was pretty strong. The *Los Angeles Times* had even obtained a "partial" list of 73 couples who had stayed overnight in 1993 and 1994; it reported that 27 of these had donated a total of $3 million to the Democratic Party in the 1992 and 1996 campaigns. The fact that some of these contributors gave money significantly before, and significantly after, their overnight stays did not alter the basic premise: The underlying motivation for their invitations to, and stays in, the Lincoln Bedroom was to convince them to make a contribution or to make another contribution.

The only thing left for us to do, it seemed, was to release the actual list of names of people who had stayed overnight in the Lincoln Bedroom. This would have completed the factual story reported by the *Los Angeles Times*. In fact, the *Times* reporters had asked me to help them fill in the blanks. Had we freely pushed out all the documents and all the information concerning the perks-for-cash Phipps memo, including the Lincoln Bedroom story, with a few on-record comments about how unshocking all this was, arguably that would have been the end of the story. There would have been nothing left to discover or report. In fact, Glenn Bunting had called me and pleaded with me to give him all the information, including more accurate numbers and the full list of names and the dates of overnight stays. I knew that this list would enable the *Times* to correlate an overnight stay with a particular donation, but I figured it was obvious that there was some connection between staying overnight and giving money. We might just as well get it printed now, in the full context of all the other guests who had overnighted in the Lincoln Bedroom but who had nothing to do with possible Democratic campaign donations. Bunting pointed out that we could get the full story over with and our comments included high up in the story.

Of course all Bunting was doing was recommending that we follow the rules that McCurry and I had committed to a month or so before. He was preaching to the choir. But when I crossed the street to make my argument to my colleagues in the counsel's office, I ran into a wall of resistance. Their concern, which was genuine and intensely expressed, was that the Clintons were entitled to some minimal privacy. I suggested that we simply release the names of anyone who was a major Democratic contributor who had stayed overnight, since no one was interested in a list of Chelsea's friends or of the friends and relatives of the president and the first lady. But the lawyers resisted.

I began to prepare, in any event, for the moment in time when the overnight lists would be released, because I knew it was inevitable. I probed a colleague who knew a great deal about the list, and learned that the *Times*'s number of "up to 900 donors" was way too high, and that there were hundreds of dignitaries and other public officials, as well as friends and relatives of the Clintons, on the overnight list. In short, not surprisingly, the actual facts were much more favorable than the uninformed perception—exactly the recipe for getting a story out ourselves rather than waiting for the opposition to beat us to the punch.

In early February we received the second batch of Ickes documents in the White House. McCurry and I pressed to get these out in a second dump, and to release the Lincoln Bedroom lists at the same time. But my colleagues in the counsel's office were unwilling to authorize a dump at that time because of an agreement with the con-

gressional investigating committees that we would not release subpoenaed documents publicly until we had delivered them to those
committees. McCurry, Adam Goldberg, and I continued to lobby for
release of the Ickes documents and Lincoln Bedroom lists through
the first few weeks of February, but to no avail.

Finally, we were told that the Ickes documents were due to be
delivered to the congressional committees on Tuesday, February 25,
and we could plan our second dump then. We were also told, however, that we would not be releasing the Lincoln Bedroom lists. So on
Friday night, February 21, Adam and I went to a small, stuffy office
on the fourth floor of the Old Executive Office Building and started
to read through a stack of papers from Ickes's files. We assumed that
this batch would be no different from the first, and would be spun in
exactly the same way: not too surprising that Harold Ickes was doing
politics and running the campaign while he was at the White House,
only old news here.

And then a funny thing happened on the way to our spin line.
We found a hot document—even hotter than the Phipps memo. The
good news was that as soon as I saw it, I instantaneously knew that
the Lincoln Bedroom lists would now *have* to be released in order to
get the story behind us. The bad news was that this document made
us lose our balance, our judgment, and our message because—there is
no other way to say it—this document psyched us out.

I REMEMBER THE CHAIR I was sitting in. It was classic government
surplus—a big plastic-covered easy chair with the stuffing coming
out of the seat. I had a pile of documents on my lap—mostly boring
status reports to the president, the vice president, and what seemed
like forty people in the White House, the DNC, and the campaign
committee hierarchy, written over the course of 1996. I was almost
dozing off when I came across a memorandum from Terry McAuliffe,
who had served as national finance chairman of the Clinton-Gore

campaign of 1995–96. It was dated January 5, 1993—but it was clear that the 1993 was a typo and should have read 1995, since McAuliffe did not become finance chairman until late 1994. There was some dark handwriting on the page that caught my eye. The memo was to Nancy Hernreich, who was the president's personal secretary and chief liaison to the political scheduling people. The handwriting, I later discovered, was hers. Here is what I saw:

DEMOCRATIC ★ NATIONAL ★ COMMITTEE

David Wilhelm, Chairman.

Mr. President. Do you want me to pursue #1 w/ Billy #2 w/ Erskine + Carolyn #3 Handle 3 Run it all by Erskine

January 5, 1993

MEMORANDUM TO: NANCY HERNREICH
FROM: TERRY McAULIFFE
NATIONAL FINANCE CHAIRMAN

During my recent meeting with the President, we discussed the following projects:

1. I would like three dates over the next month, about one week apart, for breakfast, lunch or coffee with the President and about twenty of our major supporters. The purpose of these meetings would be to offer these people an opportunity to discuss issues and exchange ideas with the President. This will be an excellent way to energize our key people for the upcoming year. We would need one hour of the President's time for each of these meetings. These individuals will come in to Washington from across the country.

2. The following individuals are our ten top supporters: — *overneats*

John Connelly
Carl Lindner
Skip Hayward
Miguel Lausell
Arthur Coia
Finn Casperson
Paul Montrone
Larry Hawkins
Stan Shuman
Ernie Green

Finally, if there are any opportunities to include some of our key supporters in some of the President's activities, such as golf games, morning jogs, etc., it would be greatly appreciated.

Thank you for your assistance.

CGRO-1569
Req. 2/3/97

Democratic Party Headquarters • 430 South Capitol Street, S.E. • Washington, D.C. 20003 • 202.863.8000 • FAX: 202.863.8091
Paid for by the Democratic National Committee. Contributions to the Democratic National Committee are not tax deductible.

Attached to this memo was a note from the president:

The translation of the president's handwritten note is as follows:

> *Yes pursue all*
> *3 and promptly—*
> *and get other names*
> *at 100,000 or more*
> *50,000 or more—*
> *cc: H Ickes, L Panetta, B Webster*
> *ready to start overnights*
> *right away—*
> *give me the top 10 list*
> *back, along w/ the 100, 50 [illegible]*

There are moments for those of us in the business of dealing with bad news that are a perverse combination of pain and pleasure, perhaps diagnosable as spinmeister's schizophrenia. Such a moment occurred as I read the McAuliffe memo and the president's handwritten note.

The first sensation was not quite giddiness, but in all candor it came close to that. I just sat and stared for a few minutes, my heart pounding. Then I turned to Adam, and in slow motion I placed the two documents in front of him. I waited. We loved to bet each other on how big a story would be—even down to whether it would be a right- or left-hand lead, above or below the fold on the front page. Adam looked at them, eyebrows dancing up and down, a clear sign that he was leading up to a page-one prediction. He looked up, unable to contain his excitement.

"This is going to make one big fucking story," he said. We both burst out laughing—and then immediately, mutually, felt the angst setting in.

"One very difficult story," I said, feeling guilty at our temporarily insane mirth.

And the vision of what lay of ahead of us, and for the president, and the reality of the political firestorm and press frenzy that we knew would occur, brought us quickly back to sobriety.

Seeing the list of names of "our ten top supporters" with Nancy Hernreich's word, "overnights," was, without anything more, a pretty good story. But as McAuliffe so aptly put it in his memorandum, these invitations were to "energize our key people for the upcoming year." Since the *Los Angeles Times* story had reported most of the significant issues concerning overnights in the Lincoln Bedroom, we did not expect that release of the list of names would propel the story very much higher or cause any significant damage. However, once I saw the president's handwritten note referring to "100,000 or more" and "50,000 or more" accompanied by the words "ready to start overnights right away"—well, to put it mildly, I knew that this note would "energize" the story up to the level of, say, a nuclear bomb.

Now the debate on putting out the story on the Lincoln Bedroom guests was settled. This document would unleash the entire story, and there was no choice but to put the list out (the only exceptions being Chelsea Clinton's friends) to show that the number of actual donors was a small percentage. The McAuliffe memo with the president's handwriting—which we all knew would be the major front-page story of the news cycle—would at least be surrounded by hundreds of other interesting documents and might get somewhat overshadowed by documents pretty much proving that the White House coffees were, after all, fundraisers. Having made the decision to put out the list of Lincoln Bedroom guests, we still held back on releasing all the information the reporters had previously asked for—specifically, the dates of the overnights. Again, for reasons that completely escaped me then and still escape me now, there was some thought that if you don't give reporters the dates, and if you make it difficult for them to correlate each overnight stay with a campaign contribution, then maybe, just maybe, they won't be able to write that story.

So on Tuesday, February 25, we did a document dump of the second batch of Ickes documents, including a complete list of the Lincoln Bedroom overnights. We made multiple copies, invited reporters to the Indian Treaty Room on the fourth floor of the OEOB, and waited for the reaction to the McAuliffe memo.

I stood with Adam Goldberg and Ches Johnson in the front of the room as the reporters filed in and sat around the huge table in the Treaty Room, with stacks of documents in front of them. I looked at my watch. I knew that the McAuliffe memo, with the handwritten note from the president, was in the middle of the stack where we had found it. I started to whisper to Adam a countdown, "Ten, nine, eight, seven, six . . ." A few minutes passed. Nothing. I noticed a few reporters getting to the middle of their stack. Still nothing. And then.

"Hello. Holy shit!"

Then another. "You've got to be kidding me."

And then still another, "It's his handwriting. It is."

At that, the rest of the reporters took notice, dug through their piles, and found the memo.

The frenzy had begun.

I slipped out of the room, walked across the street to Mike McCurry's office in the West Wing, and found him at his desk. He had the grin on again. "Having a boring day, Lanny?" he asked.

McCurry decided that we might as well have a full press briefing at the end of the day. This second batch of Ickes documents also contained updated spreadsheets showing that the White House coffees were all about raising money, so McCurry figured we might as well try to bury the huge Lincoln Bedroom and McAuliffe memo stories under the inevitable "Gotcha!" stories by journalists wanting to prove that the coffees were really fundraisers.

"This is going to be the mother of all scandal-story press briefings," he said, barely able to contain his glee.

"We'll just have to put up with a lot of heat on this one," I said, glumly.

"What do you mean, 'we,' Lone Ranger?"

Despite his bravado, McCurry couldn't completely escape the line of fire on this one. So he joined me and White House Communications Director Ann Lewis at the podium in the White House press briefing room as we took questions from the assembled reporters.

Referring to the president's note, Lewis told the skeptical press corps: "It was very much the president's decision that he wanted to see and connect to people who were his friends and supporters. As he has said, they were his friends; they had been with him and for him for a long time. He liked being with them, and he also felt when he talked with them he learned things about how the world was going on."

We insisted that the president's note and the Lincoln Bedroom overnights for donors were not part of an overall DNC and Clinton-Gore campaign fundraising program, but rather, were more about welcoming and thanking "friends and supporters." "Not surprisingly," read the formal statement, released under McCurry's name but written by the White House lawyers, "some of these friends were also active supporters of the president. In no case was staying overnight at the White House contingent upon a political contribution."

In retrospect, the circumlocution here is so transparent that it is amazing that we thought we could get away with it. We denied that anyone had been invited to stay overnight "contingent" upon a political contribution, obviously begging the question as to whether the big-donor overnight guests would be expected to give more money shortly after leaving the White House complex. We never admitted that dozens of the names for Lincoln Bedroom overnight invitations came from the DNC's finance department—and that, as far as anyone knew, no one at the White House ever vetoed any of those names.

It was left to me to defend this position that night on ABC's *Nightline*. A very skeptical Ted Koppel questioned me about the plain meaning of the president's note and the intentions of inviting big donors to stay overnight in the Lincoln Bedroom. When I launched into the "friends and supporters" explanation, Koppel was having none of it:

> I don't see anything in either Mr. McAuliffe's memo or in the president's notation referring to friends. This is strictly money that we're talking about here. . . . There is no reference there to doing anything but, apparently, energizing those who have already given and, presumably, suggesting to others who might be inclined to give that, you know, if you give, you may end up being invited to the White House, you may end up jogging with the president or having coffee with the president or playing a round of golf with the president. I'm not suggesting there's anything illegal about that, but I'm just wondering why you keep putting it in terms of friends. This has nothing to do with friends. This has to do with fundraising.

Koppel had put his finger on the key point. In his frustrated out-burst to me, he summarized what should have been my message. *"I'm not suggesting there's anything illegal about that. . . . This has to do with fundraising."* Exactly. This was almost precisely the "good spin" mes-sage that we had crafted prior to finding the president's note. But instead, by insisting on the euphemistic "friends and supporters" mantra, I was left hanging on national television with a message that essentially accepted the antipolitical, moralistic premises of the Ethics Apparat. I refused to agree with, much less defend, the proposition that there was nothing illegal about using the aura of the White House to raise money.

Chris Bury, *Nightline's* regular investigative reporter, did a set-up piece prior to my interview. Bury, like most reporters covering the campaign finance story, relied heavily on the core premise of the Ethics Apparat—that "appearances" matter more than legal rules and that the use of the White House and the Lincoln Bedroom violated appearance standards more than legal ones. To confirm that thought, he quoted Fred Wertheimer, former chairperson of Common Cause: "There's no question that Clinton set the tone, but he did more than set the tone, he led the charge. He grabbed the flag and raced out onto the field. He was more aggressive, more active, more involved in going after this money than probably anyone else in this whole operation."

How terrible! I thought to myself as I heard this. The president, as leader of his party and up for reelection, was "more aggressive" in going after donations than probably anyone else. So what? So what else is new? We didn't violate any laws, only Fred Wertheimer's sensi-bilities. Anyway, that's what I thought. But I didn't say it.

IT'S ONE THING TO ACKNOWLEDGE the obvious. Facts are facts, and we have seen that two plus two adds up to four and no amount of spin will make them add up to five. But some facts lead to irrefutable inferences; others lead to debatable ones. What I learned from the Lincoln Bedroom controversy was that effective damage control requires knowing the difference between the two—between inferences that are objectively undeniable and those that are subjectively arguable. As Woodward said to Bernstein in the movie version of *All the President's Men:* "If you go to sleep at night and there is no snow on the ground, and you wake up in the morning and there is snow on the ground, then you can be pretty sure that it snowed overnight" (irrefutable inference). But Bernstein replied to Woodward: "If you are listening to the radio and you hear music without commercials, then it must be FM and not AM" (debatable inference).

So the real art form in damage control, I learned, is to be able to judge how far along the spectrum of credible inferences—from irrefutable on the one end to debatable on the other—a particular set of facts would place me. It's one thing to avoid denying those inferences from a given set of facts that are beyond dispute or close to it. But the Lincoln Bedroom example showed that it is also important to avoid damaging oneself unnecessarily by being too willing to concede the validity of a debatable inference—especially if the inference is derived not from objective standards but from the subjective judgments and values of one's critics.

The temptation to concede too much is greatest in the middle of a bad story where there is a high embarrassment factor—meaning when I was worried about the perceptions of others and trying to find a message to mitigate those perceptions. Often without realizing it, it was as if I were living through an *Invasion of the Body Snatchers*—my opponents and critics seemed to be taking over my mind. I started to think like them, I looked at myself and my actions through their eyes. In short, I was buying into their premises, their prejudices, even their self-righteousness. And this led me to the double-whammy error of damage control: I was denying the irrefutable inference and conceding the refutable one—the worst of both worlds.

With the Lincoln Bedroom story, we were reacting to the world seen through the prism of the "tacky factor"—as well as through the eyes of the Ethics Apparat, who saw the necessities of political fundraising and what it takes to win elections in America today as, well, unseemly. Once we bought into those premises, we were done for—our strategy was to concede that there was something wrong with inviting big donors to the Lincoln Bedroom to stay overnight; therefore we had to try to camouflage what really happened with euphemisms and linguistic gymnastics.

It took me a long time, but I learned that the best way to resist this invasion of my mind by my critics was twofold. First, I had to recognize what was happening to me and resist it. I had to fight to get my mind and my judgment back. I had to have the strength to return to my basic convictions and values, regardless of the critical perceptions of third parties. And then I needed to develop an affirmative response—a strong statement of why I *needed* to do what I did, knowing that my subjective judgment as to what is "right" or "proper" is just as valid as those of my critics.

But the hardest part came next. I had to be willing to defend my position completely and consistently—following its logic to its fullest extension without apology. Being half pregnant doesn't work here any more than it does in real life; trying to split the difference leads to serious trouble.

I remember first learning this lesson when I was preparing for my Moot Court appellate-argument competition at Yale Law School in the spring of 1969. I was asked to argue that a taxpayer, solely in his status as a taxpayer, did not have "standing" to file a lawsuit to challenge the constitutionality of a religious chaplain offering a prayer before each opening session of Congress. In a legal context, to have "standing" means to have sustained a direct, personal injury sufficient to be recognized by the courts as qualifying for some legal redress. I had to argue that the amount of the individual's taxes used to pay a portion of the chaplain's salary was too *de minimis* to constitute a sufficient personal injury; thus, a taxpayer had no legal "standing" to sue on this basis.

During a practice argument before the final competition, one of the judges on the panel—the late Professor Alexander Bickel, one of the great constitutional scholars in U.S. history—asked whether I differentiated the right of a taxpayer to sue if the chaplain gave a short, generalized prayer, as opposed to a prayer that openly proselytized for one particular religion over all others.

"Yes, of course," I answered.

"Oh, I see," Professor Bickel said. "You have enough injury for a taxpayer to have standing to challenge a very religious prayer but not enough injury to challenge a little religious one. Which is your constitutional test of standing—how do you decide how much is too much religion in the prayer?"

I felt a little queasy, sensing I was walking into a trap.

"Well, I suppose if the injury to the Constitution is egregious enough, then there must be some remedy for a taxpayer to be able to challenge it."

"Oh, I see," said Professor Bickel, sensing it was time to swoop in for the kill. "So how do you decide what is or is not 'egregious'? If the chaplain says 'God' once in his prayer, would that be egregious?"

"Possibly not," I tried, now knowing I was sliding down the slope with no one to rescue me.

"What about three times?"

I was silent, struggling. "Maybe."

"How about five? Seven? Ten? Tell me what your constitutional rule is, Mr. Davis."

I was more than queasy. I was in a panic. I knew I was done for.

After the practice argument was over, Professor Bickel called me to his private office and gave me some good advice—applicable, as I now realize, not only to legal appellate argument but also to all effective damage control.

"Lanny, either accept the premise of your argument and believe it enough to ride it to its logical conclusion, or try another one that you *are* willing to ride. But you can't ride two horses at once."

I knew he was right. While I had stated the strict doctrine of standing—that there had to be more than a *de minimis* injury from the misuse of a minuscule amount of tax dollars paid by a taxpayer in order to challenge a governmental act—I hadn't been willing to defend it all the way in its practical application. Instead, I had essentially bought into the premise of my opposition: that for serious constitutional wrongs, there simply must be *some* legal remedy, regardless of the absence of a substantial, individual impact on the plaintiff claiming judicial standing. So I tried to split the difference, and tried to have it both ways.

The next night, during the actual final competition, the late Supreme Court Justice Potter Stewart, who was presiding as chairman of the panel of judges for the Moot Court final competition, asked me a question very similar to Professor Bickel's first question. This time I was ready.

"Mr. Davis, are you really saying that there would be absolutely no legal remedy for a taxpayer to be able to sue to stop a congressional chaplain from insisting that there is only one legitimate religion in America today?"

"That is correct—there would be no legal remedy. There would be no standing solely based on a taxpayer's status. Under our system, not every wrong has a legal remedy—no matter how egregious."

"No remedy at all, Mr. Davis?"

"Not a legal one. But there is a political one, Mr. Justice Stewart. Voters could demand that our representatives fire the chaplain."

Mr. Justice Stewart nodded at my answer.

If I had remembered the lesson Professor Bickel taught me, which was reinforced by Justice Stewart's nod of the head, this is what I should have said to Ted Koppel that night on *Nightline*—and, more broadly, how we should have handled the Lincoln Bedroom story with the media.

First, acknowledge the obvious:

"Sure, we used the White House to raise funds. We were rewarding our donors, hoped they would give us more money, and if they didn't do so beforehand, we sure asked them to after their stay in the White House."

Second, trump the opposition's premises:

"There's nothing wrong or inappropriate about making use of the White House to reward our contributors and motivate them to keep giving. No policies were changed as a result of these stays. And we're not the first White House to reward big givers with access to the White House; check out how many in the Republican Eagles Club were invited to the White House for special dinners and meetings and given special access to Presidents Reagan and Bush.

"Rewarding big donors with special access is about as shocking in American political history as allowing gambling in Rick's casino in the movie *Casablanca*. Give me a break!"

Third, label any criticism as pure politics (our ultimate message and the core theme):

"Remember—it's President Clinton who wants to end the influence of big money in politics by effective campaign-finance reform and it's the Republicans who oppose it. Even with our use of the White House to raise money, the Republicans still outraised us in 1995–96 by $220 million. No wonder they oppose reform."

This is what I call good spin. Each of these arguments is based on established facts—and is also based on reasonable inferences to be drawn from these facts. But most important of all, this approach would have allowed *our* message, not a reaction to the opposition's message, to frame the story. If we had had greater confidence in our own message, we could have saved ourselves a lot of grief.

5

Unconnecting the Dots

AS EACH NEW CRISIS PLAYED ITSELF OUT INSIDE THE WHITE House and in the newspapers, I came to realize that all of us, myself included, were children of Watergate. The *Washington Post* reporters Carl Bernstein and Bob Woodward, whose investigative reporting broke the Watergate story, had set new guidelines for the practice of journalism and politics alike. In the wake of their success, news organizations have developed investigative agendas and funded teams of reporters to pursue them. The result is often the creation of news stories, which then drive events and generate further reporting and investigations by other journalists.

Obviously there is still an important need in our society for investigative journalists. Government wrongdoing is not likely to be discovered easily. As Bernstein and Woodward demonstrated, journalists often have to rely on circumstantial evidence to suggest that one event caused another event and have to quote unnamed sources in order to ferret out the truth from recalcitrant government officials. Mistakes will inevitably be made in this process, but many would argue that this is a price at least occasionally worth paying.

However, it is also true that since Watergate, increasing numbers of reporters and news organizations have forgotten the dangers and limitations of investigative reporting. There is the obvious over-reliance on anonymous sources. The more subtle danger is inherent in the investigative process itself. Once a news organization or reporter chooses a subject area to investigate, it becomes difficult to avoid trying to prove a predisposed hypothesis. This is done, some-times unconsciously, through choices in researching, writing, editing, and headline writing—and by omitting or downplaying evidence that tends to undermine the hypothesis.

A related post-Watergate trend is the movement away from objective reporting toward what my colleagues and I called "connect-the-dots" journalism. By this we meant the reporting of apparent facts ("dots")—facts arranged, juxtaposed, and edited in such a way as to lead a reader to connect them—to infer a cause-and-effect rela-tionship even though there may be no direct evidence to support it.

The Latin expression for such fallacious dot-connecting is "*post hoc, ergo propter hoc*"—literally translated, "after this, therefore because of this." A more colloquial way of putting it is: "First, the rooster crows. Then the sun rises. Therefore, the rooster *causes* the sun to rise." I saw this syllogistic fallacy at work again and again during the campaign-finance story. A campaign contribution was reported, a policy decision was made at some later date, and through suggestive phrases and juxtapositions, the reader was influenced to conclude that, *ergo,* the contribution *caused* the policy decision, though no direct supporting evidence was offered and, indeed, contrary evi-dence was ignored.

I discussed this connect-the-dots technique with many reporters, and I was surprised at how many agreed that this was a serious issue—although most would point to others as being more guilty than them-selves. Tim Berger, then a reporter for *Legal Times* and now with the New York *Daily News,* provided me with a critical understanding of the problem: it's the failure by reporters to differentiate between "cor-relation" and "causation." An example of facts that correlate would be a liberal Democratic donor who gave money to a liberal Democratic congressman, followed by the congressman voting for a liberal Demo-cratic program. One cannot say that the contribution "caused" the vote; rather, there is a philosophical correlation between the liberalism of the contributor, the liberalism of the congressman and the congress-man's support for the liberal program. The same holds true, naturally, for conservative donors and politicians. In covering the Clinton White House, reporters almost never suggested an innocent correlation between facts (or even entertained the possibility that there might be one). Instead, they usually relied on inference and innuendo, vir-tually demanding a cause-and-effect relationship and thus an infer-ence of wrongdoing. It was very difficult to untangle the logic and hard evidence behind such stories, but that was the job I was hired to do.

Sometimes my task seemed Herculean indeed. When Mike Kranish of the *Boston Globe* called me on the morning of January 15, 1997, and told me of a set of facts that he believed he had established, even I instinctively connected these dots:

- In June 1995 President Clinton endorsed the recommendations of a commission on legal immigration reform chaired by the late congresswoman Barbara Jordan. One of the recommendations would have eliminated the "sibling-preference" category under U.S. immigration laws, which permits brothers and sisters of natural-ized citizens to immigrate to the United States. And then . . .
- On February 19, 1996, John Huang, controversial fundraiser, sent a memo to the president urging him to oppose a bill that would eliminate the sibling-preference category. Defeating this bill was called by Huang a "top priority" of the Asian American community. And then . . .
- That same day, $1.1 million was raised for the Democratic Party at an Asian American fundraiser chaired by John Huang and attended by President Clinton. And then . . .
- About four weeks later, Clinton reversed his policy toward the legal-immigration bill, which included a provision eliminating

the sibling-preference category. The effect of his reversal was to retain unchanged the sibling-preference category—the very provision advocated by John Huang on behalf of the Asian American community.

I asked Kranish if he would fax me a copy of the Huang memo, and he did. Dated February 19, 1996, the same date as the fundraiser, it did seem rather unusual, patently presumptuous. It reported to Clinton that attending the fundraiser that night would be some eighty to one hundred Asian American donors who had given a minimum of $12,500 each, totaling $1.1 million, to the Democratic National Committee. A section headed "Heads Up" stated that the "top priority" of Asian Americans at the dinner was the assurance that the U.S. government would continue to allow brothers and sisters of naturalized citizens to immigrate to the United States. "Brothers and sisters are considered part of the 'immediate family' in the Asian Pacific American community," the memo stated. "As such maintaining the [sibling] preference is of extreme importance to the APA community."

I looked back at my notes. Kranish had told me that about four weeks after this memo was apparently sent to Clinton, the White House had reversed its earlier support for eliminating the sibling-preference category and, instead, favored retaining it.

My first reaction, I must concede, was that the chain of events outlined by Kranish strongly suggested that Huang had caused or at least influenced the flip-flop. A politician takes a position, then a fundraiser raises money and asks him to change, and then the politician changes to the position advocated by the fundraiser. . . . Q.E.D. How could I blame Kranish for connecting those dots when I instinctively found myself doing the same thing? This could well be the smoking gun, the *quid pro quo,* money-for-policy story that we had feared from the first days of the Democratic campaign-finance allegations.

Then, I realized: I had been seduced by the same connect-the-dots, presumption-of-guilt logic for which we at the White House had criticized journalists on the scandal beat. It was so easy to jump to negative conclusions when it came to money and politics.

Kranish asked me whether the White House confirmed or denied that John Huang's influence was at least partially responsible for the flip-flop. He also asked me whether President Clinton had ever seen the Huang memo and whether we had any explanation for the change in policy on the legal-immigration reform legislation such a short time after the February Asian American fundraiser. I told him I would call him back.

This could be very serious, I thought; if there were any basis for finding a nexus involving the memo, the fundraiser, and the change in position, it was not excessive to imagine that it could lead to the appointment of another independent counsel to investigate the president. Ken Starr's ongoing Whitewater investigation was tough enough to deal with, but the independent-counsel statute hung over the head of and terrorized every member of the senior White House staff with whom I worked. It was always in the back of our minds, affecting daily judgments concerning every possible breaking story and how to deal with the press about it. It empowered the lawyers in the White House, because no one wanted to be responsible for making the mistake that would trigger the horrific consequences of the president suffering another independent-counsel investigation. In my position, especially, one mistaken comment by me to a journalist, one story written slightly wrong or out of context, could produce such a result. This made me even more fearful than most people in the White House. The concern about unjustified connections between factual dots that suggested wrongdoing by President Clinton was therefore not just the stuff of critiques of the press and case studies for journalism schools. It was about a criminal investigation, about potentially millions of dollars of further legal fees for the Clintons, even about possible impeachment. It scared the living daylights out of me, all the time, that one mistake by me in the press could provoke Ken Starr's legions and lead to that nightmare.

My first priority was to start gathering as many facts as possible, starting with the reasons why the White House apparently changed its mind from opposing sibling preferences to favoring retaining them. Obviously it was my hope that I would find a reason having absolutely nothing to do with John Huang or his fundraiser. One obvious strategy was to prove that the president had never seen the Huang memo or had never known about the Asian American community's opposition to elimination of the sibling preference. But I knew the latter would be difficult, if not impossible to prove. How do you prove the negative in a situation like this—that the president did *not* read a memo, or did *not* have a conversation with John Huang at the fundraiser on the immigration issue, almost a year before?

It quickly became apparent to me how Kranish had put this story together. I couldn't help but admire the reporting that got him there. First, I figured, he must have gotten the Huang memo from among the 3,000 pages from the DNC's finance department produced pursuant to a Republican-sponsored congressional subpoena and then released to the press. But all the other journalists in town had the same memo. And it was more than likely that most had read it, given Huang's notoriety. But to his credit, Kranish took the further step of looking at the White House's record on the immigration issues advocated by Huang in the memo.

Kranish must have researched the immigration issue, trying to determine whether the administration had ever taken a position consistent with Huang's memo after the February fundraiser. With a quick LEXIS-NEXIS search, and a few phone calls to congressional Republicans, he must have hit the jackpot and found the president's general statement in support of the Jordan commission's recommendations, which included eliminating sibling preference. The administration supported such elimination in an immigration-reform bill under consideration early in 1996. But then on March 20, 1996, a month or so after the memo and fundraiser, the White House announced its opposition to permitting a vote on the legal-immigration-restriction provisions, including sibling preference.

Kranish naturally connected the dots: It certainly looked as if Huang's money-raising caused or at least influenced the president to change his policy. There was no doubt in my mind that he would write a story suggesting that causal relationship—unless I could find facts showing there were other, independent reasons for the president's change in position.

S O ONCE AGAIN I BEGAN my journey as a fact-finder, acting like an investigative reporter myself, interviewing those involved and trying to get at the truth. I knew that to combat the connect-the-dots mind-set, I needed facts—facts that established without any doubt that the reason for the president's change on the sibling-preference issue was based on the merits—and not on anything connected with John Huang or raising political money. Because of the serious ramifications of this story I didn't want to be delayed, so I decided to continue on my own for a while before asking for help from the White House counsel's office.

I made a few calls and learned that Rahm Emanuel, senior counselor to the president, had been one of the political aides in 1996 who was most involved in the immigration issue and the congressional legislation dealing with it. I visited him in his small, cubicle-like West Wing office, next door to the president's private study. I told him briefly about Kranish's possible story, and asked him why President Clinton had reversed his position, from eliminating sibling preferences to allowing them to continue, just weeks after the fundraiser.

His response was an unbroken string of expletives that I found simply awesome in their diversity and creativity. The last one best summarized his position: "That's complete bullshit!"

Emanuel is intense, dark-haired and dark-complexioned, and

when he is angry, even darker. I took a breath and ploughed on. "But the president supported the Jordan commission's recommendations, at least generally, and then he supported legal immigration restrictions, including eliminating sibling preferences, in the 1996 bill. Then suddenly he switched his policy—after the fundraiser. Why?"

"We didn't change our policy at all," Emanuel said. "We supported elimination of sibling preferences then and we still do today."

"Say that again?" I said. I was surprised. I looked at my notes. Kranish had definitely used the expression "changed policy" and "reversed policy" several times. That was the heart of his story.

"We did not change our policy—we made a tactical retreat," Emanuel explained. "We were under pressure from congressional Republicans as well as Democrats to separate the illegal-immigration measures from the legal-immigration restrictions." The legal-immigration provisions cut down on the numbers of legal immigrants permitted to enter the United States each year, he explained, whereas the illegal-immigration provisions included tough measures for policing U.S. borders and increasing enforcement resources. While the illegal-immigration restrictions had broad support, the legal-immigration measures were opposed by a broad coalition, from the Catholic Church to Microsoft Corporation to Republican majority leader Dick Armey and leaders of the Hispanic community, especially the conservative Republican Cuban community in South Florida.

"You can hardly say that the Catholic Church and Dick Armey wanted us to separate the legal-immigration reform provisions from the ones cracking down on illegal immigration because they wanted to please John Huang," Emanuel sputtered in disgust. "So what we ended up doing was supporting a separate vote on the legal-immigration provisions of the bill—to save the provisions restricting illegal immigration."

I was still concerned. I anticipated that Kranish and others would disbelieve that the reason was purely tactical. "Any documentation to show that we were in favor of eliminating sibling preference even after the Huang fundraiser?" I asked.

Emanuel phoned a young aide who had helped him on this issue the previous year. Shortly thereafter the aide appeared with a letter dated March 13, 1996, from Deputy Attorney General Jamie Gorelick to Speaker Newt Gingrich, stating the position of the Justice Department on behalf of the administration on the legal-immigration-reform provisions of the bill. The letter, written a month after the Huang memo and fundraiser, indicated that the administration continued to support "suspension" of all future applications filed under the sibling-preference category. And as to the more than one million applications in the backlog, Gorelick would only say that the administration would "reach agreement with Congress on an appropriate and equitable" solution.

How could the *Globe* publish a story suggesting a changed policy resulting from the Huang memo if a month later the administration notified Speaker Gingrich that it still supported eliminating sibling preferences—the opposite of what Huang advocated?

So now I tried to determine whether I could prove the negative—that Clinton had never seen the Huang memo. I asked Emanuel whether there was any way we could confirm this. Again, Emanuel uttered a string of expletives that in their multisyllabic virtuosity was nothing short of impressive.

He pointed out that it was not exactly fair to expect the president to remember definitively whether he had read a memo almost a year before. Moreover, it was extremely unlikely that such a DNC memo would ever get to him, since paper flow from any source outside the White House is strictly controlled by the staff secretary, especially if it is coming from a fundraiser who works for the DNC. This sounded right and logical, but I still wanted a more direct answer.

"Why don't we ask the president directly whether he remembers reading the memo?" I asked Emanuel. He demurred, saying that it wasn't practical to go to the president every day with "bullshit questions" like this from the press.

I asked Emanuel how we could track down the senior political aides and advance men who attended the February 1996 Huang fundraiser. I knew they might remember whether the president had read any background memo prior to the event or had been briefed about the immigration issue. I talked to one of them, who was pretty sure he had attended the Huang event with the president, and who was just as certain that the subject of sibling preferences or immigration reform had not come up before or during the event.

I also took a stab at trying to get a direct answer from the president that I could quote—even if (as I expected) he said nothing more than that he could not remember. I knew I could not talk directly to the president on something like this without going through the White House counsel's office, for the fear of triggering the independent counsel statute was still uppermost in our minds. I asked a top official in the White House counsel's office whether we could get an answer directly from the president. The official responded with a categorical No, for the reasons I had anticipated. We couldn't and shouldn't ask the president of the United States a question like that about something that had occurred so long ago. Even if he thought he could remember, we could not consider his memory reliable, given that it was almost a year ago, and his answer could be used against him by Ken Starr.

I was still disquieted by the thought that I couldn't even say to Kranish that the president did not remember, and I had a passing, uneasy thought that I was doing this job without having direct, independent access to the president. This bothered me and reminded me of my earlier unease about the proscription on my doing independent fact-finding. But then I thought, I've got to get the job done before Kranish's deadline. In other words, I wimped out.

It was early in the evening by the time I finished the fact-finding. I was now completely convinced that there was no causal relationship between the Huang memo and the fundraiser and the change in position. As Emanuel had pointed out, there were numerous Republicans in Congress who wanted the deletion of the legal-immigration reform provisions in order to get an illegal-immigration bill passed, and who had pressured the White House to back off its support for the restrictions on legal immigration. They weren't indebted to John Huang.

So I had my spin—good spin, as it were, because it was based on facts of which I was reasonably certain. I even had myself convinced that I could talk Kranish out of writing the story, since without a connection between Huang's lobbying and any policy change in position there was no news value to his story.

But when I called Kranish, it was clear he was not backing off his theory, even in the face of the facts I was giving him.

"What about Gorelick's March 13 letter?" I asked. "Doesn't that show that the Justice Department took the lead on this and that the administration stuck to our position to eliminate sibling preferences, even after Huang's lobbying and the fundraiser?"

"But you guys backed off that position," he countered. "One week after that—on March 20—the White House flip-flopped and announced that it favored a separate vote on the legal-immigration restrictions from the bill, which you all knew would ensure their defeat. That left the sibling-preference provisions on the books unchanged." He told me that congressional and other supporters of the legal-immigration restrictions were accusing the White House of caving in to the influence of Huang and his Asian American donors.

"That's completely baseless and ridiculous," I responded.

"Well, isn't it true you changed position within one week?"

"Yes—but we also took a position contrary to what Huang had advocated, as can be seen by Gorelick's letter, a month after the fundraiser. And, to repeat, we did not change policy—the change was a tactical one, based on the desire to save the illegal-immigration provisions and under pressure from Republicans as well as Democrats in Congress."

"Can you confirm that Clinton never saw the Huang memo?" Kranish asked.

"No I can't—but it would be impossible to prove the negative," I answered. I tried to explain to him why, given the tight controls within the White House on paper getting to the president, it was unlikely that a memo to him from a DNC fundraiser would get through to him. I reminded Kranish that there are literally thousands of notes, letters, or memos sent to the president all the time, none of which he ever sees. Prior to an event, he'll sometimes scan a briefing memo prepared by a staff person concerning who will be there, seating arrangements, and the like, but we could not locate any such memo for this particular event. So there was no way we could definitely prove that he had not seen a particular piece of paper a year ago, and we wouldn't want to try.

"Did you ask the president whether he remembered seeing the memo?"

I launched into a five-minute speech, along the lines of Emanuel's and the White House counsel's explanation as to why we couldn't or wouldn't do that. I left out Emanuel's profanity, though.

Kranish promised me that he would use my denials of the linkage between Huang's fundraising and the changed position on the immigration bill in the story. When I hung up the phone, I called Emanuel back. "I think we're going to be okay on this story, Rahm," I said.

I was wrong.

The next morning, January 16, I found the Kranish story on page one of the *Boston Globe* and read the headline and the first two paragraphs with growing disbelief and anger:

Clinton Policy Shift Followed Asian American Fundraiser

President Clinton made a last-minute about-face last year on his immigration policy, a reversal that brought the White House in line with the top priority of Asian Americans who had paid $12,500 each a month earlier to attend a fund-raising dinner with Clinton that generated $1.1 million.

Clinton made his reversal after the Democratic National Committee vice chairman, John Huang, waged an intensive effort to influence Clinton's immigration policy, according to documents reviewed by the Globe.

It was a classic example of connect-the-dots, *post hoc, ergo propter hoc* journalism. Each dot was essentially factually accurate, but they were strung together in such an order, bridged by suggestive words and phrases, that the inference to be drawn by any reader was unavoidable: The Huang memo sent to President Clinton and Huang's fundraising activities had at the very least influenced the Clinton White House to change its position to favor the one advocated by Huang and the Asian American community.

And it was at least misleading in its characterization of the change in position as a "policy shift," despite my repeated statements to Kranish that there had been no change in policy.

To appreciate why Kranish's connect-the-dots conclusion—a money-for-policy corrupt scheme—made sense to so many people, it is important to understand the context of the time in which it was written.

As we have seen, a series of articles describing Democratic campaign fundraising abuses, most involving illegal foreign money coming into the Democratic National Committee, was published beginning in September 1996 and increasing to a torrent in November and December, after the election. At the center of most of these early stories were John Huang, the DNC's finance vice chairman; his sponsors, the Riady family of Indonesia; and their multinational conglomerate, the Lippo Group.

Driving most of the journalism from the earliest days of the Democratic campaign-finance story was the search for evidence that

Huang's (or the Riadys') money had caused the Clinton White House to make policy decisions favorable to the Riadys' and Lippo's commercial interests. As we saw in Chapter 4, that search and suspicion was behind the *Los Angeles Times's* front-page story impugning Bruce Lindsey's characterization (which Lindsey vehemently defended) of the September 1995 meeting in the Oval Office between Clinton and James Riady as "basically social" and not about policy. It was also behind the calls by prominent Republican politicians, the *New York Times* editorial board, Common Cause, and others for the appointment of an independent counsel to investigate the Clinton campaign and the DNC on these campaign-finance matters.

Thus, the journalistic chase was on to find an example of money purchasing not only access but policy decisions, especially ones favorable to Huang and the Riadys. For investigative reporters, that story was the big enchilada. For the Clinton White House, the stakes were high, very high.

In December 1996, the Democratic National Committee was forced to turn over to a Republican-controlled House subcommittee more than 3,000 pages of documents from the DNC's finance department, most of which were made available to the press. For an investigative reporter on the campaign finance story, these documents represented a cornucopia for new reporting. Within the pile of memos, letters, fundraising spreadsheets, telephone-call sheets, and invitation lists to fundraising events was the February 19 memo from John Huang to President Clinton.

Therefore, with this background, the *Globe's* readers would undoubtedly infer that Huang's "intensive effort" and the $1.1 million fundraiser had caused or influenced a "policy reversal." The clever use of the "before" and "after" words—"Policy Shift *Followed* Asian-American Fundraiser" and came "after" the Huang memo was sent— was a classic use of the *post hoc* inference. What's more, Kranish did not include my categorical denial that there had been any policy change until eleven paragraphs into the story, and even then he wrote that I had "acknowledged" that there had been a change in course—a word chosen to convey that I had conceded something, when I was doing exactly the opposite. He reported that I had denied that the "changed course" was a result of pressure from Asian Americans. But what I had said—which was the key point—was that there had been a change in *tactics*, supporting a separate vote on the legal-immigration provisions of the bill in order to be able to enact the illegal-immigration provisions of the bill.

When I finished reading the story, I went over to see Mike McCurry. As I walked into his office, he was holding the phone away from his ear, and from across the room I could hear Rahm Emanuel's unexpurgated opinion of the Kranish story. McCurry laughed, winked at me, and said, "Okay, Rahm, we'll praise the *Globe* today at the press briefing." He hung up.

"I'm going to go after the *Globe* on this one, big time," McCurry told me, referring to that afternoon's briefing in the White House press room.

In my fourteen months at the White House, I don't think McCurry ever used harsher language at his daily press briefing about a particular article written by a journalist than he used that day about the *Globe* article.

McCURRY: Look, this really borders on being outrageous. I mean you were all here, you covered this debate. You know exactly the reasons why we separated out legal immigration from illegal immigration. You know why we were keen on getting measures that would help this country fight illegal immigration. And the only way we were going to preserve those would be dropping out the provisions that dealt with legal reform. And that—the Senate Judiciary Committee agreed. They voted twelve to six to do exactly that, because they saw the same situation develop. So it was a legislative strategy, had nothing to do with the so-called sibling immigration issue. In fact, our views were those that were set forth by Deputy Attorney

General Gorelick in her March 13th letter, and we can get that for you, and they have not changed. And the suggestion otherwise is crazy.

Q. But Mike, I think the question people are asking is the timing of this. I think—

McCurry: The timing had only—only—to do with the legislative fight on the Hill. There's not a single person here who worked on this issue who knew a darn thing about a John Huang memo. No one had ever seen it before. No one knew it existed to my knowledge here. And they wouldn't have cared if it had, because we wouldn't have asked him at the DNC to provide counsel to the people who were working very hard here on immigration policy. And you know who they all were, and you had them here, and you talked to them every single day. . . . And to kind of suggest it somehow had something to do with . . . Huang . . . is laughable.

He then repeated my denial that the White House had reversed its policy or had been influenced in its "changed position" by Huang.

McCurry: It's categorically not true that the fundraising done by the Democratic National Committee had any impact whatsoever on the president's thinking with respect to immigration reform. . . . I'm not suggesting that those who contributed funds didn't have concern. We know that. They had every right to express that concern. . . .

Q. But, Mike, it is true that over the course of seven days the administration reversed its position—?

McCurry: That is not true. What I'm categorically saying is wrong about the article, among other things—we took a position, we set it forth. The only thing that changed was that we had to agree, and there was sentiment in Congress to do this, that if we were going to save the illegal-immigration portion of the bill we had to separate in the bill the aspects dealing with legal [immigration] reform from those that dealt with illegal immigration.

McCurry faced the same problem of proving the negative about whether the president had ever seen the Huang memo. He said he hadn't asked the president "personally" but that there was "no indication at all it was given to him." He did concede the possibility that Huang or the Asian Americans might have talked to the president about the subject at the event (though, as I mentioned earlier, we could not find anyone who was with the president that night who could remember that).

> McCURRY: The briefing materials given to the president are those that are compiled for him by the staff secretary's office. And not to my knowledge do we routinely include any document that comes from the DNC. John Huang no doubt wrote a memo thinking that he could somehow or other get something in to the president that would alert him to the concerns of the group he was seeing. And I'm sure that people have told the president, look, here's a group of people and this is among the concerns they're going to have. . . .
> Q. Wait, wait, wait. Mike, do you know if this memo was given to the president or not?
> McCURRY: There's no indication at all it was given to him. I haven't asked him personally whether he recalls ever having seen it, but no one recalls here having ever seen it. . . .
> Q. Could you check and see if the president received this memo from John Huang. Can you do that?
> McCURRY: I didn't say it was unreasonable to check, and I will check on that.

And then, he hit directly at the "connecting-the-dots" journalism that was at the bottom of what was wrong with this story:

> Q. Mike. . . . you seem to be expressing concern that there's going to be a whole series of reports linking people who sent memos with donations.
> McCURRY: That's right. And we—

Q. What's wrong with that?

McCURRY: I'm just saying that a lot of—I'm concerned that there's going to be a lot of misreporting if people start putting together— they're going to look at chronologies and come up with wrong answers, as has happened in this case. And I'm concerned about that.

Q. Why would that necessarily, in and of itself, be misreporting?

McCURRY: Because it suggests a causal connection between one event that happened here and another event that happened here that does not exist. And that misleads people who read the article.

In the world of investigative reporting, the one universally accepted measurement of the worth of a story that attempts to break new ground is whether other news organizations follow it up with their own reporting. That is the instantaneous report card for investigative journalists. It doesn't matter what Mike McCurry thinks of a story, but rather whether other reporters see enough validity in the story to pursue additional leads so that they can extend the story further with their own investigative journalism. On the other hand, it is sometimes possible for journalistic peers to be wrong in their failure to follow up on a rival's investigative reporting. Carl Bernstein and Bob Woodward spent a number of lonely months breaking stories on Watergate before other news organizations began to take the story seriously and devote resources to pursuing it themselves.

Very few news organizations followed up on the *Globe's* story, leaving Kranish to believe (as he subsequently told me) that McCurry's briefing had killed any press interest in pursuing it. As I saw it, the briefing was certainly the main factor—but only because the press recognized that McCurry was right and that the *Globe's* suggestive writing and editing created an incorrect inference: that the Huang memo and fundraiser were behind the administration's change in position.

Kranish's story in the *Globe* the next day, February 17, essentially corrected the record. It was headlined, "Policy Shift Over Fundraiser Is Denied," and for the most part it faithfully tracked McCurry's comments at the press briefing. I had to wonder why the headline on the previous day had not been the same, since I had given Kranish the same categorical denial.

I LEARNED AN IMPORTANT LESSON from watching McCurry that afternoon as he fought back with facts and context in order to disconnect the dots. Even a very fair reporter like Mike Kranish, who was in fact one of the best and most balanced reporters I dealt with at the White House, even when intent on writing an accurate and balanced story, could get caught up in a presupposition. He had a thesis driving the facts, rather than the other way around. As Jung Chang wrote in her 1991 memoir *Wild Swans*: "Where there is a will to condemn, there is evidence."

Some time after the story was written, I mentioned to Kranish that, in retrospect, I considered this story to be a classic, egregious example of connecting-dots journalism. He challenged me to find any factual assertion that was inaccurate, claiming that he had set out the facts and it was up to the reader to draw his or her own inferences. He had a point—the story was essentially accurate (putting aside that he had used the term "policy change" and I had used "tactical change"). But he was missing the subtlety of how certain editorial choices affect how the story is interpreted by most readers. Particularly in the case of a money-followed-by-policy-change story, a news organization must exert extra care to ensure that no unfair inferences are made. It is not enough simply to set forth the "first this, then that" factual chronology. Headlines, the order of the facts presented, the placement of the denial, and other uses of suggestive words and phrases must be taken into account.

The best technique I have found to defeat such a mind-set is to find facts that trump the inferences—that is, by becoming a reporter myself within the White House. If I couldn't find the facts myself (as with Clinton's having seen or not seen the Huang memo), I could still succeed by challenging the absence of direct evidence to prove the causal relationship. Getting into a dialogue with the reporter, convincing him to look for plausible alternative theories, and even pricking his conscience with the possibility that he might be wrong and doing grave damage to his subject, are all worth trying. The problem, as I discovered with Kranish, is that if the presupposition is strong enough, the reporter will be impervious to all these techniques, even if that reporter is usually fair and meticulous. Few of us can resist a compelling story line.

The danger in a story that depends on chronological sequencing to create an inference is the same danger that lies in any legal case dependent on circumstantial evidence: The inference that an earlier event causes or influences a later event might not be valid; there may be an alternative explanation—including coincidence. This was certainly our contention in the John Huang-immigration policy story.

But before I get too sanctimonious, there still is a reasonable argument why connecting dots may sometimes be a journalistic necessity, even if it means that once in a while innocent people get injured. In *All the President's Men*, Bernstein and Woodward conceded their reliance, at one point, on a questionable connect-the-dots lead:

> The two lead paragraphs with their sweeping statements about massive political espionage and sabotage directed by the White House as part of a basic re-election strategy, were essentially interpretive—and risky. No source had explicitly told the reporters that the substance represented the stated conclusions of the federal investigators. . . . Hopefully, the story would push the missing examples into the open.

In this instance, the reporters knew about a young lawyer named Donald Segretti who had engaged in various dirty tricks to interfere with the campaigns of various Democratic presidential candidates. They knew about other instances of such dirty tricks. And that was just about all the direct evidence they had. But they still decided to lead their story with a paragraph that tried to connect all the dots to create a more understandable (and journalistically significant) story. They hoped that by stretching their story beyond the facts the real facts would follow.

Bernstein and Woodward also showed that such interpretive investigative journalism was necessary to reveal a unique government cover-up. In such an instance, some would argue that the ends justified the means since, ultimately, they got it right on Watergate even if they made mistakes along the way. I certainly remember cheering them on when I knew it was Richard Nixon in their crosshairs. Now I realize that there are great dangers to reporting beyond the facts, even if the end result is justified. At the very least, journalists should remember the important trade-offs to employing an inferential, connect-the-dots technique: the desirability of catching government officials who are hiding their wrongdoing versus the risk of getting it wrong once in a while and hurting innocent people.

In the final analysis, however, even when an interpretive factual stretch can be justified—and it should be used only as a last resort— it is mandatory for exculpatory denials and facts, if they exist, not only to be included in the story but to be played prominently under the leads. It is also imperative to avoid suggestive headlines and editing, and for reporters to constantly challenge their writing and their attitudes to avoid the virus of the *post hoc, ergo propter hoc,* logical fallacy.

The irony of my experience on the Kranish/*Globe* story is that at the very same time I was learning the hard way about the difficulty of changing the direction of an investigative journalist's story, I encountered another journalist who was intent on connecting dots after months of investigative efforts. That time, however, there would be a somewhat different result.

6

Invisible Skeletons

ONE SET OF FACTS, TWO REPORTERS, AND TWO DIFFERENT STORIES. John Solomon of the Associated Press and Paula Dwyer of *Business Week* were working on a story in late 1996 that had the following factual dots on the wall:

- In the late 1980s, a federal investigation had begun of energy and utility companies and their lobbyists thought to have attempted to bribe members of the Oklahoma Corporation Commission, which was supposed to regulate them.
- Among the targets were executives who worked for Arkansas-Louisiana Gas Company, Inc. (Arkla Inc.), a $3-billion natural-gas company headed by Thomas F. "Mack" McLarty III, President Clinton's lifelong friend who in 1993–94 served as his first chief of staff and then became his senior counselor and special envoy to Latin America.
- The Clinton-appointed U.S. attorney for Oklahoma, who oversaw the key decisions made in 1993 and 1994 not to prosecute Arkla or its executives, was later nominated by President Clinton and then confirmed as a U.S. District Court judge.

- In November 1993, two Hawaiians, Nora and Gene Lum, with close ties to former DNC chairperson and Commerce Secretary Ronald H. Brown, bought a tiny Tulsa, Oklahoma, natural-gas company and then immediately settled a lawsuit that might have produced testimony referring to Arkla, McLarty, and the bribery investigation.

How were these factual dots connected? What did they add up to? And how could I be sure the story got written right—with inferences drawn from these facts that would be both reasonable and fair to Mack McLarty?

Solomon wrote a story that reported all of the above facts but that made no suggestion of taint or wrongdoing by Mack McLarty and that made no mention at all of the Hawaiians and the settlement of the lawsuit. By contrast, Dwyer wrote a story headlined "Skeletons in Mack McLarty's Closet?" reporting that McLarty had lost his chance at a cabinet position or ambassadorship because of a taint from the Oklahoma bribery-scheme investigation, and suggesting through innuendo that the Lums settled the lawsuit in part to protect Mack McLarty.

I have thought often of these two stories. They speak volumes about the way reporters are driven to connect factual dots through innuendo rather than through fact. They tell us about the advantages of working with a reporter on a bad story. And most important, my experience here proved to me that despite a substantial investment in investigative reporting on the subject a reporter can actually have his or her mind changed by new facts, by an understanding of a broader context, and by the trust that comes from having been dealt with forthrightly.

SOON AFTER NEW YEAR'S DAY, 1997, John Solomon called me at the White House to say that he had spoken with Mack McLarty's top political aide, Steven Ronnell, who had told him to call me.

Solomon said he was about to run what could be a potentially damaging story about Mack McLarty.

I called Ronnell to ask whether it was okay for me to work with Solomon on the story. Ronnell told me that McLarty's lawyers, William W. Taylor III and Leslie M. Berger, were working with a *Business Week* reporter, Paula Dwyer, on what appeared to be the same story sourced by the same people. They had already talked with her several times. Ronnell knew that I had been working with Solomon and other AP reporters on various campaign-finance stories, so he suggested that I be Solomon's point of contact and keep in touch with McLarty's attorneys.

An hour later, Solomon arrived at my office. "I want to show you everything we have," he said. "That's the way we operate—so you can fairly react to everything. I'm trusting you to keep it close. But I'm a little nervous about leaving you any copies at this point."

"You have my commitment that I won't share any information you show me with anyone other than Mack McLarty or his lawyers," I said, respecting his proprietary work product. This seemed to relieve him.

He handed me what appeared to be transcripts of conversations. I scanned them and quickly realized that they were derived from telephone wiretaps or recordings. Solomon explained that the transcripts were of meetings and telephone calls between Robert Anthony, a commissioner on the Oklahoma Corporation Commission, which regulated state utilities, and various lobbyists and individuals who worked for those utility companies. Solomon told me that Anthony had been an FBI informant at the time. I read with fascination as Commissioner Anthony listened to various corporate executives talking about "influence buying," delivering money to regulators, and providing names to be used to disguise the payments as legal donations.

"This is all very interesting," I said to Solomon. "But what does this have to do with McLarty and the White House?"

He said there were three questions suggesting possible vulnerability for McLarty. The first was how much he knew about apparently illegal campaign donations to Commissioner Anthony by top Arkla officials, payments that the FBI thought were bribes. The second area of vulnerability was whether McLarty knew of White House or Justice Department pressure on the U.S. attorney in Oklahoma to refrain from indicting Arkla executives or Arkla itself in return for receiving an appointment as a federal judge after only a year in the job. The third was whether McLarty was in any way involved in causing the settlement of litigation in Tulsa, Oklahoma, that might have produced public testimony regarding Arkla's and possibly McLarty's involvement in the bribery scheme.

We sat down on a couch in my office, and he spread some documents on the coffee table.

He showed me photocopies of sixteen $100 bills and a copy of a check for $500 made out to Commissioner Anthony's 1988 campaign committee and signed by T. Milton Honea, who was then president of an Arkla division. Honea would succeed McLarty as CEO and chair of Arkla after McLarty went to the White House as Clinton's first chief of staff in 1993. The documents showed that in February 1989, some three months after the election, Honea and two Arkla vice presidents visited Commissioner Anthony and discussed making campaign donations to help retire the commissioner's campaign debt.

Three months later, in April 1989, according to the documents, the two Arkla vice presidents returned to visit Anthony, this time without Honea. They delivered $1,600 in cash and another $1,000 in checks, including a $500 check from Honea. Solomon showed me a transcript of Anthony warning them that these payments were illegal under Oklahoma law, which, Solomon explained, barred regulated utilities, like Arkla, or their representatives, from making any campaign contributions to members of the commission. Anthony was wired by the FBI and recorded the conversation. According to the transcript, he told the executives that they should be "awful careful about . . . letting any word get out" about the payments. One of them, Dick Moore, responded: "I can assure you you'll hear nothing out of Mr. Honea."

I studied the photocopies of the sixteen $100 bills and the Honea check and found myself impressed that Solomon had gotten them, as well as the wiretap transcripts. That was some leak, I thought admiringly.

"But at least Honea delivered a check—which was traceable," I pointed out to Solomon. "That shows he probably did not know it was illegal to make such a donation to reduce Anthony's campaign debts."

"You're right, except for one thing," Solomon said. "The check was subsequently returned by Commissioner Anthony, and it was replaced by cash—delivered by Arkla's lobbyist. Surely Honea knew that check had been returned."

"But not necessarily that it was converted to cash," I responded. Solomon agreed.

"I wonder why McLarty wouldn't have known about this visit to Commissioner Anthony by top managers of his company?" Solomon argued.

"That's a reasonable question," I conceded. "But isn't it possible, even likely, that a CEO would have no knowledge of this type of meeting in another state—and that this one was below McLarty's radar screen?"

"Yes," he said. I promised Solomon he would get a direct answer to his question about whether McLarty had any knowledge of these events.

I realized that Solomon and I had crossed an important line together. He had conceded an open-mindedness, despite his initial predisposition to connect the dots, and I had conceded that he was reasonable in his predisposition, based on the facts he knew. The fragile but indispensable build-up of credibility capital between an investigative journalist and the damage-control press person—in both directions—had begun.

We moved to the second issue raised by Solomon—whether or not the decision in 1993–94 by the U.S. attorney, a Clinton appointee named Vicki Miles-LaGrange, not to prosecute Arkla executives was reached to protect McLarty in return for an appointment to the federal bench. "Admittedly, this is mostly circumstantial," said Solomon. "But sources tell me that the FBI and others very knowledgeable about all this cannot understand why the Arkla executives were never indicted. For Miles-LaGrange not to indict anyone, what with the tapes and the cash in envelopes, it makes no sense."

Having heard, and used, the line that "a prosecutor can indict a ham sandwich" more times than I wanted to count, I had to admit to Solomon that it didn't make much sense to me either, given the transcripts and documents I had just seen. Solomon nodded, acknowledging my concession, another upward credibility notch recorded. He pointed out that the decision not to prosecute the Arkla executives was all the more suspicious because an Arkla lobbyist, William Anderson, had been convicted in 1994 for offering a bribe to another commissioner (who was also convicted) on behalf of another regulated utility company, Southwestern Bell. Anderson's attorney had even filed a motion alleging that the prosecutors' failure to indict Arkla and Southwestern Bell itself was an example of "impermissible discriminatory political considerations."

I pointed out to Solomon that it still seemed far-fetched to me that a U.S. attorney who was well regarded professionally would choose not to prosecute for political reasons, with the payoff being a federal judgeship. Moreover, I pointed out that he had not a shred of evidence that McLarty or anyone else in the White House or the Justice Department had influenced Miles-LaGrange's decision in any fashion. Solomon agreed. But Solomon also read me a quote, which he said was on the record, by Commissioner Anthony. Anthony told

Solomon that Miles-LaGrange had apologized to him when their paths had crossed at a subsequent event for there not being more prosecutions in the bribery case, and that she had said something like "We just had to cut it off."

I agreed that such a comment sounded ominous. "But she could have meant, 'We couldn't keep the investigation going forever' as opposed to 'We were under political pressure to cut off the investigation before getting to the Arkla officials.' Isn't either one possible?" I asked Solomon. He agreed.

Finally, as to Solomon's third issue—I asked Solomon what he had showing that McLarty was involved in settling a lawsuit that might have implicated himself or Arkla in the bribery scheme.

"That's the weakest piece of this, I have to admit," he said. He proceeded to tell me a bizarre and very complicated story. In late 1992, two Hawaiian Democratic Party fundraisers, Nora and Gene Lum, arrived in Oklahoma to buy a tiny natural-gas company, the Gage Corporation. They had raised money for the Democratic National Committee between 1989 and 1992 while Ron Brown was national chairperson, and continued to do so after Brown became commerce secretary in 1993. As part of their deal to buy Gage, they agreed to settle a lawsuit filed by the company against the largest natural-gas company in the state, Oklahoma Natural Gas (ONG). There were unconfirmed rumors that had the case gone to trial, the names McLarty and Arkla would have come up in the context of the bribery scheme. Another twist that investigators believed pointed to possible White House connections to the settlement of the case: the Lums retained a Little Rock attorney from Bruce Lindsey's old law firm to negotiate the acquisition agreement. Lindsey is a longtime friend of President Clinton who had since become a senior White House attorney and presidential adviser.

I again pointed out to Solomon that there was absolutely no evidence that the Lums were trying to help McLarty when they settled the case. It was much more likely, I said, that they settled the case to make peace with ONG, and that ONG had its own reasons for wanting to settle the matter. Solomon still thought there was some connection between the White House and this entire strange transaction, given the Lums' close ties to the Democratic National Committee and their association as fundraisers with its former chair, Ron Brown. I argued that he had no evidence that there was anything untoward here, although I conceded that something looked very strange about these two Hawaiians suddenly parachuting into Tulsa, Oklahoma, to buy a little energy company and settle a lawsuit.

I told him I now needed to sit down with McLarty and his lawyers. Solomon said that he had heard that *Business Week* was working on a similar story and he was worried about getting scooped. I told him I would get back to him as soon as possible.

MY NEXT STEP WAS CRUCIAL: I had to gather the facts, do my in-house investigative reporting, and develop a credible counterpoint message. Fortunately, I had a soulmate to help me do it right—as well as a subject (in Mack McLarty) ready to cooperate in every way possible.

Steven Ronnell, a thirty-year-old Arkansan, was then McLarty's top political counselor. Ronnell, a graduate of the University of Texas, had served as legislative assistant to Arkansas Senator David Pryor. He joined the White House staff in 1996. Ronnell and I met during my early days at the White House, those days of frustration when I was having so much trouble getting information reporters were asking for. From the first minutes of talking with him, I knew he understood the damage-control rules that McCurry and I were trying to follow. He recognized the inevitable intersection of legal issues, press needs, and politics. Specifically, he understood the value, from the standpoint of our client, of helping reporters write stories and getting all the facts rather than making things difficult for them.

As soon as Solomon left, I called Ronnell and told him every-thing I had heard. We immediately went to visit with McLarty in his ground floor office in the West Wing. Reading from my notes, I went through the facts that Solomon thought he had and the questions he wanted answered. I knew McLarty only slightly as of then, having met and talked with him at a few social occasions. My impression of him then, and even more so now, is that he is a decent, kind-hearted man, intensely honest, and ready to fight to protect his reputation for integrity. He was widely respected within the White House, in the business community, and by congressional leaders of both parties. The admiration and affection that the presi-dent and the first lady have for him was also obvious. Since at that point I did not know McLarty well, I looked closely at his body lan-guage and eye contact to assess his truthfulness—as I was trained to do as a lawyer. Within minutes, I was convinced he was telling the truth: he knew absolutely nothing about the 1989 meetings between Arkla executives and Commissioner Anthony in which possible illegal contributions were made. He was genuinely horrified when I told him about the $100 bills and categorically denied that he had any knowledge of those transactions. Then he erupted with real anger when I asked him about suspicions of possible political influences on U.S. Attorney Miles-La Grange, leading her to decline prosecution of the Arkla executives. "Hell, no," he said. "If anyone had ever sug-gested to me to do such a thing," he said, "I would have called the sheriff."

He repeatedly stated that if he had known about anyone in the company making illegal contributions, he would have fired that per-son. I gently cross-examined him. "How could such a meeting take place, with Arkla's executives involved in passing cash payments to a commissioner on a regulatory body, without your knowing it? Isn't that hard to believe?"

"Because a lot of things go on in a big company that the chief executive does not know about, and I knew nothing about these meetings or contributions—that's the unvarnished truth," he answered emphatically, eye contact crystal clear and unwavering.

I asked McLarty whether we could look through his White House files and records to see if we could find anything relevant. I knew Solomon was interested in looking at the telephone records, to determine whether McLarty had had conversations with Arkla officials during the 1993–94 time period when they were apparently still targets of the criminal investigation. I also wanted to check for possible calls to the Justice Department or correspondence that might relate to the appointment of Miles-LaGrange to the federal judgeship or to any contacts with the Lums. He said that of course Steve Ronnell and I could have full access to everything, a response that further fortified my impression that McLarty had nothing to hide.

Over the next several days, Ronnell and I reviewed various files and message slips and found nothing whatsoever connecting McLarty to the Oklahoma investigation, to Miles-LaGrange, or to the Lums. We also spoke with McLarty several more times with additional questions from Solomon.

The Miles-LaGrange accusation still bothered me. It was a dangerous example of *post hoc* logic: She decides not to prosecute Arkla and its executives; then she is appointed to a federal judgeship; therefore, she got her federal judgeship because of her decision not to prosecute. I reviewed my notes of my conversation with Solomon, looking for additional facts that could counter those that had driven him in what I saw as the wrong direction. Then I saw it—in fact, I couldn't believe I had missed it. The key meetings at which cash had been exchanged between Arkla executives and Commissioner Anthony had occurred in February and April of 1989. At any time from that point until January 1993, the then U.S. attorney, who was a Republican appointee, could have brought the indictments. He certainly had enough evidence, with the wired conversations and the photocopies of the $100 bills. And yet he didn't. Indeed, for the next four years, until Miles-LaGrange was appointed U.S. attorney by President

Clinton, no indictments were ever brought. Why? Maybe the answer was the same for that Republican-appointed U.S. attorney as it was for Miles-LaGrange and her team in 1993–94: the difficulty of proving bribery under federal law, which requires evidence of specific intent and the commitment of a specific *quid pro quo* in exchange for the money. Perhaps both U.S. attorneys believed that all they had was, at most, a violation of the state's campaign-contributions law—which did not fall under federal jurisdiction.

I called Solomon, trying to convince him that it would be unfair to include in his story the reference to Miles-LaGrange's appointment to the federal bench in conjunction with a reference to her nonprosecution decision without also mentioning the nonprosecution decision of the Republican U.S. attorney's office for almost four years prior. He wasn't buying. He said sources explained to him that the prosecutors and investigators wanted to continue the investigation—and especially wanted not to blow Commissioner Anthony's cover, and that was the reason for the delay.

But four years is a long time, I argued. They could have prosecuted in order to squeeze people, if they were looking to go to higher levels. "Well, at least you have an obligation to mention that the predecessor to Miles-LaGrange had declined to prosecute in the previous four years," I said. He said he would think about the point I was making.

I tried another tack. "So far, I have not seen a single document or conversation transcript in which Mack McLarty's name came up," I said. "Therefore it would be very unfair for his name to be in your story at all." Lots of luck, I thought, but nothing ventured, nothing gained.

"His company and his management colleagues were targets of a federal bribery investigation," Solomon answered. "But I'll call you back—I think I remember seeing his name mentioned in one of Anthony's wiretapped telephone conversations."

An hour or so later Solomon called me back. "The only reference to McLarty in all the documents and transcripts I have is by Commissioner Anthony," he said. I held my breath, fearing this could be the smoking gun. In a telephone conversation with a friend that was intercepted by the FBI, Solomon said, Anthony was talking about his attendance at Dick Moore's funeral in 1991. Moore was the Arkla vice president who had participated in making the $100-bill cash payments to Anthony two years before. Anthony said that he had "visited with" McLarty, Milton Honea, and other top Arkla officials at the funeral.

I waited for more. There was none.

"That's it?" I asked.

"Yup—that's the only mention of Mack McLarty in all the documents and transcripts," Solomon responded.

"Commissioner Anthony talked to McLarty at a funeral—that's all you can find?" I asked again, incredulous. "That should tell you a lot."

By then, Steve Ronnell and I had completed our review of McLarty's files and we were now ready, with confidence, to draft a strong, unqualified denial statement. We sent it over to him. After he consulted with his attorneys, he approved it with minor changes. In his statement, he denied having any "knowledge whatsoever of any alleged bribery scheme or illegal campaign contributions involving Arkansas-Louisiana Gas Company officials until these allegations became a matter of public record in June 1993." He also denied "any contact at any time" with Miles-LaGrange "or any other member of the U.S. attorney's office in Oklahoma regarding these matters." And he further denied that he had any "information as to their prosecutorial decisions regarding any individuals or entities" or any knowledge of "efforts to influence the prosecution of any individuals or entities associated with the alleged bribery scheme."

We debated about adding a denial specifying McLarty's lack of knowledge of the Lums' acquisition of the Gage Corporation and the settlement of litigation with ONG. I was initially in favor of adding such a denial, fearing that it was an issue that Solomon was going to raise. But we decided that it was such an absurd theory, with not a shred of connection to McLarty, that to issue a denial would be to dignify the allegations.

WHILE RONNELL AND I WERE having these conversations with McLarty and Solomon, McLarty's attorneys, Bill Taylor and Leslie Berger, had been doing their best to work the story with *Business Week*'s Paula Dwyer. They were giving her the same factual information and making the same arguments that I was offering to Solomon. But Dwyer seemed stuck on making a connection between McLarty as chief executive of Arkla and allegations of a bribery scheme involving Arkla and its Oklahoma lobbyist. The lawyers surmised the direction that Dwyer was heading, and they tried to convince her, as I had tried to convince Solomon, that there was no evidence of any such connection.

The competition between the journalists came to a head late in the afternoon on January 10. I had just sent McLarty's statement to Solomon, when he called me back to say that he was rushing to put the story out over the wires, because he had just learned that *Business Week* had put out a press release on its story, although the magazine itself would not be published for a few days. He checked a few more facts with me and was kicking himself for not having written the piece earlier. I asked him to call me when the story went out on the wire. In the meantime, I learned that *Business Week* had further jumped the gun on the AP by posting its story on its Internet Web site. At around 5:30 P.M., I found it and printed it.

When I saw the headline, I was aghast. And the more I read the more outraged I became. For starters, there was the headline—in all caps, "SKELETONS IN MACK McLARTY'S CLOSET?" Then the subhead, just as irritating: "Troubling questions about the Arkla ex-CEO and old Clinton pal haunt the White House." What "skeletons"? What "troubling questions"? I quickly scanned the story for new information beyond what Solomon had told me. There was none.

Actually, the story did have one new twist, which was utterly false but nonetheless formed the overall premise of the article: that McLarty's "efforts" to be named commerce secretary or ambassador to Mexico had been sunk as a result of the "questions surrounding" the bribery investigation. The lead stated:

> Around the Clinton White House, he's known as "Mack the Nice"—one of the few presidential pals from Arkansas who hasn't been ensnared in an ethics controversy. But it turns out that there are troubles in the past of Presidential Counselor Thomas F. McLarty III, a wealthy businessman who served as Chief of Staff in the first 18 months of Bill Clinton's Presidency. And those woes may have disqualified him from a higher-ranking Cabinet post.

I noted the conditional word, "may," in that last sentence. But in the next paragraph, it had become transformed to an asserted fact: McLarty's efforts to gain a cabinet post or ambassadorship "sank" under the "weight" of the "questions surrounding a bribery scheme." I looked for the credible substantiation of that assertion. There were only two sources—both anonymous and both ambiguous, so ambiguous that it wasn't clear whether there was one source or two, or what was the basis of their opinion either that McLarty had been considered for these posts or that the White House had failed to nominate him because of these allegations involving the Oklahoma bribery scheme. Dwyer did quote from a letter sent by McLarty's attorneys that "it is patently false to suggest that Mr. McLarty was prevented from being named to a cabinet or ambassadorial position in the Clinton Administration."

I called around to everyone who might have had any knowledge of McLarty's having been considered for nomination as either commerce secretary or ambassador to Mexico. Since McLarty was very popular among Senate Republicans because of his close ties to the energy industry and his popularity in the business community, I found it hard to believe that he would have had anything but a clear sail through the Senate for either of those two posts. Everyone I talked to at senior levels in the White House agreed. Everyone. When I later asked Solomon whether in all his reporting he had anyone tell him that McLarty might have had difficulty getting confirmed because of the Oklahoma allegations, he replied that he had never heard that, and that with all the calls he had made on the Hill and elsewhere about this story, one would think he would have picked it up from a credible source, if it was out there.

I also learned from McLarty himself that he had been asked by the president about his possible interests in the commerce and Mexico posts and that he had said he was not interested.

Factually, the *Business Week* article tracked pretty closely the facts and documents that Solomon had discussed with me concerning the bribery investigation. But when I got to the second half, I was chagrined to see that Dwyer had chosen to outline in detail the story of the Lums' acquisition of the Gage Corporation and its pipeline division, Creek Systems, suggesting that their settlement of the litigation with Oklahoma Natural Gas had something to do with protecting McLarty. Indeed, the article's last paragraph is a classic example of connecting-the-dots innuendo:

> ONG, Arkla, and McLarty all say [that] the idea that ONG arranged a sweetheart deal to benefit itself and Arkla, save McLarty from scandal, and line the pockets of powerful Democrats is preposterous. But some federal investigators, an Oklahoma regulator, and former employees of Creek believe just that. The irony. If the deal was designed to shield McLarty, it failed.

I read and reread this paragraph with amazement. Dwyer had not presented a single fact, even anonymously stated, that linked McLarty in any way to the settlement. All she had were anonymous people (not necessarily unbiased) expressing their beliefs. Even the fact of McLarty benefiting from the settlement was not established. The only apparent basis for this was the reporter's assertion that the "case could have resulted in testimony embarrassing to McLarty [and] Arkla," but the only backup for this is hardly persuasive: one of the co-owners of the Gage Corporation saying only that the discovery process in the case "came up with quite a lot of mention of Arkla." That's it.

I called Steve Ronnell and he had the same reaction to the article as I did. He was furious with the "hatchet job" of the *Business Week* story and frustrated at how far beyond the facts the reporting went, notwithstanding the information given to the reporter by McLarty's lawyers. Steve asked me to call Solomon to check in with him as to when his piece would hit the wire. Solomon was not happy with the news that *Business Week* had raced to post its article on its Web site, undoubtedly because it knew through the journalistic grapevine that the AP was about to send its story over the wires. He told me his piece was still being edited, and it would be a while longer.

Ronnell and I waited. We hadn't the courage to show McLarty the *Business Week* article that night. We hoped the AP version would be fairer, so we decided to let him go home; we would show him both stories in the morning. As we waited, Ronnell told me that, two days earlier, McLarty's lawyers had written Dwyer the letter she'd quoted in her story after she had told them the thrust of what she was going to write.

By 10:00 P.M. the AP story still hadn't hit the wires. Ronnell decided to go home. I was stubborn and waited. Around midnight, Solomon called. "We're putting it out now," he said.

I brought it up on my computer, and printed.

On the whole, the story was balanced, factual, and fair, although I was not entirely happy with the lead. It mentioned McLarty, which I thought was unfair since he had nothing to do with the bribery scheme. But the words were factual and accurate: "A federal bribery probe in Oklahoma implicated two prominent utilities, including the company once headed by Clinton confidant Mack McLarty, but neither utility was prosecuted."

The entire story was composed of a series of factual statements consistent with what Solomon had shown and described to me. The next reference to McLarty, in the tenth paragraph, stated correctly that the "alleged wrongdoing by Arkla occurred while McLarty was still Arkla's chairman." Then in the eleventh paragraph came the denial by McLarty of any "knowledge whatsoever of any alleged bribery scheme or illegal campaign contributions" involving Arkla until the probe surfaced in the news in 1993. I was unhappy that our denial was in the eleventh paragraph, so far down in the story. I thought it should have been immediately under the lead that first referred to McLarty.

I was further annoyed that the reference to Miles-LaGrange—that as the U.S. attorney she had overseen the decision not to prosecute Arkla in 1993 and 1994 and that she was later appointed by President Clinton to a judgeship—was placed in the fourth paragraph, higher than the McLarty denial. This meant that Solomon or his editors gave credence to the suggestion that there might have been a political motive to her decision or a reward for her decision. But there was no substantiation at all of this incredibly serious charge. I looked to see whether at least Solomon had remembered to include my rebuttal—that the Republican predecessor to Miles-LaGrange had not chosen to indict Arkla or any Arkla officials for over four years after the alleged bribery incidents. And there it was—buried in the final paragraph, separated from the innuendo about Miles-LaGrange by 23 paragraphs: "Several federal law enforcement officials, speaking on condition of anonymity, said the FBI pushed for more and quicker action in the case but was rebuffed, both under the Republican U.S. attorney who started the case and the Democratic one who finished it."

I was also disappointed by Solomon's decision to quote from the FBI-intercepted telephone conversation by Commissioner Anthony in which he said he "visited with" McLarty at a funeral. On the other hand, Solomon had noted that this reference was the "only time McLarty came up in court documents" and the paragraph was placed far down in the story, toward the end. That reinforced the impression that overall the AP did not consider McLarty a key part of the story.

Then I realized, with relief, that Solomon (or his editors) had chosen not to include the Lums/Gage Corporation–settlement piece of the story. "I tried to find a connection," Solomon told me later. "I did a lot of investigative reporting on the subject, and there were lots of people, knowledgeable people, telling me they believed that the settlement was at least partially motivated by a desire to protect Mack McLarty. But I didn't have any factual evidence to support that. And when you don't have it, you don't write it."

Here we have two news organizations given the same set of facts, arguments, time, and attention by me and by McLarty's lawyers. Yet the contrast between the two stories could not have been greater— one based entirely on hard facts, leaving readers to draw their own inferences; the other while reporting many of the same facts, heavily relying on suggestive words, speculation, juxtaposition, and anonymous sources.

Though I was far from thrilled with the AP story, at least my unhappiness was not over its inaccuracy. I couldn't find a single paragraph that was factually inaccurate. I could only criticize what were essentially editing decisions—the placement and order of the facts reported.

Although I know McLarty would rather not have been mentioned at all in Solomon's AP story (and I believed that there was a very weak journalistic basis for any reference to McLarty in the story), at least Solomon had minimized McLarty's role, and made no suggestion whatsoever that he was involved in the bribery scheme or had suffered any political consequences from the perception of such involvement. When we visited McLarty the next morning, his anger remained focused on the *Business Week* story—a testament to Solomon's middle-of-the-road reporting. (The following week, the magazine printed three letters—from former Georgia senator Sam Nunn, from Mike McCurry, and from Sol Linowitz, former ambassador to the Organization of American States—condemning the piece as inaccurate and unfair. Of course, letters to the editor do not even come close to the impact of a headlined story in the magazine.)

The negotiating process I had gone through with Solomon—dialogue, mutual dissection of the evidence, debates over what are reasonable inferences from facts and what are not, and occasional concessions to the other's analysis—taught me that this process is critical to effective damage control as well as to good journalism. It is the only way that the initial potpourri of rumors, sources, facts, and speculations can be sorted out and narrowed down to accurate, complete, and balanced reporting; the only way to get the waterfall, as Mike McCurry once said, narrowed down to go through the garden hose; the only way to keep the dots connected by facts, not by innuendo.

But I also learned that this back-and-forth dialectic between the reporter and me could be very fragile. It hung on the thread of mutual credibility and trust. The minute either one of us felt manipulated, deceived, or disrespected for doing our job, it would all be over.

That wouldn't be good for either one of us.

7

Been There, Done That

DON GOLDBERG STEPPED BACK FROM THE HUGE ERASABLE BOARD that was nailed to the wall of his office in the Old Executive Office Building. Clearly he was admiring his handiwork: a kaleidoscopic array of columns, lines, and neatly scrawled words and phrases in various marking pen colors. He walked slowly to the board and took out his red marker. Under the heading "Issues," there were seven items. Next to each of them was another column, with small printing in a different color, under the heading "Answers." A third column had miscellaneous notes, smudges, and doodlings in still more colors. He drew bright, thick red lines around the first two items. He stared at the board for a few minutes. We waited for him to say something—something profound, insightful, cerebral about the meaning of it all.

We weren't disappointed.

"If Fred Thompson gets the red done, we're fucked," he said.

IT WAS EARLY MARCH 1997. The Senate Governmental Affairs Committee, chaired by Senator Fred Thompson, Republican of Tennessee, would not hold its first hearings on campaign-finance abuses in the 1996 presidential campaign for another three months. A few of us were assembled in Goldberg's office for yet another meeting to try to figure out a strategy to counter what Senator Thompson and his fellow Republicans were planning. We knew the hearings would be nationally televised.

We were worried. For the previous four months we had been in the vortex of a feeding frenzy by the scandal-press machine trying to find new stories about Democratic fundraising abuses and their possible impact on Clinton administration policies. We saw no end in sight—and we worried that public interest could peak just at the moment when Fred Thompson went on national television.

Goldberg, thirty-nine years old, a former investigative reporter, was a Capitol Hill veteran. He had been the chief Democratic investigator during the 1996 House of Representatives oversight committee hearings on the so-called "travelgate" investigations, which involved alleged impropriety in the firing of the White House travel-office managers. In late 1996, he joined the White House staff to monitor the congressional committees that were driving the campaign-finance investigations. Early on I recognized Don Goldberg as a philosophical soulmate. He was trusted and well known to the Washington press corps, had excellent political instincts, and understood how to get information out of the White House through indirect but appropriate methods. Because of his close relationships on the Hill, he was able to encourage Democratic staffers there to help the press write stories, and then we would be in a position to react by confirming or supplementing the early reporting. He and I and my deputy, Adam Goldberg (no relation), worked closely together, especially as the congressional hearings approached.

It was not an artistic bent that caused Goldberg to use an erasable board. It was fear of a subpoena—and lawyer's fees. It is a sign of our times, dominated as they are by investigations and subpoenas—by the independent counsel, by the Justice Department, and at one point by more than twenty Republican-controlled congressional committees—that people working in the White House are deathly afraid of writing down anything that might be subject to a subpoena. Which is to say, people in the White House are deathly afraid of writing anything down at all.

Goldberg stood in front of us, ready to practice the Socratic method.

"If you were Fred Thompson, what's the worst story for the White House that you would be looking for? And what would be our answer?"

It was an important exercise—in fact, the critical first step—in effective damage control: putting yourself into the opposition's shoes and making an educated guess as to what their most damaging messages might be—and then coming up with your own strategy and message to trump theirs.

"Money buying access," one person volunteered.

Groans. "Come on," someone else said. "Don't tell me the Republicans have any credibility complaining about big donors getting special access. Big donors actually get more access from the politician they give to than nongivers? How shocking!"

"How about when money buys policy—you know, bribery?"

Jeers. "Try proving that a campaign contributor gives money, the senator votes for the bill, and therefore, the money caused the senator to vote for the bill," someone said. "Fat chance. Let the press chase that one. There's always a reason on the merits why the vote can be explained."

As we talked, Goldberg would write down our words on the board in shorthand sound bites, using different colored markers according to a formula that only he understood.

For this one, he wrote down the acronym QPQ—for *quid pro quo,* otherwise known as bribery. We knew this was the big enchilada of the campaign-finance-scandal press corps: Trying to find an example of Bill Clinton taking money and in return changing a policy.

"What about using the White House for fundraising?"

This was a sore subject with me, given the implausible denials I had been offering to the press that the White House coffees had nothing to do with raising money.

Same groans, same reaction. "Remember the Republican Eagles [a club for six-figure donors] coming to the White House and getting wined and dined by Reagan and Bush?" someone else asked.

"They'll certainly hit us on Harold Ickes and the rest of the White House essentially converted into a campaign headquarters."

"Right," was the quick response. "And what about Jim Baker during the 1992 presidential campaign? The only difference between him and Harold Ickes is that Baker virtually openly announced he was running the campaign from the White House."

"How about renting out the Lincoln Bedroom for $50,000 a night?"

Silence.

"That one isn't very good," was the comment.

More silence.

"Well, it may be a bit over the line." (*Laughter.*) "But don't tell me Newt Gingrich and Tom DeLay didn't sell Republican lobbyists seats at the table to write special interest legislation—most people understand that Republicans trying to argue that they're purer at raising political money than Democrats is a joke."

That was it—we all recognized it at once—the overall message for the hearings, indeed, for the entire campaign-finance so-called scandal. No matter how you cut it, the pundits and the press corps didn't get it. The American people were pretty smart. They would see that the Republicans were basically using congressional investigations for political partisan purposes—not because they really cared about passing campaign-finance reform.

It would be our job in the coming months to point this out—*ad nauseam*. And whenever the accusation came—as it inevitably would—that we were falling back on the discredited argument, "Everybody does it—that makes it okay," our answer would be, "Yes, everyone does it, but it's not okay. That's why we Democrats support campaign-finance reform. It's the Republicans who oppose it—which is why their criticism of us cannot be taken seriously."

There was a sense of relief in the air. We were on territory we all knew. Politics—this is all about politics, nothing more or less, Republicans bashing Democrats to elect more Republicans. That would be our battle cry.

More important, this would be our strategy for raising the bar on measuring the success of the Thompson committee hearings. The two tests, we would say to the press corps, are whether Senator Thompson could produce bipartisan hearings that would investigate both Democratic fundraising and Republican fundraising equally *and* whether he could produce a vote recommending comprehensive campaign-finance reform.

We knew that the more committed Republicans would never allow either to occur. We would set the bar at a level that we knew Senator Thompson could never reach. This was cynical and manipulative—we knew—but also right on the mark.

Goldberg had been writing down each of the five likely lines of attack on the board, with our proposed "push backs" (spin jargon for counterattack) next to it. We noticed he numbered them from 3 to 7: "Money buys access"; "Money buys policy—QPQ"; "Fundraising at White House"; "Campaigning from White House"; "Renting Lincoln Bedroom."

Then he said:

"It's time for the two nuclear bombs."

He wrote the number 1 and then: "Foreign (Chinese) money."

We all knew this issue was very dangerous. The first scare had begun with a story broken by the *Washington Post*'s Bob Woodward on February 12, 1997. Woodward had reported that, according to intelligence and other anonymous sources, the Chinese government "planned" to make covert campaign contributions to influence the 1996 U.S. elections. The rest of the story was about Asian American fundraisers and their foreign business connections, particularly John Huang and his sponsors from Indonesia, the Riady family and the Lippo Group. But somehow the Woodward story, which initially worried us, seemed to have fizzled out. Most of the reporters who usually would be driven to do further reporting after Woodward broke a big story told me that they were left cold on this one. The sources looked thin, the new facts negligible. No one could quite figure out what Woodward had, what the story was about, or why the *Post* had hyped it so big as to make it a page-one lead—except for the fact that anything Woodward wrote was regarded as justifying major play. As one of the most respected Washington investigative reporters on the scandal beat said to me the next day, "What's news about a plan? There are a lot of plans. Where is the evidence that anything actually happened? There are very few new facts in that story, just speculation."

Okay—foreign money coming into U.S. politics could be a bad issue. But I just couldn't worry too much about it—at least, not based on what Woodward had reported.

Goldberg wrote the number 2. "And what's the second nuclear issue—maybe even worse than the first?" he asked.

Someone blurted out: "Well, if you really want to get ridiculous, you could take all the worst possibilities and put them all together: campaign money compromising foreign policy, intelligence agencies, and national-security concerns."

Goldberg wrote it down on the board, using his now familiar red marker—of course:

"Money/Foreign Policy/National Security."

That's when he drew the red lines around numbers 1 and 2 and delivered his punch line about Fred Thompson.

"That's completely ridiculous, it'll never happen," I said. "You've seen too many Fred Thompson spy movies."

ABOUT A WEEK LATER: 8:00 P.M. on Friday, March 14. I had just finished returning my last call, had cleaned off my desk, and was on my way out the door when the telephone rang. I turned and hesitated. I was tempted to keep going, pick up the message the next day. But, as usual, I couldn't resist. I picked up the phone.

"Davis. Frisby."

It was Michael Frisby from the *Wall Street Journal.*

Uh oh, I thought. Must be trouble.

"What do you have, Frisby?"

"How about this: Campaign money, foreign policy, the White House, National Security Council, Don Fowler [Chairman of the Democratic National Committee] and—get ready—the CIA!"

The CIA!? Perversely, I thought again of Fred Thompson in one of his CIA movies.

"You are not serious, Frisby—you don't have this on record, do you?"

"Sorry, old buddy. I've got it all on record. Sit down for a few minutes. I have a story to tell you."

Did he ever.

"Let's talk about Roger Tamraz," he said.

The name Tamraz evoked an immediate sensation of uneasiness—as if it was a bad dream that I wasn't surprised was about to come true. My memory flashed back over the previous two months—back to late January 1997 when I had first heard of Roger Tamraz in connection with an international Interpol warrant for his arrest.

His name was one of the hundreds on the lists of White House coffee attendees that we had released to the press. After we released all the names, the reporters began a massive research sweep of all these names, hoping to find attendees with checkered pasts. This became the source of a good deal of the investigative journalism of the next several months in the Democratic campaign-finance-scandal stories.

A search of Tamraz's name on the NEXIS database had turned up a trove of interesting articles about his past activities. Tamraz, a native of Lebanon who had been educated in the United States and who subsequently became a naturalized citizen, had been involved in various business ventures, primarily in the oil business. He had been kidnapped during the Beirut civil strife and had allegedly been tortured. He had had dealings with the Israelis and with western business interests.

It seemed that Tamraz had recently been involved in promoting an oil pipeline to bring the substantial oil reserves in the Caspian Sea area to warm-water ports in the Mediterranean. I had a vague impression from the clips that this was a controversial venture, since it seemed that Tamraz wanted to secure the backing of the U.S. government for his own pipeline route as opposed to any other routes.

The clips also had many references to an Interpol warrant, issued in June 1989, for Tamraz's arrest. It seemed that he had been accused by an Islamic religious court in Lebanon of embezzling $200 million in the aftermath of the failure of a bank where he served as chairman of the board. Tamraz disputed the charges, claiming that they were in retaliation for his connections to the West and his sympathies for Israel.

With this kind of information in the NEXIS clips, it was not surprising that Tamraz was soon the subject of press requests for WAVES records. During late January at our morning strategy meetings, Don Goldberg, Adam Goldberg, and I pressed for a comprehensive disclosure about Tamraz—not just the bare-bones date of the visit and the event or office visited, but also any information we had about the purpose of the visit as well as any correspondence between Tamraz and the White House.

It was pretty obvious that there were enough exotic aspects to Tamraz so that sooner or later reporters would get this information. The Senate investigators would undoubtedly issue subpoenas for those records, just as they subpoenaed anyone else in the campaign-finance story who became controversial through news reporting.

Ches Johnson retrieved the Tamraz records, and Adam Goldberg went to be debriefed by the White House attorney who was assigned to review them. When he returned he reported to me that there had been only a handful of visits in 1995–96, apparently mostly for social or political receptions, but there was one curious meeting with someone identified only as an "NSC staffer." I remember a flicker of concern, as I told Adam to find out more about that meeting, and about what business Tamraz had with the National Security Council. When he returned, he said there was a shutdown on any further information about Tamraz's contact with the NSC staffer. Now I had more than a flicker of concern. All my antennae were vibrating that there was something going on here that could lead to a big story.

On January 30, I reported at our morning strategy meeting, presided over by deputy chief of staff John Podesta, that the press was going with the story about Tamraz's Interpol warrant—and was asking me for comment as to why the National Security Council staff had not reported the warrant to the White House before Tamraz was allowed to attend a White House coffee with the president. I also reminded everyone that there was increasing pressure for the release of Tamraz's WAVES records.

After the meeting, I sat in the outer reception area of the White House counsel's office in the West Wing, waiting for a response from the attorney assigned to help me. I noticed this attorney huddled with a high official of the National Security Council staff. I noticed that the official was holding a folder on which the name Tamraz was written in red marker. They were whispering rather nervously. This guy Tamraz, I thought, may be more than just another Democratic donor.

The White House attorney then walked over to me.

"We're not giving any information out on Tamraz—except to say we knew nothing about the Interpol warrant," the attorney said.

"Not any of the WAVES information?" I asked. My heart was sinking.

"No."

The next day's stories were just about the Interpol warrant issue, and all I could say was that we were reviewing our screening procedures. "There is an effort under way to improve the standards as to who is properly at the White House with access to the president," was my official, authorized comment.

I also warned reporters that Tamraz had insisted that the court indictment and the Interpol warrant were bogus. "Don't treat the guy as if he's a criminal," I told a number of them.

The next development in the Tamraz story occurred a couple of weeks later. It was actually a nonevent: the decision by the White House not to volunteer additional information about Tamraz because the wrong question was asked.

Shortly after his election in 1996, President Clinton announced the nomination of his national security adviser, Anthony Lake, to serve as Director of Central Intelligence. The nomination immediately generated controversy among some conservative Republican senators, particularly the chairman of the Intelligence Committee, Senator Richard Shelby. It was said that Lake's past included involvement in the anti–Vietnam war effort, and that he had failed to sell some of his energy stocks, despite possible conflicts of interest.

In early February, Senator Shelby asked for NSC file documents referring to suspicious campaign donors who had been cited in connection with the campaign-finance scandal. Most of the names were those of the Asian American donors who had been the subject of the news articles in the closing weeks of the campaign and thereafter. I reviewed the list provided by Shelby to the White House, looking for the name Roger Tamraz. It wasn't there.

I walked into the office of a friend of mine on the NSC staff. "Didn't Roger Tamraz visit someone on the staff of the NSC in the 1995–96 time period?" I asked. The official looked at me blankly.

"Why do you ask?"

"Because we're about to send a whole bunch of information up to Senator Shelby about political/donor contacts with the NSC," I said. "We might as well get Tamraz's NSC contact out now—in the middle of all the other documents we're sending to Shelby. It's going to come out at some point anyway—of that I am certain."

The official shrugged and said, "They didn't ask us to produce anything on Tamraz."

"But that's just because he hasn't had a lot of press yet—just the Interpol story," I responded.

"That's being decided at a higher pay grade than mine," the official responded. "We're giving Shelby exactly what he asked for—and we're not volunteering anything more."

On February 14, we released the National Security Council documents to the press at the same time as we sent them to Senator Shelby. Nancy Soderberg, staff director of the NSC, Adam Goldberg, and I sat in her OEOB office working the phones with the press. Soderberg was serving as Tony Lake's unofficial confirmation-campaign coordinator. She answered reporters' questions about the NSC warnings concerning those fundraisers visiting the White House. Adam and I backed her up with information on the campaign-finance-related issues.

Our message, which we worked out ahead of time, was simple: "The NSC, under Anthony Lake's leadership, did its job to warn the White House political people about allowing too much White House access to the controversial Asian American fundraisers. In any event, no policy decisions were ever affected by such access."

The press, naturally, was skeptical. Several reporters called me to talk "off the record."

"If I were you, Lanny, I'd pull back on your push that there were no political contacts with the NSC—it could blow up in your face," one of my closest press friends told me.

"Why—what do you know?"

"Just rumors—but I'd be careful if I were you."

Again I thought of the scene in late January of the White House attorney huddling with the NSC official with the file marked "Tamraz."

No, I thought. I'm going to block that out. I'm being paranoid. Tony Lake had been my friend for more than two decades. Our message was clearly the truth: Lake would not stand for the National Security Council being compromised by political pressures.

The next day's news coverage reflected our message perfectly. The NSC was given credit for *resisting* political pressures—just as we had hoped. "NSC Gave Warnings About Asian Donors," was the *Washington Post*'s headline; similarly the *New York Times:* "Clinton and Gore Received Warnings on Asian Donors."

A successful day of spinning, I thought—good spinning, pushing facts out and giving them a reasonable interpretation favorable to a client.

We knew that by giving the NSC credit for warning the White House off allowing the Democratic donors too much access we were at least implicitly criticizing the political side of the White House. But this was a trade-off we were prepared to accept—because our objective was to help Lake get confirmed.

I stopped by to see Nancy Soderberg that morning to congratulate her on the generally positive press coverage. Tony Lake stuck his head in the office and was genuinely happy. If anything, we were convinced that the chances of Lake's confirmation had been improved.

We were smug. But not for long.

About a month later, with the Lake nomination still stalled before Senator Shelby's committee, the mysterious meeting between Tamraz and an NSC staff member—the one that we had been forbidden from disclosing in late January and decided not to volunteer to Senator Shelby in mid-February—was finally leaked to the newspapers.

On Friday, March 14, Michael Frisby of the *Wall Street Journal*, among other news organizations, reported that a junior NSC staffer named Sheila Heslin had met with Tamraz in June 1995 to discuss his pipeline proposal and had responded only that it was U.S. policy not to support a particular pipeline route. Frisby and the others reported that Tamraz had returned to the White House six more times after that meeting, including several social and political meetings and receptions attended by President Clinton. Frisby also reported that Tamraz had contributed $170,000 to the Democrats in the months following his meeting with Heslin. (Actually, Frisby had gotten the timing wrong in his lead: He had said that Heslin had met with a "major Democratic contributor" when, in fact, Tamraz had not given any money to the Democratic Party until after the meeting.)

Adam Goldberg and I were furious. Why hadn't we been allowed to put out this information in January along with the Interpol warrant story? Even more, why hadn't we sent this up to Senator Shelby in February and released it to the press, surrounded by other information favorable to the NSC, showing that the NSC staff had resisted political pressures? Instead of a neutral-to-favorable story, this looked as if we had been trying to hide the information about the NSC meeting, as if there were something wrong with it. Adding to that impression was the new information that Tamraz had contributed $170,000 after the Heslin meeting—as if he were paying off the Democrats in gratitude.

Apparently we weren't the only ones who read Frisby's story this way, as I learned when he called me that Friday night.

"SPEAK, FRISBY," I SAID.

"I talked to Sheila Heslin today after she read my story," Frisby continued. "She was pissed. She thought the story unfairly implied that she had done something improper in meeting with Tamraz, and that he rewarded the Democratic Party with $170,000 in return for his meeting with her. She told me that not only had she told Tamraz the administration disapproved his proposal for an exclusive pipeline route, but she also had repeatedly tried to block his future access to the White House—only to be overridden again and again by the political people. She was angry that the White House had not put out the entire story."

"Was she on the record?" I asked, disbelievingly. I thought that NSC staffers didn't usually talk to the press on the record without authorization from the highest levels. "Yes," he replied, "but she told me she's no longer at the NSC.

"And Don Fowler and the CIA?" I asked, still incredulous that the CIA was in any way involved in connection with the chairperson of the Democratic National Committee and a Democratic donor.

"My sources tell me that Don Fowler called Sheila Heslin and tried to convince her to back off on her opposition to Tamraz coming back to the White House, and to further persuade her, he arranged for the CIA to send her a document backing Tamraz's service to the agency."

"Did she ever hear from the CIA?" I asked, hoping against hope the answer was no.

"Yes—she got a report from the CIA favorable to Tamraz a few days later."

"Damn!"

Two days later—late Sunday afternoon—Frisby called again to tell me that he had talked with the DNC's Fowler—on the record— and Fowler had confirmed that he had called Heslin to try to overcome the NSC's opposition to Tamraz attending White House social and political functions. He said he was only asking for Tamraz to be able to go to group functions, not to have personal meetings with the president or anyone else. However, he said he could not remember whether the subject of the CIA had come up in his conversation with Sheila Heslin; he admitted that it was "possible."

"A nondenial denial," I said to Frisby, glumly.

The next day, Monday, March 17, the *Wall Street Journal* played Frisby's story as its page-one lead. This was unusual for the *Journal*, since it usually put political stories on its back page. The placement suggested that this was going to be a huge story—and it was.

In Frisby's story, Don Fowler repeated his nondenial denial: He did not deny that he had called Heslin, though he was foggy on the details of the conversation and on any reference to the CIA. The next day, Fowler issued a statement that he remembered talking to Nancy Soderberg and Sheila Heslin about Tamraz, not seeming to appreciate the full political implications of the chairman of a national political party calling the National Security Council to discuss a Democratic donor gaining access to the White House. In that statement Fowler categorically denied that he had contacted the CIA "in this situation, or any other" to "ask them to supply information to Ms. Heslin, Dr. Soderberg, or anyone else."

Frisby even talked to the man himself. Roger Tamraz's comment on his failure to get any help from the White House was just as telling, if unremarked upon: "People expect things, but you don't get anything, at least as far as I am concerned."

Revving the story up even more were the substantial number of questions that remained unanswered. Frisby brought together all of the strands of Don Goldberg's nightmare in one neat little paragraph:

> The tale of Mr. Tamraz and his access to the White House . . .
> could take the Democratic fund-raising controversy to a new
> level. . . . [Fowler's call to Heslin and his reference and reported
> use of the CIA] set off a flurry of internal investigations inside
> the CIA and the White House this weekend to determine how a
> political official could extend an arm deep into the nation's

cache of secrets and pull out information to help a party contributor seeking support for a private business deal. Chief
among the questions: What role did Mr. Fowler or government
officials play in shipping the CIA information on Mr. Tamraz to
Ms. Heslin, and who was contacted inside the intelligence
agency?

The immediate result of Frisby's amazing story was National
Security Adviser Tony Lake's decision to ask the president to withdraw
his nomination to direct the CIA. This occurred after several senators, including Nebraska Democrat Bob Kerrey, expressed concerns
about Don Fowler's contact with the NSC. (To this day, Kerrey has
never explained why this was Lake's fault.) That same day, March 17,
Frisby called again and told me he had soft information on another
unreported Tamraz meeting—this one with an official at the Department of Energy, again to talk about getting administration support
for his pipeline.

"Don't tell me the White House had anything to do with setting
up that meeting," I said, knowing under Murphy's law what the
answer had to be.

"Funny you should guess—some time in 1996, by Mack
McLarty," he answered, laughing. McLarty had by then become the
president's senior counselor and also served as his chief liaison to the
business community. McLarty's past service as CEO of the energy
company Arkla, Inc., might have made such a contact understandable and innocuous. Frisby faxed me some questions to fill in the
details. I went to the NSC press person, but he couldn't help me out.
Neither could the White House attorneys. The wall of silence seemed
to be in place once again.

What's going on here? I thought. This is just another little time
bomb that is going to keep ticking away until the next round of leaks.
Don't they realize that? I called Frisby back and told him I couldn't
help him. The next day, March 18, Frisby reported, with obvious

obliqueness, that "Energy Department officials" had acknowledged that McLarty had "arranged" for Tamraz to meet with them to discuss the oil pipeline, offering no other specifics, no names, no dates. Although there was little follow-up in the next several days and weeks, that didn't mean the blanks in the tale would go away.

OVER THE NEXT SEVERAL MONTHS, as we approached the start-up of the Thompson hearings, the Tamraz story seemed to simmer just below the surface. Press inquiries continued, and most of the reporting concerned the CIA's in-house investigation concerning Heslin's claim that Don Fowler had interceded on Tamraz's behalf at the CIA (which Fowler categorically denied). But, aside from the DNC-Fowler story, very little new information developed. Frisby continued to push me, however, on the McLarty–Energy Department piece of his story, which he had been unable to report fully in March. By mid-April and into May, the pressure had started to build again—as if more and more reporters were getting off-the-record leaks from the Hill; they couldn't tell me about what they knew, but they were acting as if they knew that there was still something big out there.

I too was still unable to find out what else might be out there. All my normal deep-background sources in the White House were unusually nervous about talking to me. It couldn't be just because I was awaiting my security classification clearance—which I finally got a month or so later. I kept pushing my friends in the counsel's office, particularly Charles Ruff, who had replaced Jack Quinn as White House counsel in February 1997, and Lanny Breuer to approve a selective deep-background placement in order to get whatever was left of the Tamraz story out the door. They seemed increasingly open to the idea by the end of May, because they realized that all the information on Tamraz was now in the hands of staffers for Senator Thompson's committee, and it was likely they would leak it or, even worse, wait to present it as a centerpiece of the early days of televised hearings.

I kept nagging Chuck Ruff—I saw it as part of my job description. He put up with it good-naturedly, at least most of the time. A former Watergate special prosecutor and U.S. attorney, Ruff had represented such U.S. senators as John Glenn and Charles Robb and had successfully convinced prosecutors not to pursue cases. He was brilliant, contained, cerebral. I sometimes found him very stubborn when it came to being more forthcoming with the press, and his reticence to share information with me (I'm sure because he feared I would leak it) often made my job difficult. Yet, because I trusted him and respected his integrity, I assumed that he always had good reasons for resisting my entreaties, usually reasons involving legal and factual issues that were unknown to me.

On the Roger Tamraz story, Chuck Ruff and Lanny Breuer were especially cautious about my going too far with reporters. At one point, after I pressed Ruff strongly to allow me to get the full story out on deep background before Senator Thompson did, he warned me that this one had serious prospects for triggering an independent-counsel investigation. This was the first time I realized that there really was something very damaging still out there, unreported.

In early June, with the opening of the Thompson hearings just weeks away, it was apparent from our sources on the Hill that Senator Thompson planned to make the Tamraz story a linchpin of the hearings. Ruff and Breuer approved releasing a more complete narrative of Tamraz's visits and contacts with the White House, including more information about Mack McLarty's and the president's knowledge of Tamraz and their possible assistance concerning his pipeline proposal.

On Tuesday afternoon, June 3, we decided to release additional Tamraz information, but only to the six major print news organizations that had devoted most of the investigative resources to the Tamraz story: the *Wall Street Journal*, the *New York Times*, the *Washington Post*, the *Los Angeles Times*, *USA Today*, and *Time* magazine. Breuer and his legal team had assembled all the information, and a White House special counsel, Buzz Waitzken, was assigned to help me give the proper background to the reporters. I called the six reporters and set up a conference call for 7:00 P.M. that night.

Shortly before seven, I was handed the three-page statement I was about to issue. I had not seen it before, and I was not happy with the very short time I had to prepare before talking to the reporters. I quickly realized that it was written legalistically, without disclosing much new information. We had filled in some blanks on what Michael Frisby had previously reported in March and had issued a complete list of Tamraz's WAVES records, which showed a total of seven visits. We finally filled in the blanks about McLarty's introduction of Tamraz at the Energy Department. Tamraz had talked briefly about the pipeline with the president at a March 27, 1996, DNC dinner, and that the president (according to my background briefing sheet) "later asked Mr. McLarty, his designated liaison to the business community at the time who also had a background in the energy field, to follow up with Mr. Tamraz." Then again, on April 1, McLarty "spoke with Mr. Tamraz . . . for a few minutes . . . [and Tamraz] outlined his pipeline project, including mentioning that Bethlehem Steel would be providing the steel for the pipeline project and that the plan therefore would result in many new American jobs." According to my statement, McLarty then requested that Kyle Simpson, an Energy Department official whom he knew from their days in the private sector and in the energy business, look into the Tamraz matter and determine whether there was any new information to justify Energy officials' meeting with Tamraz. A few days after the April 1 coffee, McLarty had forwarded to Simpson some Tamraz brochures on the pipeline. Afterward, my statement said, McLarty "briefly mentioned to the president that he had looked into Mr. Tamraz's pipeline proposal, and that it did not warrant further attention." That was it, as far as White House intervention on behalf of Tamraz; a nonstory, as far as I was concerned.

My continuing reaction, of course, was: Why hadn't we put out this relatively innocuous information before now? My next reaction was: There were still a lot of questions that we weren't answering. Why hadn't we earlier disclosed everything about the contacts between the CIA and Sheila Heslin? Why did the National Security Council's opposition to Tamraz returning to the White House fail to get communicated to the rest of the White House political hierarchy? Above all, were there any additional political pressures put on Heslin—by the White House or by anyone else—to relent in her opposition to Tamraz?

I told the White House attorneys that some reporters had told me, off the record, that Heslin had been pressured by someone in the Energy Department. I could tell by the looks on some faces that it was true. "We need to get it all out now," I said.

I sensed reluctance—something was worrying them. I left the room and returned a few minutes later. Then I was told two new facts that I could divulge during the briefing, but again only on "background": First, another Energy Department official, Jack Carter, had met with Tamraz in May 1995 to discuss the pipeline proposal—a month before Tamraz's conversation with Sheila Heslin. This meeting had been arranged by the U.S. ambassador to Armenia, whom Tamraz had also lobbied on his pipeline proposal. (This guy sure gets around, I remember thinking.) And the second fact was the real bombshell: Jack Carter, who I was told had been a Texas Democratic party fundraiser before his appointment to the Energy Department, had actually called Sheila Heslin, with whom he had previously worked on a pipeline task force, and allegedly tried to pressure her to remove her opposition to Tamraz attending White House receptions.

As I conducted the press briefing, I remained certain that I still hadn't been told everything. The lawyers' body language, the pattern of dribbing and drabbing, had conveyed to me that we were still holding something back. Something big, I felt.

Later that evening, after deadlines, Mike Frisby and *USA Today*'s Ed Pound separately called me. Both had heard that Heslin had told Senate investigators in a deposition the previous week that Jack Carter had mentioned to her that Tamraz might make additional campaign contributions if he got support for his project from the administration.

I was stunned. If anyone at a high level of the White House had known about such a statement, it could lead to appointment of an independent counsel. I'd say this was a piece of information that we should have been told about—if it was true.

"I have no information on Carter mentioning money to Sheila Heslin," I told each of the reporters. "They would not have put me out there tonight with all that I told you and hold back something as important as that. Of that I am certain."

Next time, don't be so certain.

That was my first thought the next morning, June 4, when I read, disbelievingly, Ed Pound's story in *USA Today* detailing Tamraz's *quid pro quo* offer, i.e., that Carter had raised the issue of Tamraz's willingness to give more contributions in his conversation with Heslin. Pound had obviously done some independent reporting beyond what we had given him the night before, I assumed a leak from a congressional staffer. In the *Wall Street Journal,* Mike Frisby laid out the implications of this new information: "If Mr. McLarty, Mr. Simpson or Mr. Carter referred to Mr. Tamraz as a major contributor in their conversations or mentioned that he might make more contributions . . . it could force Attorney General Janet Reno to call for an independent counsel."

How come Pound and Frisby had gotten this information and I hadn't? I was perplexed and angry. Obviously someone—probably one of the Republican staffers on the Thompson Senate committee who was deposing Heslin and everyone else relating to the Tamraz story—was starting to leak the information. Since Sheila Heslin wasn't talking to us but was talking to the Senate investigators, it seemed we were at the mercy of such leaks—demonstrating, once again, the disadvantage of letting the opposition control the release of information.

Two days later, John Solomon of the Associated Press faxed me a note, in which he wrote that he had sources from the Senate telling him that White House officials had Sheila Heslin's notes of her conversation with Carter, notes that explicitly detailed Carter's reference to Tamraz's donations in his call to Heslin.

Now the leaks were turning into a torrent—and yet I was still in the dark. My colleagues in the counsel's office again refused to answer any questions about Sheila Heslin and her notes of her telephone conversation with Carter. I couldn't get a confirmation that the notes even existed.

I fell into a black mood, and turned to Dr. McCurry for medicine. The cure, we both knew, was obvious. We needed to get those notes of Heslin's out and complete the Tamraz story once and for all. But how? With full deniability for all? I went to each of my favorite sources in the counsel's office and begged, stamped my feet, cajoled and shouted, but to no avail. Even Lanny Breuer, who was very sympathetic to the need to get this story fully written, was unable to help me.

Then, a few days later, I literally bumped into one of my favorite people on the NSC staff, someone who had both foreign-policy expertise and political instincts and, most important, someone who understood the value of disclosing information to the press yourself before the other side does it for you.

"Anything more you can tell me about Sheila Heslin that hasn't been reported?" I asked.

The staffer hesitated. I persisted.

"Look, you know as well as I: This stuff is all coming out anyway. The only question is—do we let Fred Thompson frame the story or do we get a chance to do it ourselves, with our own imprint on it?"

There was a long pause. Then the staffer seemed to be making a decision.

I waited. I knew instinctively that I had struck a nerve, that there *was* something else, something that might have been the basis of the nervousness I had seen in the White House attorneys from Day One in January when the name Roger Tamraz first came up.

"Follow me," came the reply, the decision obviously having been made.

"Do you know about the Heslin notes of her conversation with Jack Carter from Energy?" the staffer asked me, closing the office door.

"I just heard about them from an AP reporter. Some reporters have written that money was mentioned," I said.

The staffer went to a desk drawer, leafed through some notes, and picked up a piece of paper, saying that just to be on the safe side, the staffer would only summarize Heslin's notes.

Here is what I heard:

Carter . . . Tamraz, DNC . . . $400,000; $200,000; $600,000 . . . McLarty . . . Pres want.

That last one was new, and explosive. I took a deep breath: this was the first mention of the president in association with a donor who is promising to give more money in return for help on a commercial project. Why would Carter mention the president and McLarty in the context of more money from Tamraz? How dumb was that?

Of course the White House lawyers, and possibly the president's personal lawyers, must have been aware of this from the earliest days, since they had access to Sheila Heslin's notebooks. So it was Heslin's notes of her conversation with Carter that, from the beginning, lay at the core of the counsel's office's nervousness about the Tamraz story going all the way back to the first day in January when we first responded to questions about his Interpol warrant.

This cannot be true, I thought. I could not believe that Mack McLarty, much less the president or anyone at the White House, would allow campaign donations to be discussed in connection with governmental policies. But if this story were leaked without our having a complete opportunity to knock it down, it would take us a long time to catch up with the truth.

I called a close friend in the press. I needed help.

How much can you tell me about what is still unreported in the Tamraz story? I asked him.

How much do you need to know?

I need to know what Thompson and his staff have on Heslin's notes—and whether we can be sure they're going to get them out anyway.

He paused. Okay, he said, here's what I can tell you: They are planning a big headline for opening week, and it's going to include the contents of Heslin's notes of a conversation with a guy from the Energy Department.

That did it.

I sped back to McCurry's office and found him in his professorial mode, feet on his half-circle desk, his now familiar Cheshire-cat smile on his face. Hey, what's up? he asked, his usual opening for most of our conversations.

"Houston," I replied, "we have a problem."

It usually didn't take more than a few minutes for McCurry and me to decide strategy. I would tell him only the minimum of what I thought he needed to know. He would speak in half-sentences and elliptical phrases. And that would be it.

I then went to Lanny Breuer's office, closed the door, and had a careful conversation with him to ask his advice, but without revealing specifics. I had an understanding with Lanny: I would never allow him to be blind-sided by any placement I was about to make, but on the other hand, I had to be careful not to tell him too much to avoid compromising his obligations to his colleagues in the counsel's office and his commitments to congressional committees and others regarding premature release of information. So I had to walk a fine line, telling him just enough, but not too much. My method was to ask him a series of hypothetical questions, à la Socrates, aimed at assessing the risks and ramifications of a particular deep-background private placement. I trusted his intelligence and political sensitivities to pick up my message and then to signal me in his own way if he had a serious problem with my going forward. This is the approach I used on this occasion.

As I walked out of Lanny's office, I knew exactly what had to be done. And I knew I had to do it on my own. I had to report the story myself.

I made several calls to people associated with the key players who would figure in the story, such as Mack McLarty and the NSC's Nancy Soderberg. I was able to definitively knock down the notion that McLarty had ever mentioned money when he referred Tamraz to his friend Kyle Simpson at Energy, and could confirm that McLarty never discussed the president or money with Jack Carter. I also confirmed that Nancy Soderberg had strongly supported Sheila Heslin in resisting the pressures allegedly applied by Carter. The open question, of course, was why Carter said what he said (if he said it)—but that was, fortunately, not a White House problem.

The final step was to get a denial that the president had ever expressed himself on the subject of Tamraz's pipeline—beyond his *pro forma* referral to Mack McLarty to follow up after the March 27 dinner. I went to someone very close to the president, a high-placed staffer who could ask the president directly. That staffer called me back and told me the president had no idea why someone wrote "Pres wants," but it had nothing to do with anything the president had said. That was enough for me.

I could have called reporters Ed Pound or Mike Frisby, who deserved to get the rest of the story, but I wanted a "predicate" story to be written on a subject as important as this one—a story that would tell the full story, in context and from beginning to end, a story that would have such credibility that everyone else in the press would use it as the basis for all future reporting. I also wanted a reporter whom I trusted to write it fairly, and John Solomon of the Associated Press fit the bill perfectly. He also seemed to know about the Heslin notes from other sources.

The AP was also a perfect vehicle for this story because I wanted to get it out to everyone at the same time, so that everyone would be writing off the same predicate story for the same news cycle. This, too, would maximize the chance that the subsequent reporting, at least in the first round of stories, would be consistent—hopefully, as balanced as the AP story on which everyone was forced to rely. And the major newspapers hated to reprint AP stories, so they usually ran them on the inside pages.

"I've got a deep-background private placement for you, John," I said.

"Heslin's notes?" he guessed right.

I told him I could only describe to him key words from the notes. "Have you seen them?" he asked me.

"No. But I completely trust the person who summarized them to me."

Per our agreement, the AP released the story at 2:10 A.M. on June 11. This meant that everyone would be working off the same story the next morning—one written comprehensively and fairly. The Heslin notes were summarized completely. Solomon had also included my flat-out denial that McLarty had ever mentioned Tamraz's status as a donor in his conversation with Kyle Simpson or that the president had ever expressed himself on the merits of Tamraz's pipeline proposal. Most important, there was a denial by a "senior White House official" (guess who?), stating that "in the end, nothing was ever done to help Tamraz"—the good spin.

The story set off a firestorm, as I knew it would: dozens of press calls flooded into my phone within the first few hours. For the most part, I simply referred the callers to the AP story and refrained from further comment—exactly the advantage of a good predicate story.

FINALLY, I THOUGHT, THE TAMRAZ story had now been written. Not a pretty one, to be sure. An emblem, perhaps, of the worst of the Democratic campaign-finance story: money buying access, brazenly so, but producing nothing. Tamraz didn't get his pipeline deal, and that was the most important point.

Better still, we had succeeded beyond all expectations in our pre-emption strategy involving the list of hot issues on Don Goldberg's kaleidoscopic marker board. The effect of our campaign to get bad news out the door as quickly and completely as possible had been to turn the bad news into old news—and that made it less damaging to the administration. In fact, after the first day of Thompson's hearings, on July 10, the *New York Times*'s Francis X. Clines wrote: "The day was rich in partisan fencing but virtually devoid of fresh disclosures. Much of the testimony rehashed earlier news accounts of financing abuses rather than any new ground being broken." That reflected a comment made a few days before by the spokesperson for the Thompson committee, Paul Clark, to *Washington Post* reporter John Mintz: "It's unfortunate for us. They've clearly tried to minimize the impact of all this bad news. . . . It takes away the surprise of any hearing. We want to keep our powder dry, and present it to the American people." And then there was Senator Thompson himself, who a few weeks later had this exchange with a counsel to President Clinton's legal-defense fund:

SENATOR THOMPSON: You consulted with Mr. McCurry and our good friend, Mr. Lanny Davis, too, I believe, didn't you?
MR. CARDOZO: No, I spoke with Mr. Davis the day of my December press—
SENATOR THOMPSON: Did he tell you this was old news? (*Laughter.*)

Despite this, I knew that to a great extent we had lucked out. There had been four critical junctures when we could have made full disclosure of all the facts surrounding Tamraz—the first Interpol-warrant story at the end of January; the Anthony Lake disclosures on political contacts with the NSC in mid-February; the mid-March Michael Frisby story concerning Sheila Heslin, the CIA, and Don Fowler; and our early June proactive disclosures concerning Tamraz's brief conversations with the president and Mack McLarty, and McLarty's referral to the Energy Department. On each of these occasions, for reasons that seemed quite legitimate at the time, the White House chose to put out less than the full story. We let the story come out in pieces and out of context. Thus, as the story dribbled out, it appeared to be bad and growing worse. Because the press perceived that we were reluctant to be forthcoming, they naturally sensed that there must be something even worse. And because Adam, Ches, and I were not given access to all the facts all at once, we had to think like reporters, too—forced to try to connect the dots, pushed into thinking that things must be very bad if people seemed so paranoid about us finding out the facts—which ironically led us to believe that things were much worse than they turned out to be.

This is a classic demonstration of the advantage of putting out the entire story yourself, good and bad facts together and in context, versus the adverse consequences of letting the story leak out and then trying to catch up to the negative spin being put on it by your opposition.

In retrospect, I can appreciate the serious concerns of the White House attorneys about any casual disclosures to the press regarding Tamraz. Certainly the Sheila Heslin notes alone, referring to "$600,000" and "Pres wants," looked like the basis for triggering the appointment of an independent counsel. But ironically, the reasons for the attorneys' (and my own) nervousness about the Tamraz story turned out to be exaggerated or unjustified. The Tamraz story started out in all our minds as potentially the nuclear story of the year—and then, once all the facts had come out and Tamraz's testimony before the Thompson committee was completed, the actual story was a great big fizzle. We had all bought into the opposition's premise: that there was something terrible about a wealthy businessman blatantly buying access to try to influence decision makers. We overestimated the political and legal dangers of the story, even the Don Fowler–CIA component.

As bad as some aspects of the Tamraz story were—and I cannot defend the decision by DNC Chairman Don Fowler to communicate with Sheila Heslin, nor explain why Jack Carter said what he allegedly said to Ms. Heslin regarding campaign contributions—the fact is, the coverage of the Tamraz story remains a classic example of a scandal-press corps that focuses more on appearances and innuendo than on substance and the facts. The reality was that no policy had been changed; Tamraz, for all his money and puffing, walked away empty-handed. All he got for his $300,000 in donations (the ultimate total he gave in 1995–96) were a few meetings and social contacts at the White House with the president.

The climax of the Tamraz story—or more aptly, the anticlimax—came when he finally appeared before the Thompson committee on September 18, 1997. What was most remarkable is that Roger Tamraz came across as refreshingly honest, remarkably unthreatening, and—unfortunately, for what it said about the American political system—typical of most political donors to both parties.

In one of the most telling exchanges in the Thompson committee hearings, Senator Joseph Lieberman focused on the issue of money for access:

LIEBERMAN: As you look back at the $300,000 you gave, do you think you got your money's worth? I mean, do you feel badly that you didn't get any change on the pipelines, for instance. . . . So do you think that you got your money's worth? Do you feel badly about having given the $300,000?
TAMRAZ: I think next time, I'll give $600,000.

The committee and the audience were unaccustomed to such unbridled candor. The room burst into laughter and some applause.

MONEY BUYING ACCESS IS AS OLD as democracy itself. The sanctimony and double standard being applied to the case of Roger Tamraz was apparent to many people in the hearing room. The story fizzled because, at the end of the day, there was no there there.

During one of the breaks, I was upstairs in the press gallery above the Senate hearing room when I heard Tamraz's familiar thick accent. I walked down the hall and watched him, diminutive, smiling, surrounded by reporters, answering questions, soaking up the attention. At one point, someone asked, "What is your opinion of the Clinton White House people after all the money you spent trying to get in?" His answer:

"They stiffed me. I paid and paid and paid, and they stiffed me. They were polite. But they stiffed me."

I remember thinking to myself: Once again, a victory for the obsession with appearances over reality. My mind raced backward, like a videotape rewinding over the previous six months, a montage of images and emotions and crises all centered around this rather unremarkable, small man and his big pipe-dream of cornering the Caspian Sea oil market: the Interpol warrant; Tony Lake's failed nomination to head the CIA; Sheila Heslin's notes; the heavy breathing and hype of the press; and the real possibility that Don Goldberg's thermonuclear bomb—money plus foreign policy plus national security plus compromising the CIA plus the chairman of the DNC— was about to detonate.

And instead of a thermonuclear bomb, one great big . . . dud. Pfffft.

8

Nunsense

BY THE TIME IT WAS OVER, AL GORE PROBABLY WISHED HE HAD never heard of the Hsi Lai Buddhist Temple.

On October 17, 1996, three weeks before the presidential election, the story broke in several major newspapers that John Huang, the controversial Democratic fundraiser, had sponsored an event on April 29 of that year at this Buddhist temple in the Los Angeles suburb of Hacienda Heights, California, with Vice President Al Gore as the guest of honor. Not only had the attendees contributed $140,000 to the Democratic National Committee—a newsworthy fact in itself, since religious institutions were supposed to be off limits for partisan fundraising—but, as first reported by Phil Kuntz of the *Wall Street Journal,* some of the nuns and devotees admitted to participating, albeit unwittingly, in an illegal conduit scheme to disguise the source of political contributions to the temple event. The nuns, who had taken vows of poverty, apparently had written checks in their own names and then were immediately reimbursed by temple leaders with cash payments of up to $5,000. Later stories reported that the illegal reimbursements had totaled $58,000.

The stories generated a political and journalistic firestorm concerning the propriety and legality of Vice President Gore's attendance. Certainly the "tacky factor" was a political issue for the vice president, since using a religious institution as a location to raise campaign money, never mind using nuns to make donations, seemed inappropriate at best. There were also two potential legal issues: first, if the vice president or his staff had had any knowledge of the alleged illegal conduit scheme, that could expose them to criminal liability; and second, if they had participated in the use of a tax-exempt institution to raise political money, that could be a civil violation of federal campaign and tax laws. The press and the Republicans demanded to know whether or not Gore knew that the event was a fundraiser, beforehand or while he was there, or knew anything about the alleged conduit scheme. Five days later, on October 22, the vice president offered Nina Totenberg of National Public Radio a categorical denial:

> The DNC set up that event, asked me to attend it. It was not billed as a fundraiser. It was billed as a community outreach event. . . . But as I understand it, after the fact, the contributions came in too soon after the event to say that it was anything other than an event directly tied to it. I did not know that at the time.

For the next eleven months, the scandal-press corps dug out every conceivable element of this story in order to refute Gore's denial. They interviewed nuns and devotees and the temple's leaders. They reviewed thousands of pages of documents released by Republican-controlled congressional committees and by Gore's legal and communications staffs. The Republican-controlled Senate and House committees searching for Democratic campaign-finance abuses saw this issue as a way of damaging the presidential prospects of the vice president. They took numerous sworn depositions and held days of public hearings on the subject, even dragging the nuns before the bright lights of national television. All these combined journalistic and partisan efforts were aimed at one objective: To prove that Vice President Al Gore was lying when he said he had not known that the Buddhist temple event was a fundraiser or about the alleged illegal contribution conduit scheme.

A FTER THE VICE PRESIDENT'S initial denial to Nina Totenberg failed to cool interest in the controversy, Gore's staff realized that they would not be able to stanch the flow of bad news but would have to adopt a policy of proactive disclosure to make sure that the developing story was placed in its proper context. Their task seemed daunting at first blush: The Republican-led congressional committees had subpoenaed DNC documents that referred to a fundraising event to be held in Los Angeles in late April 1996, to be attended by Vice President Gore. And by early January 1997, the newspapers were reporting that prior to the event John Huang had communicated to DNC staffers (and perhaps to members of the vice president's staff as well) that the Buddhist-temple luncheon was expected to be a fundraiser.

Lorraine Voles, the vice president's communications director, realized that she was less informed than the reporters about the DNC documents on this subject, so early in January she visited the DNC to review the documents herself. She returned to the White House and informed her colleagues that the briefing memorandum prepared for the vice president prior to the event had clearly indicated that the temple luncheon was sponsored by the Asian Pacific American Leadership Council, a DNC-financed group organized by John Huang. The memo indicated on the first page that membership in the Council required a contribution of $2,500 per person or $5,000 per couple. However there was no reference in the memo to a price tag for attendance at the luncheon itself, nor was there any reference to fundraising or fundraising objectives associated with the event.

After some discussion, it was the consensus of Voles and others on Gore's staff that the vice president should go beyond his statement to Nina Totenberg that the Buddhist-temple event was a "community outreach event." Thus in early January 1997, Gore told Dan Balz of the *Washington Post* that the event was also a "finance-related event" because he recognized that it was "sponsored by the Asian Pacific Leadership Council of the DNC." He said it had been a "mistake" for him to attend such an event at a Buddhist temple. But he clearly reiterated his denial of any prior knowledge that the event was a fundraiser: "It was not a ticketed event and I did not see any money being collected . . . [or] solicit[ed]." And "there were not only members of the council present but political supporters and [others] from the surrounding neighborhood."

Five days later, Gore reiterated to Katie Couric on the *Today* show, "I did not know that it was a fundraiser," but he confirmed that he did know that "finance people . . . were going to be present." Therefore, it was "inappropriate" and a "mistake" for him to have attended an event at a temple "sponsored by a council that required a contribution for membership." And then he repeated: "But I was not told it was a fundraiser, and that's a fact."

Gore had clearly repeated his categorical denial that he had any knowledge that the event was a fundraiser. Yet he received little credit for going beyond this denial and volunteering that he had made a mistake in attending an event at a temple that had been sponsored by a DNC-financed group. Rather, he was derided by pundits and Republicans, among others, for his use of the phrase "finance-related event," which, it was said, was an overly cute euphemism for "fundraiser." And the truthfulness of his denial continued to be challenged in the press and by congressional Republicans.

Within the White House, there were mixed reactions to Gore's decision to admit to having made a "mistake." The day the Balz article appeared in the *Post,* January 9, I was called into the Oval Office to join in a briefing of the president and the vice president prior to a "press availability" event. When I entered, the president and vice president were sitting on the two yellow chairs on the far side of the

Oval Office, opposite the president's desk, with various senior White House aides sitting on the two facing couches or standing nearby.

"What's the reaction of the press corps to the vice president's admission of a mistake in attending the Buddhist temple event?" Mike McCurry asked me as I walked into the room.

At this point I was not responsible for handling any press stories pertaining to the vice president. But since the matter of the temple event had arisen in the context of the press's efforts to report the campaign-finance scandal, I was receiving a lot of calls about the Buddhist-temple issue, all of which I referred to the vice president's staff. Nevertheless, I had had numerous off-the-record conversations with reporters and had some sense of their mood.

"They're feeling somewhat vindicated," I said. "I mean, they see it as a vindication of their suspicions that the vice president knew the event was a fundraiser, and that's the opposite of what he first said. I think we should push back hard that the vice president had no idea that Huang had converted that event into a fundraiser."

As I walked out, one senior presidential aide pulled me aside and said: "This is a good lesson. If you try to placate the press, you get no credit for it, they just keep pounding you."

I thought about that as I walked back to my office. My first reaction to the news of Gore's statement was to appreciate his candor and to assume that he would get a lot of credit for it. That would be the end of the story, I thought. Then I realized that such a thought was naive, to say the least.

For the next several weeks, the Buddhist-temple story simmered, with most of the press corps chasing the more explosive revelations of White House coffees and Lincoln Bedroom overnights in the wake of the Harold Ickes document dumps. I continued to refer any calls concerning Gore and the Buddhist temple to Lorraine Voles and to the vice president's deputy press secretary, Ginny Terzano.

However, from the few questions I received about Gore, it was obvious to me that the press's strategy was to find as many examples as possible of DNC officials and Gore's personal staff having known that the event was a fundraiser, and then leaving it to the public to infer that Gore must have known, too.

This line of attack was first fueled by documents that were sent to Senator Richard Shelby, chairperson of the Senate Intelligence Committee, on February 14, 1997, in the context of the committee's consideration of the nomination of Anthony Lake as director of Central Intelligence. Shelby had sent to the White House a subpoena requesting all documents relating to donor contacts with the National Security Council, the same subpoena that had led to so much consternation over Roger Tamraz. Among those papers were various e-mails and memos exchanged by members of the National Security Council staff and the vice president's national-security staff on the possible adverse foreign-policy implications of the vice president's attendance at the Buddhist-temple luncheon. The issue was whether China would be offended, in light of the Hsi Lai Temple's affiliation with Taiwan. Gore was given the green light to attend by the members of the NSC and his own national-security staff, so long as there was no identification of the event as being related to Taiwan. However, one member of Gore's national-security staff, John J. Norris, did refer to the event as a "fundraising lunch" in an April 19, 1996, e-mail to an NSC staffer, Robert Suettinger, seeking advice on whether Gore should attend. (Six months later, on October 16, 1996, after the story broke, Suettinger wrote a memo to the file in which he used the same phrase, but it is clear that he was only repeating Norris's characterization.)

Following our policy of releasing documents before the Republican congressmen could leak them, the Gore-NSC correspondence was released to the press the next morning, February 15, along with the other documents subpoenaed by Senator Shelby. This was the first time I had significant contact with reporters about the Buddhist-temple story. I was working with the NSC's Nancy Soderberg to talk to the press about the documents, but we referred all questions about

Gore and the Buddhist temple to Lorraine Voles. It was clear to me, however, that there was an intense press reaction to John Norris's single reference to a "fundraising lunch." Indeed, most of the major newspapers ran front-page stories about Gore and the Buddhist temple, focusing on Norris's and Suettinger's characterizations. Typical was the reporting of Alison Mitchell of the *New York Times,* who wrote that the "computer messages made clear that members of the vice president's staff were aware beforehand that the luncheon at the temple was intended to raise campaign money, despite Mr. Gore's initial assertion in the face of news reports last fall that he had thought it a 'community event' and not a fund-raiser."

Buried in Mitchell's story, as well as in most of the others, was Lorraine Voles's reminder that just because one or more members of Gore's staff thought the event was to be a fundraiser does not mean that this characterization was communicated to the vice president. "Mr. Norris's description of the luncheon as a fundraising event was not inconsistent with Mr. Gore's own remarks," Voles said. "Some members of our staff may have known the event was a fundraiser, but he did not." In other words, Al Gore's statement of denial had not been contradicted. While some of his staff might have thought the event was or could be a fundraiser, Gore himself did not.

YET THAT MESSAGE WAS NOT getting through. For the next several months, the drumbeat continued that Gore did know, or must have known, or should have known—you name it. Since the story was still not my responsibility, I gave it only passing attention. But as the July 1997 Senate hearings neared, it was obvious that the Buddhist-temple story would be a prime focus, not only because all the facts and circumstances were still cloudy but because the Republicans could not resist trying to inflict political damage on the vice president, the likely Democratic presidential nominee in the year 2000.

By this time, I had become close friends with Charles Burson, the vice president's counsel, and I began spending more and more time in his second floor OEOB office discussing how to minimize the damage from the Buddhist-temple story and to get his advice on other stories.

Burson had been attorney general of the state of Tennessee for eight years and had come to Washington in February 1997 to work for his friend Al Gore. I first took a liking to Burson when, during a debate in the counsel's office over whether to do a document dump of the second batch of Harold Ickes documents, he agreed with me that we should put them out ourselves early rather than wait for them to be inevitably leaked. (I tend to like people who agree with me.) Soft-spoken, thoughtful, with a light southern accent, Burson combines a sharp, cerebral approach to the law with a good dose of political and press sensitivities and experiences—in other words, the combination necessary for a counsel to the vice president of the United States.

In late May, in the middle of preparing to send up additional documents to Senator Fred Thompson's committee, Burson and his team discovered a new document, which they immediately recognized was semi-hot, in connection with the Buddhist temple story. It was a phone message slip bearing a handwritten note by David M. Strauss, who was then Gore's deputy chief of staff. The note, dated March 13, 1996, reflected a conversation that day between Strauss and John Huang. It was apparent that the conversation was in the context of the visit with the vice president, scheduled for two days later, of the Venerable Hsing Yun, master of the Hsi Lai Buddhist Temple. Below John Huang's name and his phone number was Strauss's note:

lead to a lot of $ moving support.

I just happened to stroll into Burson's office after the morning campaign-finance press strategy meeting as Burson was reviewing the Strauss call-slip note with his colleague, Special Counsel Buzz Waitzken. They showed me the document.

"How hot?" Burson asked me.

I looked it over, asked a few questions about Strauss and the meeting with Hsing Yun, and answered, "Moderately hot. After all, there's no reference to the Buddhist-temple event itself, and there's no reason to believe Strauss had any idea that there was supposed to be a Buddhist-temple fundraiser. He probably thought that a meeting between the vice president and the venerable master could open the doors for John Huang to raise more money from the Asian American community."

Burson still winced. We knew that this cryptic note could be stretched to suggest a connection between the temple master, the temple, John Huang, and campaign donations, all in support of the presumption that if Gore's staff knew about the event as a fundraiser, then the vice president must have known. Of course, since there was no reference to the event in the note, I had a hard time believing that even a press corps intent on connecting the dots would be able to make that connection credibly.

"Have you asked Strauss what this note meant?" I asked.

Burson nodded affirmatively, explaining that Strauss could not remember specifically, but could only assume that Huang had mentioned that it would help him to raise money in the Asian American community if Gore developed a friendly relationship with Venerable Master Hsing Yun.

"Obviously Strauss's notes are not referring to raising money from the venerable master, and there's no reference to the Buddhist temple luncheon," I said.

"Is there anything else?" I asked.

Waitzken and Burson looked at each other, and I could tell there was another hot document about to be produced.

"Take a look at this," Burson said, handing over another sheet of paper. It was a memorandum from Huang—dated April 11, 1996—to Kim Tilley, the vice president's scheduler. The subject line stated: "Fundraising lunch for Vice President Gore 6/29/96 Southern California." (It was obvious that this was a typographical error; the date should have been 4/29/96.) The memo described the "proposed event" to be held at the Hsi Lai Temple, in Hacienda Heights, California.

Fundraising lunch? Uh-oh, I thought.

The memo mentioned that the temple had been the site of other political events, "for Congressmen Howard Berman, Bruce Morrison, and Lee Hamilton recently." Huang asked for an answer "ASAP" regarding the vice president's willingness to attend the event. Huang also made reference to a conference call the preceding week to discuss the event, which he said had included DNC Finance Director Richard Sullivan as well as David Strauss. This last reference was ominous, because now it appeared that Gore's deputy chief of staff was directly tied to the event and likely had knowledge that it was a fundraiser. I made a mental note that someone had to ask Sullivan for his recollection of this crucial conversation. In a postscript, Huang stated that during the March 15 White House meeting between the vice president and the venerable master, "Vice President Gore expressed his willingness to visit the temple," establishing at least a potential connection between the March 15 Gore meeting and the April 29 "fundraising lunch."

"Well," I said, after rereading the memo several times, "it certainly looks as if at least Kim Tilley and possibly Strauss knew that John Huang was planning a fundraiser at the temple on April 29."

I called deputy Adam Goldberg, whose predictions on the relative temperature of documents were unerringly accurate, and asked him to come up to Burson's office. Goldberg walked in, looked over the two documents with the seriousness of a physician examining a medical chart, and declared soberly, "Page one, above the fold."

This wasn't just a game, testing our ability to predict the newsworthiness of a new document. It was an important skill, necessary for effective damage control, honed over time, to be able to predict how big a story was likely to be. Based on that assessment came our judgment of how to handle the story—whether it to put it out ourselves generally, through a private placement, or to do nothing and not risk revving up what might otherwise by a minor story or a nonstory.

Once we agreed that these two documents would garner a lot of press interest, and that we needed to explain them and put them in the context of not contradicting the vice president's denial, we discussed various methods of getting these documents out proactively. Burson wanted to talk to his colleagues on Gore's staff. We had some time to decide the best course of action, because no documents could be released before the congressional committee had received them—and that wasn't scheduled to take place for another week or so.

And yet even after these documents had been sent to the Senate committee, there was still no decision about pushing them out. Then I received a phone call from Don Van Natta, Jr., of the *New York Times*.

Van Natta told me that he and his colleagues were doing investigative reporting on the Buddhist-temple event and had some pretty good information that Gore had been sandbagged by Huang, in that Huang had secretly canceled another fundraiser scheduled in Los Angeles for the same day and then had sent his donors to the temple event without telling Gore or his top people. He asked whether I could persuade Gore's team to share any new documents or information with him for part of the story they were writing. The documents would come out anyway, Van Natta pointed out, once they got into in the hands of Senator Thompson.

It was obvious that by this time many reporters had learned which buttons to push to get me to put out a story. I thought to myself, without saying so to Van Natta, that this could be the opportunity we had been looking for to release the Strauss notes and the Huang memorandum, buffered by the "good" fact that John Huang had sandbagged Gore by secretly converting the temple luncheon into a fundraiser.

I told Van Natta I would check with the vice president's staff, but that Van Natta needed to tell me everything he would be reporting so that I could make a complete presentation to them about cooperating. I assured him that he could trust me to treat his investigative reporting with full confidentiality. If Van Natta wanted me to help him, he needed to tell me everything he knew. He agreed.

Van Natta said that he and a fellow reporter, Christopher Drew, had pretty well established that John Huang had planned *two* events in Los Angeles for April 29: the first a fundraiser at a restaurant in Monterey Park and the next a visit to the Hsi Lai Temple in Hacienda Heights, "two valleys away," to meet with Asian American community leaders. The second event, at the temple, was not supposed to be a fundraiser, Van Natta said. He had sources at the DNC who were very categorical about that point, and Huang was told as much.

That's very significant, I thought. This is the first time I realized that the DNC, too, had been deceived by Huang.

So—all the references in the DNC documents to a fundraiser scheduled for Los Angeles on that date would have concerned the earlier event supposed to be held at Monterey Park, and not the temple, I thought, satisfied that the pieces of the puzzle were finally coming together. That also explained the basis for Gore's clear impression that the second event, at the temple, was about outreach to the Asian American community—and was not a fundraiser.

"So how did the temple luncheon turn into a fundraiser producing $140,000, with nuns being reimbursed for their individual contributions?" I asked Van Natta.

Van Natta said that the *New York Times* had confirmed that at the last minute, within a few days of the event, Huang made the decision to merge the Monterey Park event with the temple event. He did this because he had been told by the DNC that the locations were too far apart and there wasn't enough time for the vice president to attend both. Huang then told his donors that they would be going to the temple event instead. I asked Van Natta whether anyone knew yet who was responsible for the illegal reimbursement of the nuns. Was it

Huang or one of his colleagues? I asked. Van Natta said he knew that some of the nuns had been reimbursed in cash and that some of the money might have come directly from the temple account, but it was still unclear where the money had come from or who had devised the plan.

And then Van Natta filled in the final piece of the puzzle, which I had been looking for: whether the DNC's Richard Sullivan and Gore's staffer David Strauss, during the conference call mentioned in Huang's memorandum, had ever approved or discussed Huang's having a fundraiser at the temple. Van Natta told me that he had sources "close to Sullivan" who were saying that Sullivan had specifically, with Strauss listening, told Huang there could be no fundraiser scheduled at the temple, and that Huang had specifically promised there would not be. And also, he said, Huang told them that this was to be a community event, that the temple was more like a community center, and that Gore would win big political points in the Asian American community for being there under the auspices and approval of Venerable Master Hsing Yun.

That did it. As far as I was concerned, the vice president's statement of his understanding of the event was now fully corroborated— not only by confirmation of Huang's secret collapse of the Monterey Park event into the temple luncheon, but also by Sullivan confirming that he had told Huang, with Strauss listening, that the luncheon could not be a fundraiser but rather must remain a community outreach event.

I went back to the Ickes files and saw that there had always been two events for Gore to attend scheduled for Los Angeles on April 29. Now I could understand the confusion about these two events, with some staff members using the word "fundraiser" to refer to the earlier Monterey Park event, not the temple event.

I went up to see Charles Burson. He seemed especially upbeat as I walked into his office.

"What's up, spinmeister?" he asked. From anyone else, that term irritated me. From Burson, it usually made me sputter and then laugh. Among the reasons I liked Burson is that he would always find a way to cheer me up when I was having a bad day, usually by making me laugh at myself.

I told him about my conversation with Van Natta. I suggested that this might be the time to release the Strauss call-slip note and the Huang memo, surrounded by good documents showing Gore had no knowledge that the event was a fundraiser.

Burson smiled and handed me a new document.

It was a "briefing memorandum" describing the April 29 Hsi Lai Temple event. This is the piece of paper that went into Gore's "trip book," the book outlining his schedule and detailing where the event is, the nature of the event, the key sponsors and attendees, and any background information he needs to know, especially if he is expected to offer remarks. If anyone wanted the best evidence of what Gore "knew" about the nature of the event, one would look at this "briefing memo" for the event itself. It is virtually certain that Gore would have at least scanned this briefing memo prior to going to the event. Also accompanying the briefing memo was an outline of suggested talking points for the vice president's remarks at the event.

The title of the briefing memo referred to the event as a "luncheon," not a "fundraiser": "Democratic National Committee Asian Pacific American Leadership Council Luncheon Honoring Vice President Gore," and under that the location, "The Hsi Lai Temple, Hacienda Heights, California." In the first paragraph the Council was described as an organization that "requires an annual contribution of $2,500 per person or $5,000 per couple" and attendance was estimated at 125 guests.

So it was clear that right from the get-go Gore knew the temple event was sponsored by an organization which required a substantial contribution to the DNC for membership. But this is exactly what Gore had stated in the *Washington Post's* January 9 story as well as his interview with Katie Couric on the *Today* show five days later.

Significantly, there was no mention anywhere in the memo that the event was a "fundraiser" or that there would be any particular fund-raising total expected to result from the event.

"Do you have a copy of what Gore said at the event?" I asked Burson.

He smiled, and handed me another document.

The title was "Talking Points for Vice President Al Gore, Asian Pacific American Leadership Council Luncheon, Los Angeles CA April 29, 1996."

There were fourteen talking points—beginning with a standard self-deprecatory joke, with Gore kidding himself: "It's so cold back east that people who didn't know me well thought I was frozen stiff." Then he went on to talk about the difference between Democrats and Republicans, the environment, social security, and economic prosperity in California and elsewhere. He closed with comments about the great diversity and unity of the American people, with a brief reference to the contributions made by Asian Americans. It was what Gore's staff called his standard *e pluribus unum* speech. What it clearly was *not* was a fundraising speech. There were none of the comments thanking attendees for their generosity or their financial support that are always part of a politician's speech at a fundraiser.

"The dog that didn't bark proves the case," I said to Burson. He smiled, enjoying my Sherlock Holmes analogy, and said, "Here's an event when the dog did bark." He handed me another document, a briefing memorandum for the next event—an evening event on the same date in San Jose—as well as the accompanying talking points.

The memo was in the same format as the Hsi Lai Temple briefing memo, the standard document Vice President Gore normally reads before a scheduled event. Under "Event Description" is the sentence: "The event is raising $250,000 for the DNC."

The contrast with the Buddhist-temple luncheon memo could not have been more obvious. For a change, this was a hot document *in our favor,* virtually proving that Gore knew that the San Jose evening event was a fundraiser but the temple luncheon was not.

As if this wasn't good enough, I turned the page and looked at the attached talking points for delivery by the vice president at the San Jose event.

Talk about frosting on the cake. In contrast to the *e pluribus unum* speech at the Buddhist temple, Gore began this one with the opening remark that nearly all Democratic politicians use at their fundraisers: "President Kennedy used to welcome people to events like this by saying, 'I am deeply touched—but not as deeply touched as you.' Truth is, we are grateful for your contribution. Your involvement is at the very heart of our party."

I looked up and smiled back at Burson. "This does it," I said. "We have to get this out. We have a *New York Times* reporter who has nailed down the rest of the story, namely, how Huang sandbagged Gore by secretly converting the temple event into a fundraiser, in defiance of express instructions by his supervisor at the DNC. This is the perfect opportunity to put out the Strauss note and the Huang memo, sandwiched by all these documents and facts confirming the Veep's account from the beginning."

Burson seemed to agree, but said he needed to consult with Gore press staffers Lorraine Voles and Ginny Terzano, as well as others up the chain of command. Several hours later, he called and said it was a go. I called Van Natta and asked him whether it was still the case that he was writing a story about how John Huang had deceived Gore and the DNC by secretly merging his Monterey Park and temple events without telling anyone. Van Natta said Yes. I said that we would be willing to help him with that story by showing him not only additional documents that were somewhat troubling for us, but also memos and talking points proving that Gore did not know that the Buddhist-temple event had become a fundraiser. Based on that understanding, I invited him to come over to Burson's office the next morning.

Van Natta arrived with his colleague Christopher Drew. Burson had assembled all the documents and walked the reporters through each of them. He showed them the Strauss call slip and pointed out that the reference to "$ support" was vague and did not pertain to the Buddhist temple event. But Drew seemed skeptical that Strauss had no specific recollection of the conversation.

"Do you remember specifically the content of a conversation you had fifteen months ago?" I asked Drew argumentatively. He didn't answer.

Drew asked whether Strauss's call slip note showed that he and Huang had talked about fundraising in the context of the meeting two days thence between Gore and the venerable master, and at that meeting, wasn't there an agreement for Gore to visit his temple in the next month or so? Yes, Burson replied. But clearly Huang was interested in using a favorable relationship that might be developed between the vice president and the master as a way of motivating Asian American Buddhists to give financial contributions, and there never was any discussion about holding a fundraiser at the temple.

I certainly didn't like the drift of Drew's questions. I could see that he was connecting the dots between the Strauss note, the meeting with the venerable master, and a fundraiser at the temple. I knew things would only get worse when we showed the reporters Huang's April 11, 1996, memo to Gore's scheduler Kim Tilley. Naturally they focused on the subject line of Huang's memo about the "fundraising lunch" to be held at the Hsi Lai temple.

I was getting concerned that this session seemed to be moving toward yet another article suggesting that if Gore's top staff had notice that the temple luncheon was to be a fundraiser according to John Huang, then Gore must have known.

Burson then showed the reporters the two sets of briefing memos and talking points, for the temple luncheon and for the San Jose fundraiser later that evening. We explained that the two speeches were especially persuasive in proving our point, in that the luncheon speech was clearly not one delivered by someone soliciting donations at a fund-raiser, whereas the evening one included classic fundraising remarks.

Again, I noticed Drew looking over the materials somewhat skeptically, and Burson and I seemed to share the growing sense of unease.

After the reporters had left, Burson, Gore's deputy press secretary Ginny Terzano, and I sat in Burson's office to commiserate a bit. We all had the same impression—that the story would be more about the Strauss call-slip note and possible staff knowledge of the temple luncheon as a fundraiser than the "John Huang Sandbags White House" story that Van Natta had first described to me.

Feeling somewhat responsible for urging a decision to proactively give these reporters these documents, I returned to my office and called Van Natta. "I know you are going to report the Strauss note and the Huang memo," I said, "but I want to know whether the story will give greater emphasis to what you had first described to me on the phone—that Huang blind-sided Gore and the DNC on the temple event."

"Yes," Van Natta said. "That is still the essential story we are writing."

I hung up the phone, relieved, and called Burson and Ginny Terzano to tell them I thought the story would turn out fine.

It didn't.

It's not as if everything Van Natta had told me was not in the story. It was. But the story of Huang's secret conversion of the temple luncheon into a fundraiser, which Van Natta had said was to be the main subject, was detailed only in the second half of a very long article and was trumped by an entirely different story comprising the first half, as summed up by the headline and the first three paragraphs:

Early Warnings on Gore's Temple Visit

In March 1996, Vice President Al Gore had a 10-minute White House meeting with the master of a Buddhist temple. It was described as a social call, but just two days before, a Democratic

Party fundraiser, John Huang, had an intriguing telephone conversation with a top Gore aide that hinted at another motive.

"Lead to a lot of money moving support," Mr. Gore's deputy chief of staff, David M. Strauss, jotted down on a phone log recording Mr. Huang's call.

And shortly afterward, Mr. Huang followed up with a memorandum to another Gore aide, proposing that the vice president attend a "fundraising lunch" at the master's Hsi Lai Temple in Hacienda Heights, Calif., that April 29.

Two paragraphs later, Drew and Van Natta editorialized,

> [T]he contacts between White House officials and Mr. Huang in the days before the event represent the strongest evidence to date that Mr. Gore's top aides had ample warning that the lunch would be tied in some way to the Democratic Party's 1996 fundraising push.

The phrase "ample warning"—not a fact, but an inference—really aggravated me, because I thought it was clear that there was no evidence that the Strauss phone call with Huang had any reference to a possible fundraising event at the Buddhist temple. The only explicit "warning" (ample or otherwise) contained in the article was the reference in John Huang's April 11 memo to a "fundraising lunch." Actually, the *Times* reporters could have cited another previously reported example—the April 19, 1996, e-mail from NSC staffer John Norris, describing the temple event as a "fundraising lunch." And there were a few other examples that had emerged in subsequent months of midlevel Gore staffers who referred to this event as if it were a fundraiser.

Still, the only issue was what Gore himself knew, and not what his staffers knew and failed to tell him. In fact, the second half of the *Times* article—the one Van Natta told me he was going to write when he first called me—supported the fact that Gore had no knowledge and that it was Huang who blind-sided him and the DNC. The article reported that "Mr. Huang told Mr. Strauss that no money would be raised at the lunch and that he would use it only to reward past donors and to encourage prospective contributors by giving them a chance to meet Mr. Gore." It reported DNC Finance Director Richard Sullivan's direct instruction to John Huang on the phone: "John, you can't have a formal fundraiser at a temple." And, most important from our standpoint, the reporters documented that Gore and the DNC had not known about Huang's plan to convert the temple luncheon into a fundraiser. They quoted Democratic Party officials stating that Huang "kept insisting it was just a community outreach [event], and that he had never, ever billed it as a fundraiser. Of course, that is far from the truth. We just feel completely misled by him."

This second half of the story was actually great stuff, I thought as I read it. It should prove once and for all that we were the victims of John Huang's deception, that Gore had a basis for regarding the event as about "community outreach," and this should finally put to rest any suggestion that Gore knew about the event as a fundraiser. Too bad the second half of the story was buried by the headline and the first half. I only hoped that most people had the time and patience to read the whole article.

Most galling of all was that Drew and Van Natta, while choosing to lead with the highly ambiguous and cryptic Strauss telephone message, chose not to contrast the briefing memos and speeches prepared for the temple luncheon with the San Jose fundraiser that evening. The article did report, buried deep in the story, that Gore's briefing memo for the temple event did not describe it as a fundraiser and that Gore had given his rah-rah *e pluribus unum* speech, with no pitch for money. But there was no mention at all of the evening fundraising event in San Jose, nor any quotations from its briefing memo, explicitly stating the fundraising goal of $250,000, or from the classic donor-oriented speech delivered there by Gore.

After reading the article together in Burson's office, Terzano and I retired to a nearby office and called Van Natta and Drew.

The conversation was not exactly edifying. To put it mildly, voices were raised. The reporters insisted that they had not baited-and-switched on the direction of the story, as we contended. They said the article was accurate, and challenged us to point to any inaccuracies. We couldn't. It was their subjective judgment with which we disagreed.

I was especially upset because I had kept my side of the bargain, and then some, and felt that the *New York Times* reporters had not reciprocated. I had given Van Natta exclusive access to the Strauss note and the Huang memo, and I had kept my commitment even after a *Washington Post* reporter, John Mintz, told me over lunch, several hours after Van Natta and I had talked, that he too was working on an in-depth story on the Buddhist temple event.

Mintz's focus was slightly different from Van Natta's. Mintz told me that he had interviewed a number of the nuns and officials of the temple and its attorney, and he was ready to describe in some detail the means by which the temple had reimbursed the nuns for the personal checks they wrote. He asked me whether I had any new information that might shed light on Huang's role, since he also had sources (evidently similar to Van Natta's) telling him that Huang had deceived the DNC and Gore's people by secretly canceling his Monterey Park event and diverting his donors to the Buddhist temple luncheon.

I must admit that for a moment I was tempted to leak to Mintz the Strauss note and the Huang memo—better to get the information out in both the *Post* and the *Times* at the same time, since that would mean the *Post* would not be writing a follow-up to the *Times* story. But that would have been a violation of my promise to Van Natta. I called Burson and McCurry and asked them whether I was right to continue to honor the commitment to him, and both of them said I was, especially because of his promised focus on Huang's deception of Gore and the DNC.

I also felt sorry for Mintz because he had told me he was still a few days away from finishing his reporting, and I knew the *Times* would be publishing Van Natta's story sooner than that. But I couldn't tell Mintz that Van Natta was working on a similar story—this too would have been a violation of the trust Van Natta had placed in me.

I have written before of the importance, and fragility, of the trust relationship that I had to develop with a reporter if both of us were to do our jobs effectively and with integrity. The reporter had to trust me at all times to be honest, to be factual, and to protect his proprietary work product. But the trust had to be reciprocal. I had to trust the reporter not to blindside me with an unexpected angle or a cheap shot that hadn't been part of the context and understanding of our conversations. At the very least, if circumstances changed at the last minute—as the story was being crafted or edited—I would expect the reporter to make some effort to recontact me and give me a chance to comment on the new angle.

In short, since I had been the one to urge Burson and the Gore people to trust Van Natta and the *New York Times,* I felt naive and stupid. In our post-story phone conversation with Van Natta and Drew, at least Van Natta conceded that once they knew that the story would focus on the Strauss memo and the "ample warning" rather than on the Huang deception, they should have given us a chance to comment early in the story.

THE ONE ASPECT OF THE BUDDHIST temple story that had never been fully rebutted was the conduit scheme whereby the nuns had been agents for funneling money to the DNC. As the Thompson hearings prepared to take testimony from the nuns in early September, there was still no clear evidence as to who had devised and implemented this potentially criminal scheme. The one thing that was certain was that neither Al Gore, nor his staff—nor, as far as we knew, anyone at the DNC—had any shred of a hint that the conduit scheme was going on. But, taking no chances, the Gore team, with my full support, decided that they still had to make one final stab at proactive disclosure, the bad experience with the *New York Times* notwithstanding. On September 2, two days before the nuns' scheduled testimony, Gore's people assembled the scandal-beat reporters in the OEOB's Indian Treaty Room and handed out thick stacks of documents that outlined the whole story of the Buddhist-temple event. Charles Burson and Lorraine Voles patiently walked the reporters through each document to provide full explanations and contexts and to separate the vice president from any connection with the scheme, which had been John Huang's baby from start to finish.

However, Gore's top aides had decided to hold the briefing session "on background" rather than "on the record," which irritated the reporters, because all of the documents had been previously released and they believed this was simply an attempt by the White House to present its interpretation of those documents. When a reporter protested Voles told her that if she didn't like the ground rules she could leave. The already grumpy atmosphere got grumpier.

The chill continued into the next day's reporting, which played up the fact that Gore must have been terribly worried about the issue if his staff felt compelled to hold a background session on the Buddhist-temple issue. Nevertheless, the briefing succeeded in making it clear to the Republican senators that although they might still try to take political shots at Gore because his staff might have failed to read the "warning signs" that the event was a fundraiser, they should avoid suggesting that he had any knowledge about the alleged scheme involving the temple's sympathetic nuns. And that is exactly what happened at the hearings.

FOR ALMOST A YEAR THE PRESS corps and its vast investigative resources had dug out every conceivable element of this story to try to disprove Gore's denial of knowledge of the fundraising aspects of the Buddhist-temple event. They interviewed nuns and devotees and the temple's leaders. They reviewed thousands of pages of documents released by Republican congressional committees and by the White House and Gore legal and communications staffs. The Republican-controlled Senate and House committees took numerous sworn depositions and held days of public hearings on the subject, even dragging the Buddhist nuns before the bright lights of national television. All of these combined journalistic and partisan efforts had one objective: to prove that Vice President Gore was lying when he claimed not to know about the Buddhist temple event as a fundraiser or about the alleged illegal conduit scheme—or both.

Yet, with all these facts, documents, articles, broadcasts, witnesses, and televised testimony, it is a remarkable thing to note more than two years later: *Not one single fact or document ever emerged that contradicted a single word in Vice President Gore's first statement to National Public Radio the previous October denying any knowledge both that the event was a fundraiser and of the alleged illegal conduit scheme.*

Why the press and the pundits nonetheless persisted in reporting that Gore had such knowledge was of course part of the familiar connect-the-dots syndrome. But in retrospect it was also a function of the sometimes great difficulty we encountered within the White House, despite all our resources, to try to gather all the facts together in one place, early, so that they could be gotten out before the opposition had a chance to frame the story. In the case of the Buddhist-temple story, the irony was that so much of the story was right in front of our noses. We just couldn't confirm it or put it all together.

This hit home for me more than eighteen months later, when by accident I discovered an article by Rich Connell and Alan C. Miller in the *Los Angeles Times* that had appeared on November 2, 1996, more than six months before the Drew–Van Natta *New York Times* story. The Connell-Miller story contained all the information subsequently reported by Drew and Van Natta on the canceled Monterey fundraiser and Huang's decision to merge that event with the temple luncheon. However, they reported not only that Huang had originally scheduled a fundraiser at Monterey Park on the same day as the temple luncheon, but also that when Huang learned that the DNC had said there was not enough time for both events, he was angry that his fundraiser was being "ruined" by the scheduling of the temple event. They wrote that Huang redirected the donors who had signed up for the first event to attend the temple luncheon instead.

Moreover, Connell and Miller got probably the best quote of all, from our standpoint, one that confirmed Gore's statements that he had no indications at the event itself that the luncheon was a fundraiser. They even reported Gore's non-fundraiser type of speech:

> Participants say the luncheon did not feature many of the usual trappings of a fundraiser. There was no front registration table, no donor cards and no thank-you's expressed from the speaker— Gore—for the generous financial support. Don Knabe, a Republican who attended, said that, "if it was a fund-raiser, it wasn't like any fund-raiser I've ever been to."

Months later, I asked Charles Burson why the *Los Angeles Times* story had not been more widely circulated by the Gore communications team earlier in the process. He told me that despite the information in that story and from Drew and Van Natta, he and his staff were unable to get documentary confirmation of Huang's Monterey event until just before the September 1997 Senate hearings.

I learned an important lesson from this whole story: Sometimes you just have to tough it out. That doesn't mean stonewalling; what it means is sticking to your guns without apology when the facts are on your side. It's a lesson similar to the one I learned from Justice Stewart in my moot-court competition in law school. I didn't feel good about arguing that there was no remedy for citizens offended by a sectarian congressional prayer, but I was confident that my argument was right and I stuck with it. Similarly, Al Gore probably should not have acknowledged that it was a "mistake" or "inappropriate" to have attended the Buddhist-temple luncheon, given the knowledge he had at the time. He understood the event to be "community outreach," as he told Nina Totenberg in October 1996, and it was not his fault if an overzealous fundraiser surreptitiously turned it into something else without his knowledge or consent. There is nothing unusual in American politics—at least not in anyone's memory—about political events being held in churches and synagogues. And it is not unusual for those events to be attended by community leaders, political supporters, and even by actual and potential financial contributors. Every candidate who speaks at a church or synagogue hopes that the members of his audience will like what they hear and may feel motivated at some later date not only to vote for the candidate but also to give money to the cause. If that hope runs afoul of the "tacky factor" or the Ethics Apparat, well, they'll just have to get over it.

9

Dead Men Do Tell Tales

"WHAT WOULD YOU THINK," ABC REPORTER LINDA DOUGLAS asked me, "if I told you that Bill Clinton sold plots in Arlington Cemetery to raise money for his campaign?"

Nothing could be that bad, was my first thought.

Douglas told me she had just been faxed the advance galley proof of an article that was due to be published in *Insight,* the Sunday magazine of the *Washington Times,* the conservative newspaper owned by the Reverend Sun Myung Moon.

"The article reports that Democratic party leaders pressured Arlington to waive eligibility requirements for burials on behalf of big Democratic donors—cash for plots, so to speak," she said.

I must now admit that when I heard Linda say this, my first thought was that it could be possible. In fact, by this point in my White House tenure—it was mid-November 1997—I had reluctantly concluded that when it came to the Democratic party's zealous fund-raising practices during the 1995–96 election cycle, almost anything was possible.

My second thought was, Oh, shit.

I realized immediately that if this story were true, it would neatly typify the worst of the Clinton campaign finance allegations. In a perverse kind of way, the story was almost too good to be true. Selling the Lincoln Bedroom for $50,000 a night came pretty close to making the overall point. But selling plots in Arlington Cemetery to raise campaign money—Arlington Cemetery, the national symbol of patriotic service and honor—that, if it were true, had the makings of a political third rail.

Back in June, there had been two reports, one on a local Washington, D.C., television station, WJLA-TV, and the other in the *Army Times,* that Army Secretary Togo West had waived the criteria for burial at Arlington at a rate nearly triple that of the Reagan and Bush administrations. The *Army Times* story, written by George Wilson, had said that the high numbers had "generated allegations of favoritism." But Wilson did not suggest that there had been White House pressure behind any of those waivers. However, he was not able to put that possibility completely to rest, because Secretary West had refused to release the names on the waivers, on privacy grounds.

The *Army Times* story had gone nowhere, though I did receive a flurry of calls about it, and I heard that Terry Everett, a Republican congressman from Alabama, had begun an inquiry on the waivers issue. He apparently had asked West for a full list of all the waiver names. But I had heard nothing more.

However, the story Linda Douglas was telling me apparently had taken a much more significant turn: the assertion that an individual's status as a big Democratic donor had gotten him a waiver at Arlington. As always, the issue of causation was the key: whether political money had *caused,* or at least influenced, the decision on the waiver.

I asked Linda whether there was any evidence of causation in the story. "Well, there are a number of sources claiming that that's the case—and the reporter, Paul Rodriguez, seems to make that claim without citing specific evidence."

I asked her whether she was planning to report the story on ABC-TV that night.

"Not before we can independently confirm," she said. "The story is not exactly written with solid sourcing."

Talk about understatement. Douglas faxed me the galley and I sat at my desk, pen in hand, underlining and taking notes as if I were reading an examination question. Rodriquez's all-important lead, which would drive the entire story, was as follows:

> Pressure from political bigwigs at the White House and within the Democratic Party apparently helped gain coveted waivers from top brass at the Defense Department and the Department of Veterans Affairs for dozens of big-time political donors or friends of the Clintons—civilians who wanted themselves or family members buried in America's most precious grounds, the national war cemeteries, including Arlington National, *Insight* has learned.

I was struck by the word "apparently" in the second line, which tipped me off to a lot of innuendo masquerading as fact. And as I continued reading, I found a lot of anonymous sources, but precious little hard information to substantiate the charges that Rodriguez was leveling against the administration.

I was growing frustrated. I kept looking for facts, looking for corroborated information. There must exist somewhere a list of people granted waivers for burial at Arlington since Clinton had taken office. It would be easy enough to determine how many of the individuals who had received such waivers were actually campaign donors—simply by comparing the waiver list with information on file at the Federal Election Commission. But Rodriguez provided no names and no reference to a list or to a specific number of waivers. He also reported that the number of waivers granted to "civilians who had served in the military and were pillars in the private sector" had "quadrupled to approximately 60 to 75 in the last four or five years." This, he reported, was seen as "an unusual number of waivers since 1993" which had led to a "hush-hush review . . . at the highest levels of the Army."

Finally, in the second-to-last paragraph of the two-page piece, Rodriguez stated flatly that "some" of the individuals who received waivers for burial at Arlington and other national cemeteries "gave large sums of money to the Clinton-Gore campaign and to the DNC." He backed this up with a quote from another anonymous "military source" that "some gave money to Clinton." Then he added, as his own assertion, "in a few cases, tens of thousands of dollars." I looked back at the lead paragraph, and saw that Rodriguez had said that "dozens" of "big-time political donors or friends" had "apparently" been granted waivers.

I sat at my desk for a few minutes, worried—but also confused. I read the article again. And then a third time. What *facts* exactly did this reporter report himself, as distinguished from anonymous people making charges? What was the substantiation for those facts? I looked over my notes. I was amazed that there were only two actual facts reported in the entire article:

- First, that an unusually large number of waivers were granted for burial at Arlington during Clinton's term: 60 to 75, or four times the average for prior administrations.
- Second, that "some" of those granted waivers had given "large sums" to the Clinton-Gore campaign and the DNC.

I tried to cheer myself up by noting that Rodriguez had cited no evidence that the White House had applied any pressure on Arlington officials to get the donors waived into Arlington—only charges by anonymous sources. Usually reliance on such sources must be backed by corroborative evidence—or by multiple sources who can verify the factual accuracy of the assertion. That is the normal safeguard that legitimate news organizations use when reporting allegations made on "deep background." I worried, however, that in the current atmosphere, with the perception that the White House was willing to sell anything in order to raise campaign money, most reporters would inevitably draw the inference that big donors had received their waivers because of political influence, no matter how strongly I criticized Rodriguez's sourcing.

I tried to reach Rodriguez to see how many individuals on the waiver list he had been able to identify as political donors, but I couldn't get through to him. Meanwhile, I heard from several reporters that the story had been faxed all over town and that several members of Congress were already calling for investigations, most notably Senator John McCain of Arizona, who had issued an angry press release to this effect. Though the facts alleged were sketchy at best, I'm sure Senator McCain would have defended his actions by pointing out that he had only called for an investigation, and had not asserted that the reports were true. But the fact remains that a U.S. senator calling for an investigation is news, and many mainstream news organizations justified their front-page coverage of the story precisely because McCain and others had called for investigations.

I visited Lanny Breuer, briefed him fully, and he, Adam Goldberg, and I went to the counsel's office in the West Wing to tell them what was up. The deputy White House counsel, Cheryl Mills, immediately placed a call to Army Secretary Togo West to get the facts: how many waivers, who were they, were they Democratic donors, etc. West's first response was negative: No waiver list would be released, to protect the privacy of those named on it. I called several people on the political side of the White House: Did anyone remember political pressures to get donors buried at Arlington? No one did.

While I waited for answers, the calls started to pour in from the press corps, as the *Insight* article gained wider and wider circulation, hit the Internet, and then the radio talk shows. Within an hour of Linda Douglas's call to me, I had received calls from reporters as far away as Brussels, London, and Tokyo.

I knew we had little time to get a denial out, and it was critical that we do so before the network news shows aired. I went across the street to the West Wing and up to the second floor, where Mills was again on the phone with West's office.

"Can I issue a strong denial?" I asked.

She said yes, that none of the waivers had anything to do with politics or political influence. I could say that categorically. She said she was trying to get the full list from Togo West of all the waivers that have been granted since 1993.

Mills handed me a write-up describing the only four instances since 1993 in which Clinton himself had granted waivers to permit burial of noneligible people at Arlington. None of them had anything to do with White House influence on behalf of a donor. One was granted for the late Supreme Court justice Thurgood Marshall; a second was for the widow of the late chief justice Warren Burger; a third was for an active-duty Drug Enforcement Agency agent who had served in the Army and who had been killed while on a mission in Peru; and the fourth was for a Washington, D.C., police officer, killed in the line of duty, who had previously served in the Marines.

Something still bothered me. These were the four waivers that Clinton himself had granted, but what about the other sixty to seventy that Rodriguez had reported? Couldn't some of them have been the result of political pressures from the White House or from other top Democrats? I knew that we ought to go through every name and find out everything we could to be sure that there had been no political influence on Secretary West's decisions. But we couldn't do that without the list of all the waivers—which West was still refusing to produce. This is crazy, I thought. As long as West holds back the list of names, this story will clearly be driven by the innuendo that he is resisting full disclosure because there are instances of political influence behind some of the waivers.

Unfortunately, we didn't have the luxury of waiting to get all the facts before we offered a public comment on the story. With the broadcast television networks about to go on the air, we knew that we could not afford to have this cash-for-burial-plots story go out to millions of living rooms without our denial attached. So, not for the first time, I plunged ahead with the limited information I had, following the risky Alice-in-Wonderland-like rule: Denial first, facts second— and pray that ultimately the rest of the facts won't trump my denial.

Barry Toiv, the White House deputy press secretary, called to ask when we would have a statement, since the press was clamoring for some response and the networks' deadline was approaching. I left the counsel's office, raced down the stairs to the lower press office on the first floor, and ducked into Toiv's cubbyhole office. I sat at his computer, with Cheryl Mills, Adam Goldberg, and Toiv looking over my shoulder, and started to type.

> The president and this administration consider Arlington National Cemetery and other national and veterans' cemeteries across the country to be hallowed ground.

"Get to the point," Toiv growled.

> It would be outrageous for anyone to grant or influence the granting of exceptions under the rules for burial at national cemeteries because of political or fundraising considerations.

I chose the word "would" as a qualifier—just in case it turned out to be true. I then added:

> Neither the president nor anyone at the White House ever made such a recommendation because of political or fundraising considerations.

I was deliberately leaving out "personal" considerations, since I couldn't be sure that someone in the White House hadn't intervened on grounds of friendship.

"That's a categorical denial," I said. "We are denying that waivers had anything to do with political considerations or pressure from the White House. That's what the *Insight* article charges, and we're denying it." Toiv grunted assent. Then I added: "The report making these allegations is scurrilous and untrue. It is based on anonymous sources and innuendo, not facts."

I was focusing on knocking down the *Insight* article, rather than on the underlying issue of political influence by the White House—again, because I lacked confidence that I knew the whole story.

With Mills's assistance, I then specified the four instances since 1993 in which the president had sought waivers of the usual rules to qualify for burial at Arlington Cemetery—none of which, I pointed out, had anything to do with politics.

We couldn't go any further without seeing the full list of waivers that Secretary West had granted and cross-checking that list against the Federal Election Commission records of political donors. We certainly had no evidence that anybody at the White House had tried to influence West or anyone else about getting a Democratic donor or bigwig a waiver to be buried at Arlington. But we also had no evidence to prove the negative.

I went to see Mike McCurry before issuing the statement—despite the lateness of the hour and the threats from the press corps that they would have to go with the story without a White House reaction if I waited much longer. I showed him my draft statement. He stopped when he read my sentence about nobody having recommended a waiver, "because of political or fundraising considerations."

"Wait a minute," he said. "You're out a bit too far on that."

"Why?"

"Because I specifically remember Larry Lawrence's case," McCurry responded. "I seem to remember we had something to do with his getting a waiver at Arlington after he died."

"Who's Larry Lawrence?" I asked.

"He was named ambassador to Switzerland by Clinton. He was an extremely wealthy San Diego businessman, owner of the Hotel del Coronado, and a huge real-estate developer," McCurry continued. "He gave Clinton and the DNC lots of money, and he and his wife,

Shelia, became close friends of the Clintons. He died of cancer in early 1996 while he was ambassador. I think I remember his wife pushed for him to get a waiver to be buried at Arlington."

My heart sank. "On what basis was the waiver granted?" I asked.

"I remember we issued a press statement that he was in the Merchant Marine during World War II, had been thrown overboard, or something like that, and that he almost died," McCurry said. He explained that under today's rules, based on Lawrence's Merchant Marine service during wartime, and the war injury, he would probably have qualified for burial. So that's why he was granted a waiver by the army.

"So what's the problem?" I asked. "Sounds like he had a basis for the waiver, if he was in the Merchant Marine and was injured in action."

"Well, I really don't know whether anyone here helped get it done or what the real basis for the waiver was," McCurry responded. "You'd better be careful. We should check with Leon Panetta [chief of staff at the time] to find out whether he remembers making any calls on the Lawrence issue."

I went back to Toiv's office and told him what McCurry had said. While Toiv tried to reach Panetta, I reread my statement. Clearly I needed to add some hedge words to my categorical denial. I wanted to make the distinction between the White House providing "background personal information" for waiver purposes and granting waivers in response to individuals' political or financial support. But how to do that credibly? By definition, if the White House had communicated any support for a waiver for someone who was a Democratic bigwig, the Pentagon could easily have perceived it as political backing by the White House. At that point Toiv walked in and reported, "Panetta never intervened on behalf of Larry Lawrence, but we can't swear that no one around here ever did."

I called Mills, and she came down to help. After some back and forth with McCurry, we settled on the following language:

In addition, there may have been instances in which the White House provided to Army officials information regarding individuals in connection with the Department's consideration of burial requests.

Ugh! Enough hedge words to start up a hedge fund.

Later that evening, we learned that Army Secretary West had finally released more information explaining the waivers, stating firmly that the charges that they had been granted "for political considerations or, worse, for political contributions, are untrue." West had approved fifty-eight waivers since November 1993, and the president had requested and been granted four. An Army spokesman then stated that most (forty-two) of the exceptions were waivers of the rule that a veteran's widow who remarries may not be buried in Arlington. Virtually all the rest were for legitimate veterans who for one reason or another did not qualify under the current rules.

By Day Two, Thursday, November 20, there was no doubt as to what this story was about: the accusation that the White House had sold burial plots the same way it had sold Lincoln Bedroom overnights. And once again Mike McCurry was correct in his prediction that the Larry Lawrence waiver would quickly surface. By midmorning on that second day a reporter from WJLA-TV, the local ABC affiliate, called to ask for White House comment about whether Lawrence's waiver was a result of his reportedly having raised millions of dollars for the Democratic Party over the years and contributed $200,000 to the 1992 Clinton-Gore election effort. As soon as the WJLA story hit, Republican partisans and conservative talk-show hosts seized on the fact that Lawrence had been a major Democratic Party contributor and began asserting, without evidence, that he had received the waiver because of his donations. That assertion as fact, based only on the inference of the *post hoc* fallacy, spread across the mainstream press, the cable and broadcast TV networks, and around the globe on the Internet. Soon the chairman of the Republican

National Committee, the speaker of the House, and various conservative talk-show hosts had seized on the Larry Lawrence case to state flatly that waivers to be buried at Arlington Cemetery had been sold in return for campaign donations to the Clinton campaign.

This, we realized, was yet another example of the dangers of connect-the-dots journalism and the fallacy of the *post hoc, ergo propter hoc* syllogism. Dot One was that Larry Lawrence had been a big Democratic Party contributor. Dot Two was that he had subsequently received a waiver to be buried at Arlington Cemetery. The press and the Republicans could hardly resist the temptation to connect the dots by suggesting that Fact One had *caused* Fact Two, at least not after all the accumulated charges that the Clinton White House had been rented by the night in order to raise campaign money. Our only hope was to create a third factual dot that had not yet been sufficiently reported: that Lawrence had served in the Merchant Marine and had received war injuries. The danger to this strategy, however, was that as far as we knew, there might well be other examples of Democratic donors who had obtained waivers. After all, Rodriguez had said there were "dozens." And we still couldn't be certain that there had been no White House calls on behalf of Lawrence.

By midday, I was relieved to hear that Army Secretary West had finally agreed to release the complete list of the sixty-nine persons—seven more than West had stated earlier—who had received waivers of the normal rules for eligibility for burial at Arlington. In distributing the list, West also provided explanations as to why the chain of command, including himself and the director of Arlington National Cemetery, had unanimously agreed that these waivers were merited and had nothing to do with politics. As soon as we got the list of sixty-nine names, my colleagues and I tapped into the Federal Election Commission's Web site listing all contributors to the Democratic Party and to the Clinton campaign. We did a cross-check of every one of the sixty-nine who had obtained waivers. We found—and I must admit I was stunned at our good fortune, because I had expected otherwise—that the only Democratic donor on the Arlington waivers list was Larry Lawrence.

The only one.

It's a great feeling when the facts are on your side. Now we could safely push out the Lawrence/Merchant Marine story.

When I told McCurry the news that Lawrence was the only Democratic donor among the sixty-nine waivers, he smiled mischievously. "This is going to be delicious," he said.

"We've got to track down that Merchant Marine incident you mentioned to me—that will trump any suggestion that he got the waiver because of his Democratic Party or White House connections," I said.

McCurry said he was pretty sure the press office had put out a written statement shortly after Lawrence died, referring to the Merchant Marine incident. Sure enough, a "Statement by the president" on January 9, 1996, expressed the president's sorrow over the death of Ambassador Lawrence, and added, "During World War Two, at the age of 18, he volunteered for the Merchant Marine. [In 1945] he was wounded when his ship was sunk by enemy torpedoes in arctic waters. Many years later, Larry was decorated with the Medal of Valor by the government of the Russian Federation." We also learned that Assistant Secretary of State Richard Holbrooke, a friend of Lawrence's, had written a letter urging the Army to grant the waiver based on the ambassador's wartime service and injuries. Holbrooke recounted the incident in which Lawrence had been "thrown overboard into frigid Arctic waters," was knocked unconscious, receiving a severe head injury, and was taken to a hospital in the Soviet Union where he recuperated. We also confirmed, as Rodriguez himself had reported in the *Insight* article, the eligibility rules had since changed and that Lawrence would have qualified for burial at Arlington had the same incident occurred today while he was serving in the Merchant Marine in time of war.

After a brief meeting in McCurry's office, Cheryl Mills, Adam Goldberg, Ches Johnson and I worked on "talking points." Point One was that the *Insight* story, charging that Arlington Cemetery waivers had been "sold" to Democratic donors and that the White House had influenced those waivers, was now demonstrated to be false. Point Two was that this falsity was being trumpeted by partisan Republicans and right-wing Clinton haters. Point Three was that the single example of a Democratic donor receiving a waiver—the Larry Lawrence case—in fact proved that there was no political basis for the waiver decision, since Lawrence's waiver would have been granted on the merits regardless of his status as a donor. Even if someone at the White House had picked up the phone to put in a good word for Lawrence, the waiver still would have been justified based on Lawrence's Merchant Marine service.

The next day, the White House's comments to this effect were picked up by all the major papers. The American Legion admitted publicly that there was no instance of a waiver having been granted for political reasons. "It seems clear that the anonymous accusations regarding unqualified burials at Arlington were unfounded," said John F. Sommer, the Legion's executive director. Senator McCain, whom I had come to respect as one of the most honest and independent of the Senate Republicans, now seemed to regret having jumped too quickly into the fray, stating that he was "aware of no evidence of wrongdoing or impropriety."

But just when we were celebrating our public-relations victory, the press corps switched the story line.

On December 4, Don Van Natta, Jr., of the *New York Times* called me to say that investigators for Congressman Everett's subcommittee had released documents suggesting that Larry Lawrence had *not* served in the Merchant Marine—nor was he wounded in a torpedo attack on a ship in World War II. His name was not on the log of crew members of the ship or on other documents listing casualties. Indeed, Lawrence's name could not be found in any records showing that he had ever served in the Merchant Marine. Moreover, Lawrence's secretary stated that when she first started working for Lawrence twenty years earlier, his service in the Merchant Marine had not been listed on his résumé.

My first reaction was that even if it were true that Lawrence had lied about his war record, that had nothing to do with the essential falsity of the original *Insight* magazine story. Then I remembered how we had emphasized Lawrence's war record to prove that his waiver was legitimate and not based on his donor status or Clinton connections—and I realized that this would give our opponents a chance to change the subject and attack our credibility for not knowing about Lawrence's lies on his résumé.

I called Mike McCurry. "We may have celebrated too soon on the Arlington Cemetery story," I said, and I told him about Van Natta's story.

McCurry cursed.

"But that only means Lawrence lied on his résumé and we didn't catch it; it doesn't mean the original story about buying plots for cash was true," I argued. But we also agreed that the press would shift its focus to our failure to catch the mistake—and would suggest (without any evidence, of course) that the reason the résumé lies had not been found out at the time of his vetting for ambassador was because of his political connections as a major Democratic donor.

We were exactly right.

The next day's stories, led by Van Natta's, put us clearly on the defensive. At his daily press briefing, McCurry began the process of distancing us from Lawrence, if in fact he had lied about his war record. The White House's earlier comments about Lawrence's war record were based on statements by "people who were close to him and who knew of—presumably knew what his alleged record was, or what they thought his alleged record was."

Several days later, Van Natta broke another story which nailed down the fact that Lawrence had lied about his Merchant Marine service. The reporter studied a *Who's Who* entry about Lawrence and noticed that he had attended Wilbur Wright College in Chicago in 1945—exactly when he was supposedly on the Merchant Marine ship that had been torpedoed. Van Natta verified with the college that Lawrence had been there at the time of his claimed war injuries.

The press calls flooded in. "So what happened to your war hero?" was the typical question. More troubling, no one seemed to buy my argument that this latest development was not in any way a vindication of the original cash-for-plots allegations. This infuriated me, because the two stories were unrelated. If, in fact, Lawrence had lied on his résumé, then that showed that the background vetting of him had been inadequate. But that was a different issue. Clearly someone had goofed, but we at the White House were just as much the victims as those in the Senate who had confirmed Lawrence's appointment as ambassador, and those in the Pentagon who had believed that Lawrence's record merited a waiver for a burial plot. And my point was: The fact that Lawrence lied on his résumé had nothing to do with the fact that no burial plots had been sold to Democratic donors, and that the White House had never pressured Arlington to grant waivers on any donor's behalf.

Not surprisingly, the conservative *Wall Street Journal* editorial page blurred that distinction and referred to the news of Lawrence's fictitious résumé as a "second act" to the "stories last month over special dispensations and campaign contributions for burials at Arlington National Cemetery." I called Robert Bartley, the editor, to complain. "The original story accused us of selling burial plots for campaign donations—not for being sloppy about checking Lawrence's résumé. One has nothing to do with the other," I argued. I got nowhere. "The cash-for-plots idea certainly was plausible," he said, implying that because of all the other campaign-finance scandal stories, he was willing to believe any similar allegation against the Clinton administration.

I was in the right, but I could see that I was never going to win this battle.

It wasn't only the *Wall Street Journal* that employed the "even if it wasn't true it sure seemed like it was" defense. Maureen Dowd, in her acerbic *New York Times* column, weighed in with similar logic: "The horrible thing is that it sounded so plausible. It did not seem such a stretch to think that this White House, where everything is political and everything is for sale, would even peddle eternity."

Amazingly, to me at least, the only commentator to get it right was conservative pundit Pat Buchanan. "I'm going to defend Bill Clinton against the charge that he sold plots in Arlington Cemetery to fat-cat contributors. He did not. There's one character that's in there who shouldn't be in there, but Bill Clinton had no way of knowing the guy faked his Merchant Marine record." For a nanosecond I whispered to myself, "Buchanan for president."

A YEAR LATER, I had occasion to talk to Paul Rodriguez about the Arlington Cemetery story. What I learned astounded me.

"You know," he said, "if last summer the army secretary had cooperated with me or George Wilson [of *Army Times*] and let us see the list of waivers, I never would have written this story. I begged Secretary West's office to show me the list of waivers, so that I could run a check with the Federal Election Commission records of all the names to see whether there were any donors. They refused. Even if their privacy concerns were valid—and you can see when the heat was turned on they caved on them quickly—they could have let me see the names on an off-the-record basis just so I could have run the FEC check."

As I listened to him, I vaguely remembered that George Wilson had made a similar point when he was interviewed by *Nightline* at the height of the furor. I looked it up, and here is what Wilson told ABC reporter Chris Bury:

I had gone up the hill several times to try and get West to release
the names on the theory that this would clear it up for everybody. But he refused to give me the names on the theory that
the families who had been given exceptions would be harassed.

Now I realized that after all my sanctimonious trashing of the
press on the Arlington Cemetery story as an emblem of connect-the-
dots journalism at its worst, the original sin lay with the holder of all
the information relevant to the story—in this case, the army secretary's office—and not with Rodriguez or Wilson. The first mistake,
it now seemed clear to me, was holding back information from the
press, which, if provided early and comprehensively, would have prevented the story from being written in the distorted and unfair way
that it was. Togo West could have killed this story by helping the
reporters write it accurately. He could have shown the reporters all
the names and explained all the individual reasons for the waivers,
none of them having anything to do with donor status, political
clout, or White House connections. In other words, he could have
done early what he ultimately did (under pressure, of course) some
six months later, after the story broke. Regarding his concerns about
the privacy of the individuals and their families who obtained
waivers, Secretary West could have worked out an arrangement with
the reporters to protect those names. If he was worried about an
"official" decision to disclose this information as perhaps establishing a bad precedent, he could have allowed the information to be
leaked on "deep background."

Once again I had learned the lesson, amazingly valid even in the
instance of a classic connect-the-dots story, that ultimately, as Pogo
would say, "We have met the enemy, and he is us."

Unfortunately, not only did Secretary West's office plant the seeds
of the Arlington Cemetery story by refusing to cooperate with the
reporters' inquiries, but once the story broke, West's silence forced us

in the White House to try to knock down the allegations without having all the facts at hand.

In retrospect, our decision to be cute in the first day's statement, hedging our bets regarding possible White House lobbying on behalf of Lawrence, turned out to be unnecessary, since no such lobbying had apparently taken place. But more than that, I had essentially bought into the assumptions held by our opposition, namely that there must have been *some* political pressure, based on Lawrence's status as a big donor and friend of the president. In short, I too was unjustifiably "connecting the dots"—though I would never have admitted this at the time.

Clearly we should have demanded that the army secretary's office publicly release those waiver names and explanations on the first day. Waiting three days is waiting a near eternity in today's journalistic universe. And we should have been far more aggressive about getting to the bottom of the false Lawrence résumé story before the press did. Had we been able to uncover those lies ourselves, we should have—of course—put the story out ourselves, denounced Lawrence's dishonesty, and thus depicted the White House as the victim of two lies: the accusations in the *Insight* article and Lawrence's prevarications about his past.

I try to imagine the reaction of some of my White House colleagues had I been able to approach them with the information about Lawrence's phony Merchant Marine war record and announce, "Let's call a press conference and put these documents out."

There would have been near mayhem, I am sure, and mass resistance, as usual. But it would have been the right thing to do—on every count.

THE ARLINGTON CEMETERY STORY was the last scandal story I worked on at the White House—not counting my last ten days of trying to cope with the Monica Lewinsky story. In a way, it was fitting that it should be, for it contained the two major components of my experiences on the scandal watch over the previous year: The fatal combination of a press corps too quick to connect the dots in order to suggest wrongdoing, and an administration too slow to put out all the facts and to help the press get it right. Both of these elements energized what I came to call "the scandal machine."

I also realized that I had changed a lot. I would never read another scandal story in the newspaper, or watch another congressional investigative hearing, or follow the exposure of another politician under attack, in the same way again. I was not the same person I was before my White House education. Things were a lot more complicated for me now. I felt less righteous, more ambiguous and conflicted. I came to understand that my colleagues and I helped to feed the scandal machine when we were slow or overly coy in putting information out, whether the subject was John Huang's WAVES records or Roger Tamraz's determined effort to buy access at the White House. I saw over time how counterproductive it was to make it difficult for reporters to obtain facts and write their stories. We only caused them to redouble their efforts to get the information, and then the stories would always turn out worse for us than if we had cooperated with them in the first place.

On the other hand, I learned from my colleagues in the White House counsel's office, especially Chuck Ruff, Cheryl Mills, and Lanny Breuer, that the need to be proactive in putting information out was not as simple as I sometimes wanted to make it. There were serious legal issues to worry about, such as the accidental waiver of legal privileges (such privileges can be waived if privileged documents are publicly released), invitations to new subpoenas, charges of obstruction due to incomplete information, and, especially, the possible triggering of an independent counsel if our on-the-record comments were not carefully and meticulously phrased. I learned over time that there was no right or wrong in these inevitable tensions between my desire to get it all out and the legal staff's concerns to get it all right and to think through the legal ramifications before going public. I also learned that it was important to be on guard at all times when talking to reporters, to be clear on the ground rules at every meeting with them, and not to assume that they would always write the story the way I wanted them to.

My initial attitude toward the reporters on the Clinton scandal beat had also changed dramatically. When I first arrived I assumed there were certain reporters who had it in for the president—and I was going to watch out for them and stick it to them. But I learned over time that there were very few such reporters. Instead I realized that if I worked with the reporters, gave them all the facts they needed, and answered all their questions, then virtually without exception they would write fair stories and permit our characterizations or interpretations of the facts (our spin, if you will) to be reflected in the early paragraphs.

A good example of this change in my perception was my experience with Sue Schmidt of the *Washington Post*. Before coming to the White House, I read her stories on Whitewater and believed that they reflected an overly negative slant against the president and the first lady. I'm sure I had some basis for this impression. But during my year at the White House, whenever I gave her the facts she needed and answered all the questions she asked, I rarely found her reporting to be anything other than fair and balanced. I had the same experience with reporters working for two of the most anti-Clinton news organizations, the *Wall Street Journal* and the *Washington Times,* although too often I found that the *Times's* editorial page philosophy leaked onto the news pages in the form of heavy-handed anti-Clinton headlines and slanted lead paragraphs.

And of course, I learned the important distinction between good spin and bad spin—the difference between accepting the facts and dealing with them candidly versus attempting to deny the obvious or obfuscate to distract attention. I remember my epiphany clearly: My irreverent son, Seth, a journalist himself, who critiqued my White

House performance with a reporter's eye, had watched me on ABC's *Nightline* insisting that the invitations to big Democratic donors to stay overnight in the Lincoln Bedroom were only about friendship, and not about money. "Dad," he said, "even I know that you know you are full of crap."

On the other hand, I also learned not to concede too much by buying into the opposition's assumptions. The slippery, subjective slope of the Ethics Apparat had mesmerized me at first. I wanted to please those—in the press corps, at Common Cause, and elsewhere—who believed that the dirty, grimy part of political fundraising was "inappropriate" or something to wrinkle your nose at, even though it was legal. Over time, I learned that our efforts to satisfy these subjective appearance standards, such as our reluctance to admit that the White House coffees were about raising money or that money brought access in our political system, were fruitless and were pursued at great cost to our credibility.

On reflection, I was especially surprised to find that in a fundamental respect I had become less partisan in my views of the excesses of the scandal machine. I entered the White House with a firm perception that Republican congressional leaders had made a partisan decision to use taxpayer-funded investigations to bring down the Clinton White House, and there is certainly a lot of evidence of that to this day. I saw how innuendo-based news stories led to congressional hearings, which led to more stories, which led to independent counsels—back and forth and back again. And all the stories and investigations and accusations were themselves cited as evidence of guilt, as surrogates for facts and due process. It was scary stuff to me, and from my earliest days on the job I was determined to fight it.

But slowly, as I experienced the sensation of sitting in the crosshairs, I began to realize that the scandal machine was not a partisan phenomenon. I remembered that it was the Democrats, after all, who in the 1970s and 1980s had pushed for a broad Independent Counsel Act and then used congressional committees to generate pressure to appoint independent counsels to investigate officials of the Reagan and Bush administrations. And through the 1980s, it was the Republicans who decried the overuse and politicization of the Act, particularly during the six years when Lawrence Walsh was the independent counsel investigating the Iran-*contra* affair. Back then it was the Republicans who chafed at the "criminalization of political differences" and who complained about the unlimited budget and the lack of political accountability of an independent counsel. The decisions by Lawrence Walsh to indict Oliver North for using tax money for a security system for his home or to indict former defense secretary Caspar Weinberger just days before the 1992 election should have been denounced by Democrats, but were not.

During some of my worst days at the White House, when I was most angry at the press or at the Republicans, I would find humility by rereading the yellowing clips on Raymond Donovan, President Reagan's secretary of labor.

As Suzanne Garment recounts in her book *Scandal,* it was at Donovan's confirmation hearings in early 1981 that he was first accused of having links with organized crime. The hearings conducted by Senator Ted Kennedy never proved such links—never even provided direct evidence of them; rather, they just floated the suspicion. Charges of corruption and kickbacks concerning Donovan's New Jersey construction company also appeared—again based only on innuendo, never on any direct evidence. Investigations by the FBI indicated that the rumors were unfounded. Yet I remember at the time thinking Donovan was probably a crook, and rooting for the Democrats to keep up the attack.

Finally, after an accumulation of newspaper leaks and anonymously sourced stories, combined with the Democrats' repeated calls for the appointment of an independent counsel, Attorney General William French Smith felt compelled to appoint one—Leon Silverman. Between 1982 and 1987, Silverman opened and closed three separate independent-counsel investigations. Each time, he closed an investigation, he reported that there was "insufficient credible evidence" of a crime. Each time Donovan was left to try to continue his professional and personal life with that amorphous cloud still hanging over his head.

Donovan was forced to take a leave of absence; he ultimately resigned as secretary of labor after he was indicted in October 1984 by Bronx District Attorney Mario Merola, a Democrat. Merola and Assistant District Attorney Stephen Bookin briefed reporters extensively on the case. They got great press. Most readers (including me) thought that Merola and Bookin were courageous and that Donovan was guilty, of course. The matter took two years to come to trial. In the end, the jurors deliberated less than ten hours before acquitting Donovan on all counts. Donovan then turned to Bookin and asked his now famous and sad question, so emblematic of the bipartisan excesses of the scandal machine: "Which office do I go to to get my reputation back?"

So, it was now clear to me, the disease in today's scandal culture is systemic. It is not about one particular party being more partisan or more willing to misuse congressional investigations than the other. It is not about an ideological press corps out to get one political party or the other. The political and journalistic focus on scandal, and the willingness of politicians to take advantage of the destructive power of that focus for their political advantage, are now deeply imbedded within the body politic. All of us in the process—Democrats and Republicans, journalists and lawyers, not to mention a public ready to assume the worst about politicians—have combined to produce rot, horrible rot.

There are no entirely clean hands here. Certainly not mine.

IT WAS JANUARY 30, 1998. The Monica Lewinsky story was ten days old, but my time at the White House had come to an end. I completed all the miserable paperwork required before leaving, I paid my mess bill, and I turned in the security ID pass, keys, pager, and other software and hardware that accompany a position at the White House. Naturally my last stop was Mike McCurry's office, where I had begun fourteen months earlier. I stuck my head in the door.

"OK, McCurry, this is it," I announced. "You won't have me to kick around any more." We talked a bit about the Lewinsky story and the impossible position he was in by not having the basic facts to put out to the press. In a way, I was glad it wasn't my problem any more, because the normal rules of disclosure weren't so easy to apply here.

"Any parting advice for my future in damage control, McCurry?" I asked sarcastically.

He looked up and said, "Tell the truth—early and often." Then he gave me that McCurry grin.

I couldn't help thinking about the Lewinsky story, and I almost started to say, "On the other hand . . . ," but then I thought:

There is no other hand.

Epilogue

The Monica Lewinsky Story:
In Retrospect

THEN AGAIN, MAYBE THERE IS ANOTHER HAND.

It was Friday, August 14, 1998, and I was driving to a hotel in the Washington suburbs to have breakfast with a close friend of the president, someone from outside government who, I believed, would be able to tell me the truth about the president and Monica Lewinsky.

The events of the previous six months, as the president's approval ratings remained high despite the drumbeat of scandal stories, made me wonder whether this was the one case where the rules of full disclosure didn't apply. How could I blame Bill Clinton, or anyone, for wanting to conceal an embarrassing sexual relationship from his family and the world? And especially, how could I blame him for wanting to avoid full and open disclosure, which would subject his fate to the tender mercies of the independent counsel, Kenneth Starr?

Although I had left the White House in January, I had nonetheless continued to defend the president on television broadcasts and cable talk shows. I kept at it night after night, driven by a combination of loyalty, commitment, and just plain guilt over the fact that I had left the White House and the president in the middle of this crisis. I felt that I owed it to him to continue to do battle until it was over.

Even so, the memory of my brief meeting in the Oval Office with President Clinton on January 22 continued to haunt me. I could tell from his demeanor then that something had happened between him and Ms. Lewinsky that he found embarrassing. But I had also convinced myself that there had been no sexual relationship—the president's finger-wagging denial of January 26 had persuaded me of that Whatever the embarrassing issue was, as far as I was concerned it was none of my business, none of the public's business, and especially none of Kenneth Starr's business.

Then, in the morning newspapers on July 31, the news broke that Ms. Lewinsky had turned over a blue dress to Starr, and that testing was being conducted on "DNA material" allegedly on the dress. This revelation shook me greatly. I had not only denied the existence of a stained blue dress on television, I had also ridiculed reporters who had printed such rumors in the early days of the story. Now I had to come to grips with the horrific possibility that I had been wrong—embarrassingly, publicly wrong—and that the president's story might not be true.

The president had agreed to testify before the grand jury on Monday, August 17. As that date drew near, rumors reached me from within the Clinton inner circle strongly suggesting that the president would admit in his testimony to an improper relationship with Monica Lewinsky. I suppose I shouldn't have been shocked, and I guess I really wasn't, but I had been in denial, and I knew I faced a decision as to how I would react and whether I would continue to defend the president on television if he did make such an admission. That's when I called Clinton's close friend and asked him to meet me for breakfast. He heard the urgency in my voice, and I think he knew why I wanted to see him.

After a few minutes of small talk, I asked him the blunt question that he knew I was going to ask. He paused, then said, with some hesitation, "Yes."

He saw the expression on my face. "He's in a lot of pain," he said. "He needs his friends to stick by him, no matter how tough it may get. A lot of people are going to duck for cover when this hits. You can't."

"Can you tell me any details?" I asked. "I need to know everything, now. I can't do this anymore unless I know."

Funny. At that moment, I had a vision of myself sitting in my office more than a year and a half earlier, on the conference call about the White House coffees, being asked whether I knew that the comptroller of the currency had attended one such coffee along with a group of the bankers he regulated. I was told to say that it was "not inappropriate" for the comptroller to have attended that function, even though I instinctively knew that it was wrong and stupid. I had delivered the lawyer's answer without having the facts myself.

The friend nodded, understanding, perhaps observing me drift off a little. He brought me back. "I don't know details, and I don't think he will get into details," he replied. "He's going to admit to an improper relationship, intimacy. It's complicated. It's a nightmare. He's got to make peace with himself, his family, his friends, and the American people."

There was a long silence between us. I poked at my oatmeal. Filling the lull, my companion spoke of his lifelong friendship with Clinton, his feelings of empathy and sadness for the president and the first lady; his memories of them in the early years in the pressure cooker of Arkansas politics; watching them taking hard hits from the right wing, from vicious rumormongers, from the haters; and still enduring, becoming great leaders and partners and friends and parents.

He asked me how the hell I had come to take that rotten White House job handling the scandal-press corps. I told him that though I did not consider myself a close friend of the Clintons and had barely seen them over the years, somehow I felt intense loyalty to the two of them. I told him about my last year at Yale Law School, where Hillary Rodham and I first became friends. Even though we didn't spend a lot of time together, she had left me with such a strong positive impression that two decades later, after reading a harsh column about her written by *New York Times* columnist William Safire, I wrote an unpublished rebuttal, which I sent over to the White House and to other friends and supporters of the president. This, in turn, led to my doing many television shows defending the president and the first lady on Whitewater and other scandals; that ultimately led to my being offered the job at the White House. "I could give Safire all the credit—or the blame," I said, and we both laughed.

Then my companion asked me what it had been like at the White House when the story first broke. I told him about my feelings of guilt when I left on January 30, knowing that I was walking out in the middle of a crisis, knowing that working a story like this was what I did and did well. I felt a bit like a firefighter deserting the firehouse just as a four-alarmer is breaking out. For a brief moment or two I had actually thought about staying; I even told Deputy Chief of Staff John Podesta that I might reconsider my decision to leave. But I knew it was too late. My replacement, James Kennedy, who had served for years as press secretary to Senator Joseph Lieberman, had been hired, the public announcement had been made, and the very fact of my reversing my decision could be misconstrued as a sign of panic. Perhaps most important, even in those early days of the breaking story, I recognized that things were going to be very different in the White House, that the lawyers were now firmly in charge. Under these circumstances there would be no proactive-disclosure damage control operation, at least none like the one that I was accustomed to in handling campaign-finance stories. I just knew—and of course I didn't realize at the time how right I was—that I would be more useful to the president on the outside than on the inside.

I told Clinton's friend all this, and more. I also told him about my mother and father and what they had taught me about the importance of having a Democrat in the White House, and how I got them involved in Miami Beach in helping the Clinton-Gore campaign, how much I believed in the importance of fighting to preserve

Clinton's historic legacy as president and as leader of a new, centrist Democratic Party that would be able to successfully compete for the White House for years to come.

The friend interrupted me, laughing.

"You know who you remind me of when I watch you defending Clinton?" he said. "That Japanese soldier, the one in the cave, who is so loyal that twenty years later he is still fighting World War II." We both laughed. I got his point. I knew I had to continue to stay out there and do battle.

It hadn't been easy up to now and it wasn't going to get any easier.

A S I DROVE BACK TO MY OFFICE that morning, I thought back over the difficulties and frustrations of the past seven months in the face of a complete information shutdown enforced by the president's legal team. No one was surprised that the lawyers had refused to allow the president to appear at a press conference to answer detailed questions about his relationship with Lewinsky. But I was dismayed to observe that even the little things were being bottled up or denied, sometimes pointlessly, with the effect of further alienating an already alienated press corps.

The most emblematic example of this shortsighted strategy had occurred a month earlier, when rumors began to circulate that Starr had subpoenaed the president to testify before the grand jury. The reporters, who from force of habit continued to call me each day, implied that the information was coming out of Starr's office. This would be a huge story, if true—the first time in U.S. history that a sitting president under criminal investigation was subpoenaed to testify personally before a grand jury. (Richard Nixon had been subpoenaed to produce tapes and documents in 1973 during Watergate, and Thomas Jefferson had been subpoenaed in 1807 to give testimony in the treason trial of his former vice president, Aaron Burr. Jefferson declined to appear, but provided a sworn statement.)

I was appearing regularly on cable television shows to defend the president, and I wanted to be prepared to answer accurately if the subject of a possible subpoena came up. So I called Mike McCurry to see whether he had any information about the president having received a subpoena. The reply I got was No. I was on my own.

A few days later, on Friday, July 24, McCurry announced in a tightly scripted statement that the president had agreed to "provide information" that the grand jury needed to complete its investigation. McCurry would not comment any further regarding whether a subpoena had been served. I found it hard to believe that if the president had been subpoenaed, his press secretary would not have been told or could not confirm it to me on deep background.

I then called a friend and former colleague in the White House counsel's office.

"We don't talk about subpoenas," he said.

"But why?" I asked. "If Starr has issued one, it won't be news to him. And I suspect that reporters are hearing this from Starr's people. So why can't you confirm this for me—on deep background—so I don't appear stupid when I'm doing TV?"

"Because it's our policy not to talk about subpoenas, period," was the reply.

Now I knew what it was like to be a reporter dealing with this White House on the Lewinsky story.

Shortly thereafter, on a television program, I was asked whether the president had been subpoenaed. "I doubt it," I said, "or else they would have announced it by now." Admittedly I said this out of pique.

Throughout Saturday, July 25, I continued to get pages and calls from reporters asking if I could confirm whether a subpoena had actually been issued. Since I was scheduled to appear on a talk show the following morning myself, I tried again to find out the answer through various calls to the White House. Still no luck.

On Sunday morning, the *Washington Post,* the *New York Times,*

and several other papers reported from "legal sources" that the subpoena had actually been served on "Clinton's lawyer," not on the
president himself. Even in those stories the White House spokesman,
James Kennedy, refused to confirm or deny the report. It would take
three more days before a "senior administration official," speaking to
the press "on background," would finally confirm that the subpoena
had been served on the president's attorneys on July 17—twelve days
earlier.

What, I wondered, was the purpose of refusing to confirm for
about two weeks, even on deep background, that Starr had served the
subpoena? The anger among the White House press corps over being
jerked around like this for no apparent reason was palpable. And
there was frustration within as well. One White House attorney said
to me after this incident: "When an independent counsel issues the
first grand-jury subpoena for a sitting president's testimony in
this country's history, it is unconscionable that any White House
would—for no apparent legal reason—refuse to confirm and, even
worse, would dissemble about it to the press."

The only explanation I received, after the fact, was that the president's attorneys wished to negotiate with Starr for the withdrawal of
the subpoena, and did not want the news of the subpoena to explode
in the middle of that delicate negotiation. But even if that was the
case, once it was clear that the news had been leaked and was going to
be reported anyway, why not at least give reporters deep-background
confirmation? In fact, even after news of the service of the subpoena
had been made public, the negotiations continued and were successfully concluded.

IT WAS IN PART BECAUSE of that sort of frustrating experience with
this information-blackout strategy that I made the calculated decision to use the medium of television to communicate directly to the
president.

I know this sounds a little bizarre; it might seem that I could have picked up the phone and called Bill Clinton up whenever I wanted. But that of course was not possible. I had never had free access to the president even when I was his special counsel, and I surely didn't now—especially given the dangers to him, and to me, of talking directly with him in the middle of a criminal investigation.

I was asked to appear on *Nightline* on July 28, the day the news broke that Monica Lewinsky had reached an immunity agreement with Starr and that she would testify that there had been an intimate relationship between herself and President Clinton. The major subject on everyone's mind was whether the president would accede to Starr's subpoena and testify before the grand jury.

Forrest Sawyer was substituting for Ted Koppel on *Nightline* that night. "Let's say that you have the president's ear," he said. "What do you advise him to do now?" Little did Sawyer realize that I hoped to use his program precisely to gain the president's ear. I chose my words carefully, hoping the president was watching and receptive.

"I think it's time for him to come forward," I said. "I think he should do it now, rather than waiting until September. He should only do it if Mr. Starr is reasonable. I think the American people will support his coming forward and I think the American people and the president want to move on to the business of the country."

Two weeks later, after my breakfast on August 14, I realized that I had to try once again, at this critical period, to send a message to the president before he gave his testimony to the grand jury. I was scheduled to appear on NBC's *Meet the Press* that Sunday, and by that point I was utterly convinced that the best and quickest way to get the story out and over would be to publish the full transcript of the grand-jury testimony. I knew that inevitably it would leak out in bits and pieces anyway and that, also inevitably, it would leak in the form most prejudicial to the president. So, I reasoned, he might as well put it out himself, and his decision to do so would convincingly show the American people that he had nothing to hide and that he had told the grand jury the truth. (Of course the judge would have to grant permission to release the normally secret grand-jury transcript. But I assumed that if Starr joined in a motion for such a release—and he would be hard pressed to refuse if the president asked for it to be released—the judge would likely agree.)

I had urged this position on the president's lawyers, but they weren't about to agree at that point, certainly not before they knew what was in the testimony. So I wanted to speak over their heads to the president, and I hoped that the president would be watching *Meet the Press* that day.

When Tim Russert, the show's host, asked me a question about my expectations concerning the president's grand-jury testimony, I said: "I believe that that transcript of the grand-jury proceedings should be made public so that everybody can judge for themselves what the president has said and, most importantly, to allow this issue to be put to rest once and for all. I hope Mr. Starr will abide by that as well. The American people want these answers but want, most of all, this story to be behind them. What they really support is the president's performance in office, and they want him to get back to that job."

I didn't know whether my message got through, and I hoped for the best when the president went before the grand jury on Monday, August 17. That night, I watched with anticipation as the president addressed the nation. This would be the speech in which he admitted to an improper relationship with Ms. Lewinsky.

I must admit I didn't mind the speech while he was giving it as much as I did in rehearing it and rereading it. My most negative reaction—instantaneous, as I recall—was when the president said that his answers in the Paula Jones deposition had been "legally accurate." I slapped my hand on my knee in anger. "What does that mean?" I said aloud. Inwardly I thought, "That's talking like a lawyer, not like a president."

But he took responsibility and I especially liked that he admitted that the primary motivation for his deceptions had been "to protect myself from the embarrassment of my own conduct." That was honest, I thought. And surely people would empathize with his second reason—concern about "protecting my family."

When, in the second half of his brief speech, the president first expressed his concern about the excesses of the independent counsel, as intruding on privacy issues where a criminal justice investigation didn't belong, my first reaction was that this was justified. I felt that these concerns were shared by a lot of people. But then his harsh comments about the independent counsel went on too long and the tone got decidedly aggressive. By the end, I worried that the contrition and honesty of the first half had been undermined by the tone of the second half.

And he had never used the words "I'm sorry." I wondered why.

Four days later, around 12:30 P.M. on Friday, August 21, my office phone rang. It was the White House operator. "The president is calling," she said simply.

We talked for a few minutes. He had returned temporarily from his vacation on Martha's Vineyard the day before (the day of the U.S. bombings of Afghanistan and Sudan), and he sounded tired. He thanked me for my efforts on his behalf and we talked about the current legal and political situation. Then he asked me what I thought of his speech.

I knew that this would be a unique opportunity to tell him what I really thought, in person, to tell him that now was the time to get the story out and behind him and to move on. I held nothing back. I said straight off that he had sounded too much like a lawyer in his speech. I reminded him that when he talked straight to the American people and connected with them, there was no one better. I said he had to be president, not a defendant, that he should handle the politics and let his lawyers sort out the legal arguments. I said that the worst was behind him—he had told the American people and his friends and family the truth, the difficult, painful truth. Now he needed to get everything out—especially the grand-jury transcript—

and then invite over network news anchors Tom Brokaw, Peter Jennings, and Dan Rather, and spend an evening answering every one of their questions. Then it would be over for him and for his family, and the country could move on.

By this point, my voice was raised. I was sounding angry, and I caught myself short. This was the president of the United States I was talking to. This was also someone I cared about and did not want to see hurt any more. I lowered my volume as we talked for a few more minutes.

He was receptive. He was conflicted. He was sad.

When I hung up the phone, I was shaking. Had I been fair to him? Had I been disrespectful? It was easy enough for me to give this advice—I wasn't the one forced to admit publicly what most people would give anything not to admit privately. I wasn't the one in the crosshairs of a five-year investigation whose sole objective was to destroy me and put me in prison. How could I be so sure that my instinctive mantra—get it all out yourself now—was in his best interest? How could I second-guess his lawyers, who knew more than I did?

Even after everything—the Lewinsky story, the information blackout, the hostility of the press, the blue dress, everything—his approval ratings were off the chart. The economy was booming, the country was at peace, and he was still one of the most popular second-term presidents in the history of the country.

Maybe he knew something I didn't know.

AND YET . . . AND YET.

It was Friday, February 12, 1999. I was sitting in a television studio in downtown Washington, watching the United States Senate vote to acquit President Clinton on both charges and waiting to make a few postmortem comments. Amazingly, the Republican House managers had been unable to convince a Republican-controlled

Senate to cast a majority vote in favor of either article. The Comeback Kid, it seemed, had done it again. I was sure the president's poll numbers would go up another ten points.

But I felt no joy, no victory, no cause for celebration. I worried about history, about the important legacy of the Clinton presidency in which I still so strongly believed, and about the impact on the president and his family. And I couldn't help but wonder whether this painful, lost year and the House impeachment vote itself could have been avoided if the president and the White House had followed the basic rules of proactive disclosure.

Clearly, an early release of the grand-jury testimony would have accelerated completion of the writing of the story. Less obviously, it would also have strengthened the president's impeachment defense, at least on the article that alleged perjury before the grand jury. Imagine if the president's lawyers had been able to sit down with a couple of reporters who specialize in legal-analysis stories, such as Ruth Marcus of the *Washington Post* or Linda Greenhouse of the *New York Times,* during the leisurely, slow-news days of late August and early September. They could have walked the reporters line by line through the president's testimony, providing background and context for all of his answers. The likely result would have been a comprehensive predicate story, one which spotlighted that the president had told the grand jury the truth about the core issue in the investigation, admitting to an intimate, inappropriate relationship with Monica Lewinsky. Had this been done, the whole atmosphere might have changed. The House might well have rejected the grand-jury perjury article for the same reasons as the Senate did two months later, when the article was defeated 55–45. After all, it was not until the Senate trial that there was a detailed focus on the substance of the president's grand-jury testimony. Among the ten Republican senators voting to acquit on that charge were Arlen Specter of Pennsylvania, a former district attorney; Fred Thompson of Tennessee, a former criminal-defense attorney; and Slade Gorton of Washington, a former state attorney general. (It seems likely that if the House had voted down the grand-jury perjury article for the same reasons the ten Senate Republicans did, then the obstruction article—which passed by a narrow margin of only nine votes in the House—would also have gone down.)

Besides the advantages of getting the grand-jury testimony out early, what would have happened if Mike McCurry had been allowed to do his job? What if he had been given permission to disclose information and documents that had already been turned over or that were known to the prosecutors? The lawyers could not have objected that he was telling Starr something that Starr might not already know. The effect would have been to unleash the considerable forces of investigative journalism. The end result—and my thoughts began to surprise and trouble me—could well have been to force the president, despite himself, to acknowledge the relationship much earlier than he did.

Take, for example, Monica Lewinsky's WAVES records. When the president and I talked in the Oval Office on January 22, he had seemed open to releasing them, as most of the press were already clamoring for him to do. Since it was clear that Kenneth Starr would easily get access to them through a subpoena of the Secret Service, there would have been no prejudice to the president's legal position in his lawyers releasing all those records themselves. The result would have been reports that Monica Lewinsky (as subsequently reported by Starr) had visited the president eleven times between April 1996, when she left the White House for her job at the Pentagon, and December 1997—not the thirty-seven times that had been widely alleged in the first few days of the story. Those reports were obviously based on leaks from people who were just as prone to misunderstand WAVES records as the ones who had leaked the John Huang records the year before.

Moreover, if McCurry had been allowed to do what we had done during the campaign-finance investigation days, he would have tried to accompany the raw numbers shown by the WAVES-records release with complete explanations of who had WAVEd her in, whom she had visited, and how long she had stayed. In addition, McCurry would also have assembled the "mother of all document dumps": all documents, records, and materials in any way relating to communications between Ms. Lewinsky and the president, including telephone-message slips, telephone records, pager records, letters, courier slips, and, yes, even gifts. Again, all of these either already were or were soon to be in the possession of Starr's prosecutors, so the president's attorneys would have had no reason to object to such a dump.

The effect of such a document dump on the White House press corps would have been, well, volcanic. It would have driven investigative journalists deeper into the story, and driven them quicker. The volume of published circumstantial evidence that there had been a personal relationship between the president and Ms. Lewinsky would have increased dramatically. Pressure on the president to admit to the relationship would likely have reached a breaking point "sooner rather than later," in his own words. Not only would the public have been drawing clear conclusions, but the president's own staff and legal team would have become better informed and more convinced that there had in fact been an intimate relationship. Thus they would have been in a better position to help him come to terms with the truth and to figure out a way to get it out.

As I thought about these inevitable effects of a proactive-disclosure strategy, I was growing increasingly uneasy. Why? What was I really trying to do here? Suddenly I understood.

Those of us at the president's side had always spoken of the fact that Kenneth Starr and the lawyers for Paula Jones had used Linda Tripp's tape-recorded conversations with Monica Lewinsky to set a "perjury trap" for the president at the January 17, 1998, deposition. The scenario I was imagining to defeat the perjury trap would have pursued a proactive disclosure process that would have created, in effect, a "truth trap" to help the president. If the White House press office could have pushed out the facts, surrounded him with them, and backed up everything with visitor records, documents, and other evidence, then that could well have forced the president—trapped him, if you will—into admitting to the relationship much earlier in the process. Such a stratagem would have short-circuited the whole scandal-news cycle, and possibly the impeachment process as well.

Would that have been fair to him? Would it have been right to do that to someone you work for? Wouldn't it have been some type of serious breach—of duty, loyalty, something? Nevertheless, if the result of this strategy would have been to force the truth out earlier and thus avoid impeachment entirely, wouldn't that have been better for him, for his family, and for the country?

MY TROUBLING REVERIE WAS INTERRUPTED by the television producer, who stuck his head into the studio to tell me that the broadcast had run out of time and I would not be interviewed. I was free to leave.

Free to leave.

For the first time since I walked out of the White House that frigid January night over a year ago, I was finally ready to get off the scandal watch, to get my life back, to spend time with my family again—and, as I left the studio for the last time, to leave my sanctimony at the door.

Acknowledgments

THIS BOOK COULD NOT HAVE BEEN WRITTEN WITHOUT THREE people, and I start by thanking them:

Michael McCurry, the best White House press secretary in the history of the world: He taught me, protected me, and guided me through the minefields. He deserves much of the credit for any of the good things I happened to do during my fourteen months at the White House. For my multiple mistakes, of course, he has no responsibility.

Arthur Kaminsky, literary agent, adviser, and friend for thirty years: He stuck with me through various concepts, drafts, and proposals, helped shape my ideas and thinking, advised me on shirts and ties to wear on TV, and helped me find Paul Golob of The Free Press.

Which leads me to Paul Golob: He has been more than my editor, of course. He read my proposal and realized that the book I wanted to write and needed to write was a lot different from the one I had first proposed. As I wrote he helped me find what I really wanted to say and sometimes he helped me gain insight into what I had already written. He pushed me and coaxed me and was tough on me when it was necessary, and he never gave up on me. I can't imagine a writer having a better editor, one who knows better how to bring out the best in you. Thanks, Paul, beyond words.

I am very grateful to the many other people in The Free Press family who helped shape and edit and produce this book, especially

Paula Duffy, Elizabeth Maguire, Suzanne Donahue, Mary Bahr, Jennifer Weidman, Tom Stvan, Edith Lewis, and the entire production staff who worked so hard and effectively under great pressure. I am also grateful to Alys Yablon, Paul Golob's able assistant, for her patience and perseverance.

Thanks to my two colleagues at the White House, Adam Goldberg and Rochester "Ches" Johnson. They were kind enough to read the manuscript and try to catch factual errors. Of course any errors that remain are all my responsibility, not theirs. And I never could have survived or achieved whatever I achieved during my White House tenure without their support and friendship. Thanks also to Don Goldberg, my partner in politics and crisis management, which is to say, enlightened leaking. And thanks to my interns in the counsel's office for all their help and support, including Lisa Boswell, Amy Greenstein, Arian Hassani, Shelley Lambert, Carlos Gutierrez, James Hoffman, Jackson Norton, Gregg Weiss, Mara Hoffert, Liam Lynch, Joe Lorman, and Lindsey Browning.

Thanks to two other close friends and allies at the White House who helped make this book possible: to Charles Burson, distinguished counsel to the vice president, who was kind enough to read parts of the manuscript and even kinder to watch out for me during my White House days (a full-time job in itself) and to be my friend through thick and thin; and to Lanny Breuer, my fellow special counsel and special friend, who helped me shape and work the stories that are told in this book and who bridged the gaps whenever he could.

Thanks to my other colleagues in the White House counsel's office for helping me do my job, and putting up with my daily tugs and tensions, especially White House Counsel Charles Ruff and Deputy White House Counsel Cheryl D. Mills, and to the team of lawyers who backed our damage control operation: Michael "Buzz" Waitzken, Dimitri Nionakis, Michael Imbroscio, Michelle "Shelly" Peterson, Karl Racine, Sally Paxton, Bill Marshall, and, from the early days, Karen Popp; my special thanks also to Ora Theard, for always smiling and for putting up with me during my worst days, and to Ed Hughes and Brian Smith for their continuing support.

A special acknowledgment is due to my predecessors who wrote the rules that I tried to follow and who created the legacy of forthright disclosure that I tried so hard to fulfill—Jane Sherburne, Mark Fabiani, and, especially, the one and only, the Great (Chris) Lehane, who now lends his brilliant political and press talents to the vice president.

And thanks to John Podesta: You let Lanny be Lanny, even when it tested all your patience. You stood by me when I needed it most.

Thanks to the George Washington University School of Media and Public Affairs (SMPA) and its director, Jean Folkerts, and professors Jarol B. Manheim and Steven Livingston, for honoring me with the opportunity to be an adjunct professor for the fall 1998 semester and to teach a course titled—surprise!—"Scandal, Damage Control, and American Politics." They made available to me not only an office to write the early chapters of this book, but, more important, twenty-one of their best and brightest students, who were willing to be my critics, sounding boards, and human guinea pigs to help me test, sort out, and analyze most of the stories contained in this book. They are: Jeff Baxter, Matt Berger, Kirstin Brost, Scott Gastel, Jamie Harris, Rob Hendin, Jeff Ingram, Melissa Jaffe, Mike Kleinfeld, Justin Lavella, Stephanie Lutz, Cynthia Morris, Tom Mullaney, Rebecca Nielson, Jessica Pettorini, Franca Renzulli, Alexis Rice, Josh Saltzman, Nicholas Shipley, and Tracey Spector. And a special thanks to one of my students, Jason Haber, who also acted as my administrative and research assistant and counselor. And thanks to the friendly SMPA School support staff: Tessa Rottiers, Maria George, and Suzanne Clark. I am also grateful to professors Mark Siegel and Steve Roberts for giving me the idea to teach at SMPA and for their long years of friendship.

This book is about my work with the White House press corps, and I suppose every one of the reporters I worked with during my tenure was a contributor, one way or the other, to my White House education. I don't know whether I insult any of them by publicly thanking them, but here are the few who were involved in the stories described on these pages: Glenn Simpson, Michael Frisby, and Phil Kuntz of the *Wall Street Journal*; Peter Baker, Sue Schmidt, Ruth Marcus, and Howard Kurtz of the *Washington Post*; Jeff Gerth, Jill Abramson, Francis Clines, and Don Van Natta, Jr., of the *New York Times*; John Solomon, Pete Yost, Larry Margasak, and Jim Rowley of the Associated Press; Michael Weisskopf of *Time* and Michael Isikoff of *Newsweek*; Warren Strobel and Paul Bedard of the *Washington Times*; Robert Novak; David Jackson of the *Dallas Morning News*; Tom Squiteri, Mimi Hall, and Judy Kean of *USA Today*; Alan Miller, Glenn Bunting, and David Willman of the *Los Angeles Times*; Michael Kranish of the *Boston Globe*; Claire Shipman, David Bloom, and David Gregory of NBC; Bill Plante and Scott Pelley of CBS; Ted Koppel, John Donvan, and Linda Douglas of ABC; and Wolf Blitzer, Eileen O'Conner, Bob Franken, Frank Sesno, Gene Randall, and John King of CNN. Even when I argued with them, which was regularly, I continued to respect them.

And speaking of reporters, thanks to Gail Sheehy, for her advice on various matters in this manuscript; and especially to Carl Bernstein and Bob Woodward, for discussing many of the ideas and issues that appear on these pages. They were gracious guest lecturers at the first class in my "Damage Control" course at George Washington University.

Thanks to my friends and colleagues on television and radio panels who spent more time listening to me than they wanted to, I am sure, including hosts Tom Brokaw, Tim Russert, Brian Williams, Larry King, John Seigenthaler, Keith Olbermann, John Hockenberry, Geraldo Rivera, and G. Gordon Liddy; fellow guests Richard Thornburgh, Boyden Gray, Alan Baron, Richard Goodstein, Michael Zeldin,

Richard Ben-Veniste, Jay Severin, Ben Ginsberg, Tony Blankley, and Jonathan Turley; and producers Phil Griffin, Rani Brand, Izzy Povich, Marilyn Kaskel, Richard Stockwell, and Bob Petrick; and to the amazing crew of make-up artists who made me look better than I sounded.

I owe a special debt to Suzanne Garment, whose book *Scandal: The Culture of Mistrust in American Politics* (Times Books, 1991) influenced me more than any other book. It is a must-read for anyone who wants to appreciate the dangers of today's Washington, D.C., scandal machine.

Thanks to my partners and colleagues at my law firm, Patton Boggs, particularly to Thomas H. Boggs, Jr., for his support and faith in me for over twenty years; and to Wendy Williams, Heidi Tindall Saas, Ellen Price, Carol Rousseau, Ginger Varga, Denise Muse, and Amanda Rhodes.

A special thank-you to Lynne and Robert Kenney, my longtime and loyal friends, whose Martha's Vineyard home was where this book began; to Martha Handman, friend, editor, and *Paw Print Post* co-publisher; and to Stan and Suzan Gildenhorn, best friends and godparents to J.B., who stayed close through it all and who provided me with support and love over three decades. I am also grateful to Stan Gildenhorn for the hundreds of hours that he too spent on television and radio in defense of the president.

Thanks to President and Mrs. Clinton for their friendship and support, and for giving me the great honor of working for them in the White House.

My love and gratitude to my family: To my sister, Tama; to my three children, Seth Davis, Marlo Sims, and Joshua Benjamin Davis; to my son-in-law, David Sims; to my grandson, Jacob Nathan Sims; and to my mother-in-law and father-in-law, Margaret and Ralph Atwell. And a special thanks to Susanne Hudson, Joshua's best friend and the newest member of our extended family.

I wish my parents, Mort and Fran Davis, could have lived long enough to read this book. What they taught me about life and politics and fighting for what's important is reflected on every page.

And finally, my heartfelt thanks to my wife, partner, friend, editor, and critic Carolyn Atwell-Davis, to whom this book is dedicated. Thank you for everything. And you know what I mean by everything.

Index